MW00604948

Canadian Critical Luxury Studies

Canadian Critical Luxury Studies

Studies

Decentring Luxury

EDITED BY

Jessica P. Clark and Nigel Lezama

intellect

Bristol, UK / Chicago, USA

First published in the UK in 2022 by
Intellect, The Mill, Parnall Road, Fishponds, Bristol, BS16 3JG, UK

First published in the USA in 2022 by
Intellect, The University of Chicago Press, 1427 E. 60th Street,
Chicago, IL 60637, USA

Copyright © 2022 Intellect Ltd
Chapter 1: Luxury and Indigenous Resurgence by Riley Kucheran with Jessica P. Clark and Nigel
Lezama is an Open Access publication distributed under the CC BY-NC-ND - Creative Commons
Attribution-NonCommercial-NoDerivs License. You are allowed to download and share it with others
as long as credit is given. You can not change it in any way or use it commercially.

All rights reserved. No part of this publication may be reproduced, stored in a retrieval system,
or transmitted, in any form or by any means, electronic, mechanical, photocopying,
recording, or otherwise, without written permission.

A catalogue record for this book is available from the British Library.

Cover designer: Aleksandra Szumlas
Copy editor: Newgen
Production managers: Naomi Curston, Georgia Earl, Debora Nicosia
Typesetting: Newgen

Hardback ISBN 978-1-7893-8515-1
ePDF ISBN 978-1-7893-8516-8
ePub ISBN 978-1-7893-8517-5

Printed and bound by Severn

To find out about all our publications, please visit
www.intellectbooks.com
There you can subscribe to our e-newsletter, browse or download our current
catalogue, and buy any titles that are in print.

This is a peer-reviewed publication.

This research was supported by the Matching and Discretionary Research Fund, Brock University.

Contents

Figures

Acknowledgements

This volume has been long in the making. From initial conversations to planning small events for institutional and public outreach to a larger international conference to, finally, this volume, there are many people to whom we are beholden for their guidance, advice and assistance and institutions we must thank for their support and funding.

We are grateful to Carol Merriam, Dean of Humanities at Brock University, who gleaned the potential convergences in two new hires and saw fit to introduce them. It was during our first meeting, one late summer evening over wine, that we determined that the idea of luxury was the common element in our respective research programmes. We started working right away and have been fortunate to have had the continued support of our institution. We would like to thank Brock University's Faculty of Humanities, the departments of History and Modern Languages, Literatures and Cultures, the Office of the Vice President, Research and the Humanities Research Institute for the financial, administrative and moral support our project has received at all phases.

We have personally benefited from the collegiality among scholars in critical luxury and fashion studies. We would especially like to thank Riley Kucheran, who has been a steadfast friend and supporter. Our long conversations – about luxury and everything else – have changed the ways we understand our collective work. Many thanks to John Armitage and Joanne Roberts, Shaun Borstrock, Dellores Laing, Veronica Manlow, Katrina Sark and Thomaï Serdari for their support.

Many of the key ideas in this volume came out of discussions had and connections made at the 2017 conference, *Nouveau Reach: Past, Present and Future of Luxury*, co-organized with Alison Matthews David and Robert Ott. We deeply appreciate their support. We are grateful for the rich and varied contributions of our plenary speakers, Jonathan Faiers, Giorgio Riello and Jana Scholze. We're also thankful for the contributions of Toronto-area makers and thinkers Tala Kamea Berkes, Farley Chatto, Peggy Sue Deaven-Smiltnieks, Sage Paul and Anjli Patel. This invaluable opportunity to exchange ideas would not have been possible without the incredible work of Dylan Kwacz, Daniel Drak, Hayley Malouin, Jaclyn Marcus, Kate Marland and Juliana Scott.

Our production editors, Naomi Curston, Georgia Earl and Debora Nicosia, have been a great source of support since Intellect Books first approved our proposal. They have guided us through the process efficiently and with geniality. We are also indebted to the anonymous reviewers who offered critical and generous recommendations that enhanced the quality of the book. Thanks to Tania Larsson, Nadya Kwandibens and Lio Francis Keahna Warrior for allowing us to feature their striking work on the cover.

At the end of *Nouveau Reach*, a small group of participants met to form the Canadian Critical Luxury Collective. These are the contributors to this volume. We are grateful for all of their ideas, energy and stamina. Their ideas are what give Canadian luxury its meaning. Their energy is what will keep the collective active. Their stamina was essential to bring an edited volume to fruition. Personally, we are thrilled that we are able to share their disruptive ideas with the readers of *Canadian Critical Luxury Studies*.

A remarkably innovative scholar and maker in the field of wearables, Valérie Lamontagne had agreed to participate in this project before her sad passing. We are especially grateful to Brad Todd and Joanna Berzowska for helping us to share an edited version of case studies from her doctoral thesis, which brought a different depth to the key themes in this volume.

Introduction

Nigel Lezama

Canadian critical luxury studies (CCLS) represents a distinct contribution to the field by mobilizing the study of luxury as a lens to reconsider the historic 'periphery' and propose a new definition that includes a plurality of cultural practices. It does so by reconsidering Euro- and US-centric assumptions that limit luxury as a practice originating in former imperial metropoles and hegemonic economies. This volume re-angles existing scholarly perspectives, shedding light on historically undervalued and discursively marginalized sites of cultural production. In this way, *Canadian Critical Luxury Studies: Decentring Luxury* advances discussions in the field by representing the first critical exploration of the Canadian relationship to and role in critical luxury studies (CLS). Each chapter questions luxury within a specific framework: Indigeneity, geography, technology, history, class, space, fashion events and public art. The fundamental premise of the volume is that the circulation of luxury – goods, services and experiences – is neither unidirectional nor one-dimensional. Once stripped of its colonial and ideological underpinnings and released from the discourse of the cultural and political superstructure, luxury in the Canadian context demonstrates its value in more inclusive practices that counter the equation of privileged European mystification and US-styled market domination. CCLS' epistemological project is to highlight this decentred perspective on luxury.

CCLS situates luxury at the intersection of three discursive orbits. First and foremost, CCLS evaluates luxury in the context of colonial and neocolonial systems of capital so that the project of decolonizing luxury remains at the forefront. Secondly, CCLS investigates luxury as it circulates in its finished commodity form and as it is extracted, harvested or traded in its so-called raw, unrefined state. While it may function symbolically as power and economic domination for some, the circulation of commercial luxury impoverishes land and life for a great many others. The case studies in this volume highlight the double-edged impact of luxury in order to reveal the mystique of luxury that circulates through consumer culture. As much as luxury operates as the material medium of social power at the level of the individual and as a discursive expression of (soft) power at the level of nations, the capitalist circulation of luxury necessarily entails a zero-sum game. Reflecting CCLS' third discursive orbit is the acknowledgement that for the individuals, the conglomerates and the nation states whose dominance is symbolized, materialized or reified through the accumulation of raw and refined luxury, there is a real impact on the lives of individuals and groups finding themselves on the historical, ideological and political losing side of the equation.

Situating Canada on the losing side of an equation of global status may seem curious, considering the country's place in the world economic order and its presence in a number of international organizations: the G7, the United Nations, the North Atlantic Treaty Organization (NATO) and the World Trade Organization (WTO), to name a few. While Canada has an active role on the international stage among a cohort of Global North and West hegemonic states, it is nevertheless pertinent to note the perception of Canadians of their country's international status. Based on the results of a public opinion survey, a 2020 report from the MacDonald-Laurier Institute (cf. Devlen 2020), a Canadian non-partisan think tank, found that while a majority of Canadians (72 per cent) believe that it is important for their country to maintain an influential role on the global stage, only 5 per cent of Canadians believe that Canada's international role is currently an influential one. Perception and reality are often disparate phenomena, so that Canadians' perception of their status and the country's real political and economic impact differs depending on the age, gender, education and political slant of the respondent. However, the generalized perception of limited Canadian international stature reflects the political realities of the country and its particular history.

In North America, the US market dominates in all contexts: commercial, economic and, pertinent to the current discussion, cultural. In his study of Canadian cultural protectionism, Szeman reminds us that

> the struggle we have imagined as a national one is an international one: culture globally shares a common enemy, which in Canada long ago appeared in the guise of American popular culture. Our enemy is contemporary neoliberalism, an order that 'erects into defining standards for all practices, and thus into ideal rules, the regularities of the economic world abandoned to its own logic: the law of the market, the law of the strongest' (Bourdieu, 'Reasoned', 125).
>
> (2000: 225)

Compounding Canada's secondary relationship to the United States is the legacy of colonial interference. As a former European colonial possession,

Canada's development did not allow for a storied history of commodity production that could foster the growth of the country's 'soft' power. While a bountiful source of raw materials (and skilled production treated as a raw material) from first contact, Canada remained overshadowed as a luxury producer by European imperialist centres long into the twentieth century. In the context of cultural production, Canada has consistently been a secondary actor. Examining the strategy of place branding in the Canadian fashion industry, Brydges and Hracs posit, 'as a young country – which celebrated its 150th birthday in 2017 – with a young fashion industry, Canada can yield insights into the *ongoing process* of carving out a national identity' (2018: 109, emphasis added). The challenges and transformations brought to bear on luxury and luxuriousness in the Canadian context, a number of which will be discussed in the chapters that follow, demonstrate that 'constructing this identity [as an "author country"] can be a particular challenge for "tier-two" (Rantisi 2018) or "not-so-global" centres' (2018: 110). In this light, CCLS follows the logic expressed by David Gilbert that the status of fashion world cities 'involves the relationships between places, both between imagined or actual centres of influence and "peripheral" places in the geography of fashion' (2013: 13). In the context of a national luxury identity, the situating of Canada in the periphery acknowledges its colonial history and imperial relationship, in which Canada was a source of raw materials with constituent Indigenous labour required for its extraction and a settler-colonial market avid for foreign-made fineries. Later, the production-consumption relationship that binds Canada and the United States, a relationship whose imbalance has plagued Canadian foreign trade policy since the early twentieth century, further entrenches Canada as a secondary and tier-two site of global luxury production and consumption.

Critical luxury studies: An overview

Democratized luxury. Über luxury. Deep luxury. Branded luxury. Experiential luxury. What can we make of this fragmentation of an idea into these (and many other) antithetical, tautological or – often – illogical concepts? How, in fact, has luxury been 'democratized'? What distinguishes 'deep' from 'experiential' luxury? CLS, realized in 2016 with John Armitage and Joanne Roberts's field-defining volume, *Critical Luxury Studies: Art, Design, Media*, seeks to engage with these questions as well as analyse the myriad ways that luxury impacts society's functioning and how culture is expressed through its manipulation. Luxury is a broad-reaching and longstanding phenomenon. Accordingly, CLS is an interdisciplinary and transversal field that seeks answers not only to the question 'what is luxury?' but further also to the ancillary questions 'how does luxury function in society?', 'what compels luxuriousness in culture?' and 'who adopts practices of luxury, how do they and to what end?' Specialists in cultural studies, historians, literary scholars, philosophers, sociologists, social scientists, as well as luxury brand specialists, marketing analysts, economists and industry consultants have all engaged with the phenomenon. While CLS can be said to have been founded as a field with Armitage and Roberts's 2016 collection, luxury has a deeper history as a hermeneutic object. In John Sekora's (1977) examination, *Luxury: The Concept in Western Thought, Eden to Smollett*, the critic parses the history of perceptions of luxury from biblical allegory to the public debates and literary representations of eighteenth-century England. Sekora finds that moral aversion to luxury was a recurring theme up to the early modern period. It was only in the eighteenth century that perceptions began to shift to focus on political economy. To date, this remains the foundational premise in the history of luxury. Christopher Berry (1994) revisits this history in *The Idea of Luxury: A Conceptual and Historical Investigation*. Berry's analysis parses luxury by philosophically defining luxury as *qualitative* refinement (as opposed to *quantitative* accumulation). His study breaks down the barriers that tied luxury to elite consumption. In *Luxury in the Eighteenth Century: Debates, Desires and Delectable Goods*, historians Elizabeth Eger and Maxine Berg both expand and focus the discussion of luxury by tying the circulation of exotic and refined goods and eighteenth-century western consumer culture to a shift in sociocultural practices, what the historians call 'the civilising impact of superfluous commodities' (2002: 7). Their case studies highlight the impact of the growing cultural acceptance of luxurious goods – fashions, furnishings and foodstuffs – on the cultural politics of the time. For instance, in her chapter on imported Asian luxuries, Berg insists on the creation of the western idea of Asian exoticism, not arising from the goods coming from Asia, but from western commercial desire for an 'Orientalised' East that determined what goods were produced and exported from Asia. These foundational and insightful works remained relatively discipline-specific analyses.

CLS multiplied the tools of analysis available to scholars and researchers. Case studies in Armitage and Roberts's (2016a) eponymous volume came out of architectural studies, fashion studies, human geography, public health, media studies as well as philosophy, sociology and cultural management. Collectively, the volume responded to the perceived rise of a luxury-dominated cultural sphere that remained uncritical of the growing hegemony of luxury. For this reason, sociologist Pierre Bourdieu's ([1983] 1986) taxonomy of capital became a key concept in the field's epistemology. For CLS, luxury is conceived as cultural capital, that is to say a form of social value used by individuals and institutions to materialize power and assert both social and economic dominance. Under the umbrella of CLS, scholars have sought to explicate the underlying causes and effects of an imposing circulation of luxury on other cultural practices. Underpinning these analyses is a Marxian perspective that parses value in commodities and insists on a surplus value (beyond expense) that, first, creates the experience of luxuriousness and, second, is a materialization of social relations. 'Luxury goods serve as the reified and commodified expression of the social relationship of their production', asserts Ulrich Lehmann (2016: 67–68). So, for CLS, luxury always occupies a double function: personal and social. 'On the one hand, luxury is uplifting both spiritually and materially; on the other, it is seen as "improductive" and therefore useless in any society that privileges economic and social rationality', assert McNeil and Riello (2016: 4) in their study, *Luxury: A Rich History*. Focusing on personal values and valuation questions the authority of Bourdieusian and Veblenian models of luxury consumption as displays of either cultural sophistication or economic waste. Mansvelt, Breheny and Hay's investigation of consumption habits of individuals from varying economic strata reveals that all people build 'narratives of justification and entitlement to forms of luxury consumption [to] provide means of shaping identities as responsible, controlled and autonomous consumers' (2016: 104). CLS affirms that individuals can assert autonomy via luxury consumption. However, in the social field, luxury is also an instrument with which to enact dominance. Armitage and Roberts remind us that luxury unites a transnational class of wealthy consumers and functions as a means of distinction for this select group. Further, these scholars highlight the social functioning of this display and imagining of dominant luxury: 'A wider population aspires to join these elites and they satisfy their aspirations by imitating elite consumption behaviour' (2017: 29). For CLS, luxury is a complex phenomenon that can both liberate and limit individuals in society.

Luxury is also an institutional tool. By addressing the political economy of luxury, CLS has fruitfully studied the role and effects of institutionalized luxuries. Institutions, in this sense, include corporate entities, religious organizations, public place-making and para-public spaces. Historian Catherine Kovesi uncovers the relationship between religious veneration and the contemporary cult of luxury brands by harnessing Walter Benjamin's well-known theory of the aura. Kovesi likens the aura of the sacred relic to that of the luxury-branded commodity. She explicates the paradox that luxury brands materialize, shoring up the singularity of brand identity while ensuring the replicability and omnipresence of their commodities on the market (2016: 114). Analysing a 2009 court case launched by Christian Dior Couture against Copad, a discount retailer that had acquired the rights to sell Dior-branded corsetry from the luxury brand's licensed manufacturer, the historian concludes that contemporary consumer culture has elicited a sacralization of luxury. The ruling, handed down by the European Court of Justice, accepted Dior's legal argument that the brand's 'aura of luxury' was imperiled by the presence of its branded commodities in non-elite spaces, such as that of Copad. Kovesi cites part of the ruling to demonstrate that luxury-branded commodities are more than the sum of their material qualities. 'The quality of luxury goods […] is not just the result of their material characteristics', she argues, 'but also of the allure and prestigious image which bestows on them an aura of luxury' (2016: 116). Space is an integral aspect for buttressing the prestige of commodities – their aura of luxury.

Conversely, luxury also impacts space. Mario Paris's edited volume, *Making Prestigious Places: How Luxury Influences the Transformation of Cities*, approaches luxury as 'a driver of change in the city' (Paris and Fang 2017: 1). The studies in his volume consider luxury as a means to transform spaces into prestigious places. They challenge the idea that gentrification – through the increased presence of high-end and exclusive institutions, such as luxury-brand stores, cultural centres and refined public services – is one-sided development that displaces the already economically marginalized. Given the urban studies perspective in conversation with CLS, the case studies in Paris's volume generally focus on the symbolic meanings of luxury retail and cultural spaces as cultural capital, without engaging with the critical project of CLS. In their introduction, Paris and Fang privilege the commercial growth potential that luxury brings to urban space, positing that '[l]uxury is a catalyst generating several opportunities (visibility, events, new heritage and shared spaces, etc.) and not only parasitizing its historical and urban value' (2017: 6–7). A more critical approach to luxury and space can be found in architecture specialist Adam Sharr's (2016) chapter in *Critical Luxury Studies*, 'Libeskind in Las Vegas: Reflections on architecture as a luxury commodity'. Sharr examines what he calls the commodification of architecture. Specifically, he investigates the slippage of the groundbreaking aesthetic of world-renowned architect Daniel Libeskind's Jewish Museum, opened in 2001 in Berlin, into a self-referential style once applied to the design of Las Vegas's Crystals at CityCenter, a commercial retail centre, built in 2009. For his 2001 project, Libeskind developed an aesthetic of trauma that commemorated the harrowing experience of Jewish people in Berlin under the Third Reich that stood as a memorial for the horror of the Holocaust. The unprecedented style of the Jewish Museum catapulted Libeskind to 'starchitect' status, and subsequently, the aesthetic became the architect's signature. Sharr evokes the use of the 'Libeskind brand' for later projects, namely the high-end Las Vegas shopping centre, to demonstrate the flattening out of meaning when architecture no longer functions to commemorate, but to manifest cultural and economic capital. For Sharr, the formerly symbolic and complex aesthetic choices of the Jewish

Museum have become both self-referential stylistic elements and signs of the commercial domination of contemporary culture in the luxury mall while architecture slips from socially useful to socially instrumental. 'Crystals at CityCenter seeks to claim the idea of architecture as art, as a pursuit whose details and nuances exist for the appreciation of connoisseurs. [...] It connotes the idea of architecture as a signifier for high culture, becoming a device for marketing to "high-end" consumers' (2016: 171). Sharr's analysis demonstrates that luxury is not simply a change agent in the creation of prestigious places. Rather, commercial luxury can reduce the monumental and the commemorative to empty signs of consumer culture.

Aporetic luxury

For too long, luxury has been theorized and experienced as the domain of the powerful, the imperialist, the colonizer, the wealthy capitalist or the cosmopolitan consumer. Luxury as an idea is crystallized in perceptions of rarity, exclusivity and excess. In its reified form, luxury is a category defined by expense, despite a glut of luxury branded fashions and commodities on the market. In the past decade, the ensuing growth in consumer luxury spending has brought the notion of 'democratized luxury' to the fore, particularly for the field of luxury brand management (cf. Kapferer and Bastien 2009; Turunen 2017) as well as for researchers in CLS. However, as mentioned, historians of consumer culture have, following Berg (Berg and Clifford 1999; Berg 2005), already documented the imperialist and colonial circulation of 'exotic' fineries and the ensuing growth of a middling market in eighteenth-century Europe as the true beginning of luxury's so-called democratization. The idea of luxury brought down from its elite perch may conjure idealized images of commercial equality in which everyone has access to specialized commodities that satisfy personal wants and express the fluidity and multiplicity of social identity. To signal this new affirmative and psychologically reinforcing function of luxury, one could invoke Lipovetsky's (2003, 2005) 'hyperconsumer' who, freed from the constraints of Bourdieusian habitus, consumes to quell ontological anxieties yet is free to play with identity and extract personal pleasure from luxury goods. However, the contemporary global 'spirit of luxury' (Armitage and Roberts 2016c) 'should be seen as part of a long-term process involving the decline of aristocratic power, the rise of the middle classes and pressures from below for increasing democratization' (Featherstone 2014: 50). Conversely, luxury management scholars invoke a troubling neoliberal motivation underpinning so-called democratized luxury consumption. In HEC Paris professors Jean-Noël Kapferer and Vincent Bastien's (2009) work, the democratization of luxury is, in fact, decidedly *undemocratic*. Blending the jargon of microbiology and psychoanalysis with a dash of neoliberalism, these luxury management specialists posit:

> '[D]emocratic luxury': *a luxury item that extraordinary people would consider ordinary is at the same time an extraordinary item to ordinary people*. The DNA of luxury, therefore, is the symbolic desire (albeit often repressed) to belong to a superior class, which everyone will have chosen according to their dreams, because *anything that can be a social signifier can become a luxury*.
>
> (2009: 314, original emphasis)

The only thing democratic in this conception of luxury is that the neoliberal ideology of entitlement to luxury has spilled over to all levels of society. Taken to its logical conclusion, luxury in Kapferer and Bastien's conceptualization is a self-nullifying classification: ordinary to the extraordinary, extraordinary to the ordinary, luxury management empties the term of any meaning.

It is pertinent to remember that 'democratized luxury' emerged out of the imperialist project. The expansion of a so-called luxury market occurred with the labour of the enslaved, the indentured and the colonized and precipitated the damage and destruction of the natural world. In *Crass Struggle: Greed, Glitz, and Gluttony in a Wanna-Have World*, R. T. Naylor (2011) casts a damning light on luxury industries, such as gold, silver, diamond and other precious gem mining and trade. The colonial history, the neocolonial reality and the environmental and human devastation inflicted by these industries tarnish the sheen of the Cartier bangle that (as well as being made from illegally mined gold) is the reification of luxury. Contemporary production of so-called luxury goods betrays the unchanged Global North and West's domination of capital and cultural tastes. The inexorable culmination of hegemonic luxury has emerged in the wake of crises stemming from the neoliberal financialization of debt among the racialized poor, the growing reduction of the middle classes and the neocolonialism of 'globalized' supply chains, all while the wealth of a borderless class of 'super-rich' expands inexorably and behind closed doors. Picketty's recent study, *Capital and Ideology* ([2019] 2020), reveals the ideological underpinnings of global wealth disparity that have morphed economic structures so that, since the 1980s, the world is engulfed in an inequality regime that intensely concentrates both wealth and growth for a small 'über-elite class' at the cost of a numerically vast group of the world's poor. While not a treatise on luxury, Picketty's analysis makes plain that access to luxury remains profoundly circumscribed in the contemporary period. This reality extends ideas of so-called democratic luxury to the limit of the absurd. Luxury, *democratized* or not, is now a label that is applied to goods, services and experiences that strain the applicability of standard definitions of the luxurious.

However, more seriously, the so-called *democratization* of luxury masks the real entrenchment and shrinking of the domain of privilege to a very select few.

Despite the evacuation of meaning from an excessive presence in the commercial realm and the less-than-luxurious conditions surrounding the extraction of the raw materials of luxury industries, the idea of luxury has a real impact, not only for those with great economic capital or those in the cycle of consumption that characterizes the alleged aspiring and middling classes but also for the economically and sociopolitically marginalized. In this perspective, CCLS adds its voice to those who challenge luxury's epistemological Euro-American centrism and sociocultural dominance. In the recently published volume *African Luxury: Aesthetics and Politics* (2019a), co-editors Simidele Dosekun and Mehita Iqani challenge the wider hegemony of luxury in the social and cultural realm precisely because of the impact of such discourses on those without access or hope of access to the realm of hegemonic luxury. The editors assert in their introduction that

> however precisely defined, luxury very much matters. It matters in our contemporary global moment of extreme income inequality; in a world in which we speak routinely of not just 'the 1 per cent' but smaller fractions thereof and, conversely, of 'surplus' or 'disposable populations', the many (and rising) on the sharp end of 'neoliberalism's power to define who matters and who doesn't, who lives and who dies' (Giroux 2008: 594).
>
> (2019b: 4)

Like the case studies in *African Luxury*, this volume sheds light on the distinct modes that luxury can assume in peripheral markets and that add ontological value to personal and collective experience.

Armitage and Roberts remind us in their volume, 'The philosophy of luxury entails recognition that all human beings live in a world that is created by human beings, and in which they find meaning in sumptuous enjoyment' (2016b: 2). Luxury is a highly personal, symbolically imbued and emotionally charged *added value* that individuals from all socioeconomic strata can access to enrich themselves ontologically and collectively. The idea of luxury has been marshalled by former imperialist nations as a symbol of economic dominance, by fashion and luxury centres of production for its 'soft power' (viz. France's *Comité Colbert*, the United Kingdom's *Walpole* or Italy's *Altagamma*) and in urban spaces that agglomerate commercial signs and artistic representations to create prestigious places. In contrast to this hegemonic mobilization, in the geopolitical context of formerly peripheral and colonial outposts, the idea of luxury – imbued as it is with its own nationalist, imperialist and colonial history – is troubled by its wholesale and unproblematic adoption and deployment as a political and economic instrument.

With the current reign of neoliberal capitalism and so-called globalized trade, the discursive power of luxury should no longer be a surprise to anyone. However, luxury's ideological function begs the question: 'Who really benefits from luxury in this system?'

This question is at the heart of the case studies that make up *Canadian Critical Luxury Studies: Decentring Luxury*. Since Canada is a tier-two economic market and a secondary geopolitical centre of influence, luxury in the Canadian context cannot and should not be treated simply as a system of production, consumption and circulation that expresses cultural dominance or aspiration for cultural dominance. As the case studies in this volume demonstrate, luxury as an idea is an internally contradictory sign that empowers and alienates. Luxury is both personally symbolic and politically invested. Ultimately, luxury succeeds and fails as a sign of distinction and as a materialization of power. Critical luxury scholars, as much as marketers, producers and advertisers, seemingly define luxury as essentially positive for the beholder, owner or experiencer. McNeil and Riello assert that 'luxury is uplifting both spiritually and materially' (2016: 4). Acknowledging its aporetic nature, Mark Featherstone determines that 'contemporary luxury represents the sacred unconscious of the profane world' (2016: 69). Reaching further back, Lehmann finds that since the Enlightenment, 'the socio-cultural expression of [economic] dominance is luxury' (2016: 82–83). Luxury, according to these scholars, can be manipulated by individuals without adverse effect. Berry (2016), expanding on his germinal study *The Idea of Luxury*, separates the circulation of luxury in society from social positioning or personal alienation to situate luxury squarely as a source of pleasure. 'However, unless luxuries gave pleasure there would, pace Baudrillard (1988: 47) or Appadurai (1986: 144), be nothing to register or communicate' (2016: 49–50). Most recently still, in her discussion of luxury fashion, Thomaï Serdari theorizes luxury as a spiritual experience for an idealized consumer who 'is completely entranced in its beauty or when she is inspired to think about an important theme based on messages or signs the object communicates through its design' (2020: 67). To date, while questioned, analysed, historicized and theorized, luxury is broadly deemed to bring pleasure, buttress individuality and materialize liberty. In the context of European cultural power and its epistemological wake, it is possible to frame luxury as a purely humanist phenomenon. This requires, nevertheless, ignoring the colonial system of luxury that extracted raw materials, human labour and wealth from dominated geographic regions and then introduced 'refined' finished commodities as well as accompanying hegemonic discourses back into these regions. This ideological flow continues today through neocolonial systems of offshore production.

This is not to say that in secondary geographies, luxury, fed back into the system, cannot provide pleasure for the individual or demonstrate personal autonomy.

A number of case studies in this volume demonstrate the ways that individuals can reconsider luxuries as a means of personal and collective affirmation. Riley Kucheran, for example, shares the experience of care, generosity and sustainability that informs the processes of Indigenous making in his intervention in this volume. In addition to notions of tradition and handcraft, which also exemplify these practices, Kucheran asserts that 'Indigenous making is luxurious' precisely in the generosity of the exchange in which Indigenous making occurs. Valérie Lamontagne opens her case studies by commenting on the personally enriching relationships that characterize the wearables community. Her perspective deepens the idea of luxury by highlighting the relationship-building between makers, between makers and future makers, as well as between wearer and wearable. The luxuriousness of e-textiles is found in the refinement of experience that technical garments bring. Tellingly, Lamontagne expresses that the field of wearables is a luxurious space that creates surplus value. In her intervention, she asserts that 'the laboratory in itself is a research-social-materials space where humans and nonhumans and their "dance of agency" (Pickering 1995) converge and create the wearable designs of today'. The creative space itself, for Lamontagne, is more than the sum of its parts and what emerges is more than futuristic garments – the laboratory becomes a social space that enriches human experience.

As these examples suggest, the idea of luxury in second-tier contexts requires decentring to understand how non-hegemonic luxury challenges culturally dominant discourses and how the practice of extra-European luxury counters imperialist or neoliberal ideology. In Alexandra Palmer's introduction to her groundbreaking edited volume, *Fashion: A Canadian Perspective*, the curator acknowledges the difficulties of asserting a national luxury identity (this time in the field of Canadian fashion) from under the shadow of more established European commercial production. 'Canadian fashion design identity languishes unacknowledged, especially when compared to France, America, Italy, Britain, or Spain, and any success by Canadians tends to become subsumed under the more identifiable American fashion scene' (2004b: 3–4). For Palmer, however, there have been a number of attempts, both successful and less so, to build a Canadian fashion identity, which her volume convincingly argues. As Elke Gaugele and Monica Titton (2019) remind us in their excellent volume *Fashion and Postcolonial Critique*, fashion – like luxury – is a measure for cultural attainment and is used as a signal of cultural superiority. Invoking Sandra Niessen (2003), Gaugele and Titton state, 'Who has and who does not have fashion is politically determined, a function of power relations' (2003: 12). What has been deemed fashionable as opposed to unfashionable, such as traditional or ethnic dress, is a discursive distinction tied to capitalist systems and political and cultural hegemony. 'Every bit as much as imperial monuments or great exhibitions, fashion was used as a means of expressing the superiority of certain places in the world order' (Gilbert 2013: 16). The perception of who can and does produce luxury versus/as well as who consumes it, in the context of globalized and transnational capital, sharpens perceptions of cultural and economic dominance that are tainted with the history of imperialism and colonialism. This is evident in the analysis from contributors Kathryn Franklin and Rebecca Halliday that examines the problems faced by organizers of Toronto Fashion Week and determines that, for historically secondary markets, one of the impediments to forming a truly luxurious identity is that enactments of cultural production rely on international and 'imperialized' displays to the detriment of more home-grown and situated performances. A Canadian luxurious cultural identity has yet to escape the shadow of European luxury hegemony. However, contributor Marie O'Mahony harnesses examples from smaller state European craft to demonstrate ways that Canadian craft makers can use geographical closeness and regional proximity as the basis for collaborative innovation.

Luxuries in the public space occupy a nexus of power linking economic, political and social concerns that impact those who live in those spaces. Conversely to Paris and Fang's contention that when luxury is harnessed in the public realm, there is the potential to create prestigious places that materialize luxury's function as a 'traditional component of the human environment and the urban culture' (2017: 1–2), Canadian instances of public luxuries – in the form of fashionable events or public art commissions – risk obfuscating their imperialist, colonialist or capitalist underpinnings. The various case studies of the volume that privilege transnational and symbolic capital and its systems of reified economic (commercial) activity highlight the ways that these public forms of luxury effectively evade ethical questions around the impact of luxury on the urban lived space. In the case of established urban centres, luxury can easily assume the appearance of a 'traditional component' of the environment, thereby obscuring the modes of domination that luxury marshals. Julia Polyck-O'Neill examines the dynamics of capital and power in two public artworks by West Coast artists Douglas Coupland and Ken Lum, works that respond in differing ways to the history and politics of their space, in Vancouver, Canada. Polyck-O'Neill unpicks the complex network of forms of capital at play in public art commissions that can both overshadow artistic intention and buttress the sociopolitical impact on public spaces. Luxury, in the making of prestigious places, commoditizes the context(s) of the space in which it is created and displayed. In Canada, publicly funded public artworks risk being reduced to salable commodities that erase and homogenize the diverse histories of colonialism and socio-economic marginalization that artists may intend to express in their original works. As such, luxurious place-making outside of 'world cities' can flatten complex histories of domination (colonial and economic) because, similar to the phenomenon of Toronto Fashion Week, analysed by Franklin and Halliday, luxury imports established hegemonic energies that are invested in maintaining global hierarchies of power. The 'prestigious place' in London or Paris fits easily into a network of domination with singular discursive intensity. In Canada, European-styled prestigious places (as much as established fashion capital-styled events) mirror and intensify the hegemonic qualities of public luxuries. Artistic intentions that foreground marginalized histories and idiosyncratic cultural realities in secondary fashion markets can shatter against the force of this hegemonic node.

As Berry has determined, luxury is not a fixed category. 'A luxury is not something static, it is dynamic; it is subject to development as the desires, and necessarily attendant beliefs, are met and then fueled with further qualitative modifications or refinements' (1994: 18). In this way, luxury is neither immanent nor immutable. It is dependent upon the perceiver to emit its luxuriousness. Philosopher Lambert Wiesing concurs 'that luxury cannot be a characteristic of things or of actions, but that it arises through a private aesthetic experience' (2018: 78). In this light, there is such a thing as *Canadian* luxury, but it will arise from the private evaluation of surplus value. Canadian consumers, then, are well situated to increase the luxuriousness in their lives through the perception of and investment in goods, services and experiences as luxurious. Co-editor Nigel Lezama examines the creation of 'civic luxury' in the T. Eaton Company Limited's merchandising strategies during the interwar years. Contrary to what the contemporary luxury brandsphere would suggest, luxury is not limited to expensiveness (following Berry 1994: 17; Mark Featherstone 2016: 69; Wiesing 2018: 80). Luxury is a surplus value that exceeds both the exchange and use values (following Marx) attached to goods, services and experiences. As such, luxury is not only the domain of the wealthy (a postulation which, nevertheless, is contra Marx, who deems that luxury creates wealth only for the capitalist class [cf. [1867] 1972]). Consumers can invest goods with meanings that are personal or communal. In this way, while the dominant consumer culture may compel individuals to consumption as a mode of neoliberalism in the hyperconsumerist economy (in which everyone has the *right* to the pleasure of luxurious goods and services), the experience of luxury becomes personal and self-affirming and not merely determined by expense or potential status considerations. The idea of luxury is personally construed. 'Understanding place, with its constituents of local and subjective meaning, compels researchers to recognise how political, economic, cultural and environmental practices, flows and relations influence the particular ways luxury is constructed and the moralities attached to it' (Mansvelt et al. 2016: 93). Motivation for consumption is possible outside of the traditional perspective of Veblenian display, and the consumer's relationship to luxury is contingent on place – geographic as much as socio-economic.

In Canada, then, the relationship to luxury is not simply a social phenomenon, in the ways that Veblen ([1899] n.d.) or, later, Bourdieu characterizes consumption and taste as strategic or ingrained modes that embody socio-economic status for individual social actors. Nevertheless, the historical context of European imperialism and colonialism imposes symbolic values that complicate the basic meaning of luxury all the while reinforcing power structures. Gilbert explains that in the field of fashion, imperial networks of production, trade and consumption functioned to buttress European hegemony.

> The growth and systemisation of European imperialism was an important phase in the development of fashion's world cities. Most obviously this worked in terms of the relationship between the great metropolises and the colonized world, especially the world of settler colonies.

> (2013: 18–19)

The perception of luxury in 'world capitals', like London, Paris and, later, New York and their respective nations, which have sufficiently assimilated the cultural identity and economic structures of the capital, remains untroubled by cultural hegemony, if not by economic realities. This is because the cultural ideology that supported the asymmetrical bonds linking metropole and periphery asserted a 'natural' relationship tying these imperial powers to luxurious production and circulation. For example, the dominant image of Paris as the unrivaled capital of fashion did not emerge *sui generis*, but was a concerted effort, since the seventeenth century, that united monarchy, government and later the media to support economic growth and political domination through the symbolic – or soft – power of the nation's luxury industries (see Rocamora 2009). Louis XIV's finance minister, Jean-Baptiste Colbert, recognized the value of a strong fashion industry as a colonizing force and source of economic dominance when he famously (although perhaps apocryphally) declared 'Fashion is to France what the gold mines of Peru are to Spain'. What is certain is that, at the time, the French government initiated protectionist legislation to favour national production and wider consumption of luxury textiles, like Lyon silk and Alençon lace (see Steele 2017), which became the very materials of luxurious self-presentation throughout Europe.

In the twenty-first century, this imperial and colonial hegemony is sustained by neoliberal deregulation and hypercapitalist ideologies that create neocolonial conditions of production and circulation. McNeil and Riello assert that the 'capitalism of luxury has created its own world – linked to finance and global enterprise – and is fast reshaping our spatial world, that of our districts, our streets, our desires, our ambitions, and our material culture' (2016: 254). Luxury is transforming cities, from Vancouver and Toronto to New York and Los Angeles, to London, Paris and

Milan, so that there is no longer much difference in the shops that line Toronto's 'Mink Mile' and those on Paris's rue du faubourg Saint Honoré or Milan's Via Montenapoleone. Moreover, in an ironic reenactment of historical Eurocentrism, the imperialism of luxury obscures the offshore production locales of many western luxury fashions so that only the mystified fashion capital appears on the label. This volume's other co-editor Jessica P. Clark highlights earlier enactments of this 'whitewashing' in her reconsideration of Canada's fur trade, nineteenth-century wilderness tourism as well as the later deskilling of Jewish immigrant workers in the early twentieth century. Clark's chapter argues that when the racist and imperialist lens is removed, it becomes clear that marginalized people, including Indigenous women and, later, Jewish garment workers, were central to the production of Canadian luxury in ways that were erased in Euro- and Anglo-centric historical accounts. Clark's recentring of the history of Canadian luxury production demonstrates that it is essential to uncover the imperialist, settler-colonial and Anglo-centric underpinnings of society, lest one reinforce a reception and perception of luxury that buttress its commercial meanings as well as the perceived natural dominance of elite settler cultural and commercial production.

The mythology of 'Made in ...' still emits a luxurious aura for commodities that probably only have the most derisory and final aspects of their products completed in the fashion capital or that are, in fact, produced in abject conditions by undocumented foreign nationals or effectively deskilled immigrants (cf. Thomas 2007; de Bussierre 2018). In Canada, 'Made in-[insert former metropole here]' overshadows the surplus value that can be invested in the Canadian-made or in Indigenous making. Using the example of the gift, philosopher Dimitri Mortelmans reminds us, in the wake of French sociologist Marcel Mauss, that objects can be invested with symbolic value. 'As a gift, an object loses its functional or monetary character while being invested with symbolic meaning' (2005: 509), he explains. A given object or commodity can be invested with a value that will supersede use and exchange value and will carry more weight than its instrumental social function. Kucheran's discussion in this volume also underscores the deeper political investments possible in some Indigenous designers' works. He points to the important wider messages of environmental protection, food sovereignty and land reclamation that emanated from the runway at Indigenous Fashion Week Toronto in 2019. Kucheran asserts that this investment is not only politically symbolic but also materially real, precisely because of the idea of interconnectedness that characterizes Indigenous cultures. However, investment in the luxury object does not only involve the maker. Lamontagne also emphasizes how engagement with open-source design and technology is at the heart of wearables and breaks down the traditional barrier separating producer from consumer. Fashion-tech consumers, in fact, become makers and thereby personally invest in the garments through their own curiosity, interest and labour. Similarly, Indigenous making is a collective process, one that counters the western myth of the singular romantic genius, an archetype that has common currency in the fashion world, where the genius of the creative director often (but not always) overshadows the important collaborative work of the *petites mains* or the design team. To consider Indigenous making as luxurious is to rethink notions of the *griffe* (i.e. brand or label) as Pierre Bourdieu and Yvette Delsaut (1975) develop in their foundational analysis of the field of fashion, 'Le Couturier et sa griffe'. The hegemony of a founding designer, whose aesthetic and message are meant to dominate brand identity, is short-circuited because the client plays a role as important as the designer's. '"Clients" are more like collaborators engaging in mutually beneficial exchange', explains Kucheran. The fashion system's ontological question, signaled by Bourdieu and Delsaut (using the example of Chanel), is how does one make Chanel – the symbolic object, designated as a rarity by the signature – without Chanel – the biological individual whose sole responsibility is to sign 'Chanel' to Chanel products (1975: 20, translation added).[1] This, by contrast, is a question for neither the fashion-tech community nor Indigenous making. Both not only involve a community of makers but also actively involve the 'customer'. In this light, both fashion-tech and Indigenous making permit a rethinking of luxury; the maker and the consumer are equally active in the creative process, and both participants communally invest the made object with idiosyncratic value.

Luxury as community capital

The reconfigured relationship between makers and recipients highlighted in this volume counters traditional conceptions of luxury that place the consumer in a secondary role, particularly through the lens of luxury brand management. Luxury, since undergoing the philosophical process of demoralization in the eighteenth century, is defined as being autonomous yet impacted by the various contexts in which it is expressed.[2] This perspective is apparent in Armitage's most recent study, *Luxury and Visual Culture*. For Armitage, 'luxury constitutes a specific realm – the abundant – with its own logic. But, while luxury does constitute a specific realm, it is nevertheless connected to other realms, to the realm of fashion and art, photography, cinema, television, and social media' (2020: 1). In contemporary culture, luxury has become the tool with which individuals operate socially and assert themselves individually because 'luxury' is no longer the province of a hereditary caste and at the same time has been isolated from any deontological concerns because it is merely a quantifiable state: 'the abundant'. In this light, Berry's (2016) addendum to his original 1994 study is particularly pertinent. Entitled

'Luxury: A dialectic of desire?', Berry's intervention revisits the demoralization debate in order to determine whether luxury is currently, in fact, undergoing a re-moralization. Berry analyses the cogency of contemporary arguments that seek to limit the increasing dominance of luxury as a mode of existence. In the sociological perspective, he highlights the argument of consumer alienation from the Left and, from the Right, the argument of luxury's reduced meaning through the increased presence of so-called luxury commodities. Both schools see the rise of the 'citizen-shopper' as the death knell of a properly functioning society, as the structures that luxury elicits, for these opposing ideological perspectives, are 'ephemeral, inher-ently unstable and transient' (2016: 58–59). Berry then looks to the environmental arguments that construe luxury and its consumption as essentially destructive and wasteful at a time when the health of the planet requires truly sustainable modes of existence. He concludes that, while the environmental perspective may with time carry more weight as scientific data come to the aid of philosophical arguments, luxury will remain an essential part of human existence. 'On a more mundane, but, I think, conceptually more fundamental level, it also seems eminently reason-able to believe that the desire for fresh over stale bread, for "refinement" in my sense, will persist' (2016: 62–63). Ontologically for Berry, luxury is 'refinement', in line with Enlightenment philosopher David Hume's determination. As refined objects and experiences, luxury is an available ontology for all goods, services or experiences and not an exclusive category reserved for objects with specific qual-ities. This conclusion supports Berry's initial determination in *The Idea of Luxury* that luxury 'is dynamic; it is subject to development as the desires, and necessarily attendant beliefs, are met and then fueled with further qualitative modifications or refinements' (2016: 18). As opposed to Armitage's (2020) conception of lux-urious abundance, Berry attaches luxury to its *qualitative* state. Refinement is not definitive, as technology and innovation can elicit further refinements rendering earlier iterations obsolete, but it remains essential to the refined object or experi-ence and not contingent on external perception. In this way, both quantitative (abundance) and qualitative (refinement) luxury are fundamentally limitless and essentially dangerous in a world of finite resources.

When applied to luxury goods, services and experiences in the contemporary luxury brandscape, refinement has been conflated with the desire for *personal* accumulation. Analysing the complexities of consumer behaviour in the age of branded luxury in 'Le Luxe au temps des marques', luxury marketing specialist Élyette Roux (2009) notes that the shift to the excessive consumption of luxury brands from the 1980s signaled an evolution in consumer thinking that began to focus on the pleasures of ownership, of expression of individuality, of con-suming superfluous commodities and of expressing status. Luxury brand specialists Michel Chevalier and Gérald Mazzalovo determine that the growing importance of luxury consumption in the public sphere is linked (unsurprisingly) to the contemporary predominance of brand identity. They conclude that 'luxury purchasers want: To be individuals [...] To mix styles [...] To be "winners" [...] To be distinctive' (2008: 172–73). The perspective of luxury marketing and brand specialists betrays the neoliberal wish fulfilment of the hypercapitalist moment whereby the luxury status of the brand comes to stand in for the essence of the consumer. 'It is no longer the product that is rare and expensive: It is the *individual*' (2008: 173, emphasis added), conclude Chevalier and Mazzalovo. Perhaps more critically, McNeil and Riello determine a relationship of inverse polarity between luxury and consumer. It is '[a]dvertising [that] tells us that we are unique, that we need to be distinctive and that luxury is the capacity to reward ourselves with something a bit pricey but not unreachable' (2016: 229). With the devolution of luxury to the status of metonymy for *personal* surplus value, *refinement* as an idea is no longer the end, but the means, so that 'luxurious refinement' is not a quality found in the good, service or experience, but is now an expression of brand identity. In *Brands: The Logos of the Global Economy*, Celia Lury unpacks the social role of the brand in contemporary society. Lury proposes that brand identity 'is both a means of establishing the relativity or the abstract equivalence of products in space and time and it is a medium of relationality, able to support differentiation of both objects and subjects, products and consumers' (2004: 8). While Lury does not challenge brand hegemony, she highlights the role of corporate identity in social differentiation. However, refinement, which was contained in the luxury itself, has spilled out to become a social function, a 'medium of relationality'. Berry points out the problem when refinement becomes a tool for social measurement.

> Once luxury is 'de-moralised' then with the rise of mass consumption it was easily pressed into service as a guileless description to make goods 'desirable'. And once seen in this light, its salience within the lexicon of 'adspeak' can be understood.
>
> (2016: 53)

Contemporary luxury in the brandscape with its imperialist and globalized reach has co-opted meaning-making and relationality, which was the domain of the individual. Luxury is now afforded an identity and an identity-making function that was formerly the domain of humans and human relationships.

The Canadian context, while definitely not untouched by luxury's imperialism given its colonial history and neocolonial legacy, provides the opportunity to challenge this shift in refinement from an ontological essence to an instrumental quality. This entails embracing the conscious experience of engaging with goods, services or experiences as a personal act stemming from *personal* motivations that supersede *socially* instrumental reasons or brand positioning. It is the idea of *community*, as opposed to the social, that is the surplus value that makes Canadian luxury luxurious. A number of case studies in this volume demonstrate ways that luxury has been – or could be – harnessed for its communal values. Polyck-O'Neill points to the potential for public artworks, as a mode of public luxury, to represent place-specific histories often overlooked by the institutions that govern social life. Kucheran highlights the collaborative engagement required in different modes of Indigenous making. Lezama's and Lamontagne's case studies demonstrate the potential for community building on the part of the consumer, while O'Mahony points to the collaboration of both 'hand and machine' and makers and tech specialists that can bring a new vitality to luxury. Accordingly, because of the specificities of history and culture in the Canadian context, luxury circulation has the potential to operate differently than in other modern liberal states, for which 'having is constructed as an essential prerequisite of proper human being' (cf. Butler and Athanasiou 2013: 13). Some scholars have considered it of the utmost importance to foreground this liberal ideology underpinning modern subjectivity to mitigate the tendency of

> cultural studies and social history [...] to celebrate the liberating possibilities offered to individuals by consumption, but at the same time minimize the political economy of consumption and downplay the social costs that consumption has on many members of modern consumer societies.
>
> (Belisle 2003: 193)

However, by using luxury – the idea as much as the thing – heuristically, CCLS proposes that the human relationship to luxuriousness is both affirming and reifying. Luxury neither only liberates nor alienates. As both a personal experience and a sociocultural instrument, luxury sits at the intersection of political economy and cultural politics. What is considered luxury and how and by whom it is amassed, consumed, displayed or hidden depends on how the political superstructure situates the idea of luxury. Nevertheless, as this volume confirms, luxury is equally the outcome of personal engagement; individuals and groups determine value in goods, services and experiences, and are either enriched or impoverished in the experience of luxury. Furthermore, historical and asymmetrical power relations that controlled the direction of the flow of 'raw' materials and 'refined' goods as well as govern(ed) the positioning of metropole and colony, colonizer and colonized, settler and Indigenous occupant, scholar and epistemological subject also contribute to how luxury behaves both in the centre and in the periphery. CCLS is sensitive to these overarching structures that impact what is luxury and how it is experienced.

Instead of entrenching hierarchies, luxury in the Canadian context has the potential to short-circuit them. While Armitage and Roberts assert that 'it is the elites rather than the masses who offer us the most pervasive interpretations and accepted meanings of luxury' (2017: 29), Canadian luxury, when read through the lens of colonial history, problematizes these elite readings. The case studies in this volume demonstrate the ways that rural and working-class consumers, marginalized groups, diverse publics and institutions in secondary and peripheral markets have manipulated signs of luxuriousness to either positive or negative effect. The key factor in the affirming or alienating outcome is the creation of a luxury that is specific to the historical and cultural context in which it circulates. Canadian luxury, in this light, is not cultural capital in its hierarchical function, but rather a form of *community capital* (to play with Bourdieu's taxonomy) that comes out of shared values deeply related to place and common history. Kucheran crystalizes this functioning of luxury in the Canadian context when he explains the centrality of *care* in decolonizing research. Indigenous methodologies enact 'an ethics of care that is affirmed through life-long relations'. The originality of the case studies that compose *Canadian Critical Luxury Studies: Decentring Luxury* is twofold: first, the conviction that luxury circulates at all levels of society with the *potential* to enrich the lives of those who make and consume it, and, second, the focus on the impact of luxury that considers the presence or absence of a relationality that recalls or abjures Canada's colonial and social history, as central to the success or failure of luxury's surplus value to build ties linking diverse individuals and institutions.

Canadian critical luxury studies

This volume arose out of fruitful discussions held during the first Canadian conference in critical luxury studies, held in Toronto in May 2017. Among the Canadian participants, it became clear that addressing luxury epistemologically and materially from a Canadian perspective was a necessary conversation to cast light on luxury's colonial and imperialist history and its impact on secondary geographies. A number of interventions at the conference also highlighted the innovative and unique ways that luxury has been used, embodied and produced in Canada. The volume is organized into three sections, organized around the three aforementioned discursive orbits: colonial and neocolonial systems of capital; luxury's potential for failure in colonial and postcolonial sites; and futures of luxury in formerly colonized, 'peripheral' locales, including Canada. The first section presents a discussion with Riley Kucheran and case studies by Jessica P. Clark and Nigel Lezama. The opening section highlights the ontologically and socially enriching experience of

luxury for makers and consumers when cultural specificities short-circuit the alienating potential of luxury. This section also recentres the role of historically marginalized groups in Canadian luxury production and circulation by casting light on
the erasures that settler-colonial ideology and historical practices imposed to protect white Anglo privilege. The second section groups together studies by Kathryn
Franklin and Rebecca Halliday, and by Julia Polyck-O'Neill that shed light on the
failures of luxury to add value to the lives of luxury producers and 'consumers'
because of luxury's colonialist and imperialist modes of circulation. The final section
looks to Canadian luxury's future potential with analyses by Marie O'Mahony and
Valérie Lamontagne that focus on the technologies of luxury that lead the way to
the future growth of Canadian luxury at the cutting edge.

Kucheran's focus on Indigenous cultural resurgence challenges hegemonic perceptions of the exclusive circulation of capital in settler-colonial and Eurocentric
production systems. His discussion sheds new light on how Indigenous making
recentres both making and consumption and disengages the myth of the idealized creator-genius that typifies the cultural production of western modernity.
Kucheran explains how creation is elaborated through the shared knowledge and
skills of a community, emphasizing the many hands that come together to create
the luxurious object. Importantly, this intervention offers pathways to decolonizing western systems of scholarship as much as the fashion system. Clark revises
historical characterizations of the Canadian fur trade to recentre the specialized
skills of Canada's Indigenous peoples that were, in fact, of paramount importance
for the global luxury trade in the seventeenth and eighteenth centuries. Uncovering
Eurocentric hegemonic value systems that have overwritten local realities, Clark's
analysis also sheds light on the experiential luxury of nineteenth-century Canadian
wilderness tourism. The final prong in Clark's rethinking of Canadian histories
of luxury is to lay bare the Anglo-centric hegemony faced by Jewish immigrants,
highly skilled garment workers, who in the early twentieth century integrated and
introduced new skills to the Canadian fur-manufacturing industry in response to
the ethnocentrism they faced in other fine-garment sectors. Lezama's case study
of the Canadian department store the T. Eaton Company's 'Made-in-Canada'
campaign of the 1920s brings a fresh perspective to the ways that ordinary commodities can be invested with a value beyond expense or social distinction.
The Made-in-Canada movement was a wide-ranging privileging of Canadian
manufacturing that emerged out of the contentious policy of free trade versus protectionist tariffs in the first decade of the twentieth century. The movement was
subsequently adopted by elite cultural producers seeking the means to organize and
fortify Canada's cultural identity against a growing mass and commercial culture.
Lezama elucidates how Eaton's use of the Made-in-Canada discourse operated
in between these two extremes to imbue civic value into consumption, thereby

creating the refinement necessary to transform ordinary domestically produced commodities into bona fide luxuries. This section highlights alternate pathways for the creation of national luxuries that challenge perceptions of colonial, imperialist and class-based exceptionality.

The following section starts with an analysis by Franklin and Halliday of the historical and cultural context in which Toronto Fashion Week operated from its inception in 1999. In dominant markets, fashion weeks are an imperialist concentration of capital that circulates in a closed, yet totalizing system. Franklin and Halliday's case study examines the foundering of the Canadian fashion event from the perspective of glamour and luxury's failure to materialize the specificity of a smaller and culturally specific fashion market. Polyck-O'Neill's focus on Douglas Coupland's *Digital Orca* (2009) and Ken Lum's *Monument for East Vancouver* (2010) shifts the analysis to public artworks but maintains the focus on how the introduction of luxury into public space risks homogenizing marginalized histories and erasing disenfranchised communities. Polyck-O'Neill further complicates the correspondence of public artworks with public luxuries by foregrounding the political and economic dynamics that underpin art commissions. The case studies in this section highlight luxury's complex impact on Canadian urban spaces and Indigenous and immigrant people when Eurocentric and settler-colonial systems are superimposed on local lived practices.

The final section looks forward to the value creation for a Canadian context that embraces technological innovation in the making of modern luxuries. O'Mahony's intervention shares global trends that extend traditional definitions of luxury through digital innovations in design and production as well as technological evolutions for the front of house. O'Mahony suggests that if Canadian luxury is to maintain a surplus value that is immanent in the commodities as well as enriching for luxury producers and purveyors, the Canadian luxury industries will have to embrace the digital age. In the closing chapter of this volume, Lamontagne highlights the digital evolution of fashion wearables that enriches human experience. The four case studies of this intervention highlight Lamontagne's neologism 'fashion-tech' as an expression of the most contemporary embodiment of luxury as necessarily multimodal, essentially collaborative and phenomenologically centred on the human experience of being-in-the-world. The case studies introduce laboratory ateliers operating in Europe and in Québec and their projects. Importantly, however, Lamontagne foregrounds two aspects that make the fashion-tech field one of the most contemporary expression of CCLS. First, the field itself is founded on the values of collaboration and community-building, and, second, wearables' surplus value is intricately tied to human experience in that they 'offer new experiences for the body, as well as new relationships to fashion and technology', Lamontagne concludes.

The critical study of luxury is not a mystification of the power of consumption as a mode of self-actualization, but rather an investigation of how some choose to add value to their lived experience. Further still, the studies in this field consider the impact of luxury on culture and its expressions. *Canadian Critical Luxury Studies: Decentring Luxury* pushes the field further in particularly significant ways. Case studies in this volume have, at their core, the project of decolonization and the upending of accepted hierarchies based in imperialist, colonial, Eurocentric and capitalist hegemonies. Luxury is a complex phenomenon that, as this introduction has foregrounded, is neither entirely beneficial nor wholly detrimental to the persons or societies that seek it out. Importantly though, the studies that make up this book have highlighted that it is precisely *because* of the Canadian context – with its settler-colonial history; later, the Anglo-centric and imperialist slant informing cultural and capitalist activity; and more recently the country's secondary status on the world stage as a cultural producer – that luxury holds surprising and uplifting potential that merits deeper consideration. The study of Indigenous and immigrant luxury-making highlights an alternate history of agency for those who were erased from historical narratives and sidelined by political structures. By studying the successes and failures of luxury in a Canadian setting, CCLS is working to make relevant this new field for a wider swathe of people and contexts whose relationship to luxuriousness is complicated by histories of political and economic domination. This volume is an opening-up of the definition of luxury to which the editors and contributors invite scholars from a diversity of fields as well as luxury makers and specialists and those living and working adjacent to luxury to contribute. As this volume makes clear, Canadian luxury is community.

NOTES

1. 'Comment faire du Chanel – objet symbolique, marqué du signe de la rareté par la signature – sans Chanel – individu biologique, seul habilité à signer Chanel les produits Chanel.'

2. Berry (1994) outlines in excellent detail the process of 'demoralisation'. This economically modern and capitalist perspective that luxury shifted from a sign of individual weakness and social effeminacy to an engine for domestic productivity and a symbol of national strength is taken up by a majority of luxury thinkers since Berry's foundational study. Berg and Eger (2002) chart this shift in their contribution to their edited collection. Philosopher Gilles Lipovetsky (2003) analyses the movement from demoralization to habitus-freed hyperconsumption in his study 'La Société d'hyperconsommation'. Jeremy Jennings (2007) sheds light on the debates surrounding luxury's shift during the Enlightenment and its wake in 'The debate about luxury in eighteenth- and nineteenth-century French political

thought'. In CLS, luxury's demoralization is taken as the modern foundation of luxurious production and practices. In the introduction to their volume *Critical Luxury Studies: Art, Design, Media*, Armitage and Roberts assert that the project of CLS 'is necessarily concerned with morality, and the material and immaterial struggle to find and perhaps defend the meaning of the limitless' (2016b: 4–5).

PART 1

RESURGENCE AND REVISION

Conceptions of national production and consumption of luxury are underpinned with ideological positionings and a long history of cultural and economic domination. Often, nation states with widely valued luxury systems have an imperialist past to thank for an economically dominant present, or these states are imbued with a mystified history of making that links culture to mastery. Epistemologically, luxury's value is bound to a vertical system that privileges western modes of circulation. The interventions of Part 1 challenge this established perception of luxury by highlighting alternate value systems and revealing the Anglo- and Eurocentric biases at play in historical constructs of luxury as well as in contemporary histories of luxury. This section decentres hegemonic luxury in order to foreground a luxury that eschews industrial modes of production as well as one that emerges from sites and individuals not normally categorized as luxurious.

This section provides foundational understandings of luxury and economic growth in Canada. In Chapter 1, a discussion with Riley Kucheran highlights how Indigenous peoples in Canada have longstanding practices of production that are, by definition, luxurious. Further, this chapter proposes that western luxury – and western society on the whole – has much to gain by acknowledging and integrating Indigenous methodologies into established industrial practices, which, in turn, can transform consumer behaviour on a larger scale. In this way, Kucheran re-examines luxury from the perspective of decolonization to resituate production and consumption narratives of so-called secondary markets to the centre of an autonomous luxury economic system. In Chapter 2, Jessica P. Clark investigates the development of the luxury trades from the colonial seventeenth to the twentieth centuries. The chapter critically examines histories of Canadian luxury to propose a new approach that moves away from a colonial perspective of dependence upon imperial needs towards the development of a modern, diverse and inclusive luxury economy. In this chapter, Clark uncovers the hegemonic perspectives that have characterized Indigenous and immigrant activity as subordinate to colonial and settler-colonial understandings and constructions of what is luxury. Chapter 3, by Nigel Lezama, is a case study that focuses on Canada's premier but now defunct department store, the T. Eaton Company, and a curious shift in discourse in the 1920s, when the company began advertising Eaton's merchandise as Canadian-made versus the tried and true French- and British-made fine goods or the exotic merchandise from the East that regularly featured in their catalogues. The chapter subsequently sheds light on a new direction and value accorded to Canadian production and consumption at a time when the country and its political and cultural elite were attempting to foster Canadian economic and cultural sovereignty.

Canadian luxury and its study offer a fundamental shift from conventional thinking around luxury. In secondary sites of cultural influence, luxury circulation is a double-edged practice; its foreignness can express elite aspirations, but it also materializes the lack of value afforded to home-grown production. By placing Canadian practices at the centre of the epistemological project of Canadian critical luxury studies, the case studies in the first part of this volume highlight the idiosyncratic possibilities for luxury systems of production and personal investment. Extracted from Euro- and American-centric models, luxury has the potential to be differently characterized, determined as an act of fundamental generosity and having an impact that privileges the many over the few. The case studies in this first part of the volume demonstrate that luxury can have a positive impact for those who make, work, consume and receive objects and experiences that are imbued with luxury's added value.

1

Luxury and Indigenous Resurgence

Riley Kucheran with Jessica P. Clark and Nigel Lezama

Front matter

RILEY: Boozhoo ('hello')! This chapter reflects a series of conversations, engagements and mobilizations of Indigenous luxury, a new concept that has
been percolating within a growing Indigenous fashion movement in
Canada, Turtle Island and beyond. The conversational format of the
chapter reflects the movement of this idea. The dialogue between myself
and Jess and Nigel, friends and colleagues who have helped shape my
own engagement with luxury, represents a certain moment in time, a
blink in the movement. The format also models the relational aspect of
Indigenous knowledge production. In the initial writing of this chapter
I struggled with the scholarly inclination to capture in writing Indigenous
knowledge and culture that is 'dynamic – ever flowing, adaptable, and
fluid' (Absolon and Willett 2005: 111). The dialogue helped to locate
the ideas as created within the context of a community, in the hope that
this chapter honours those relations.

　　　Throughout the discussion I use the term 'western' to differentiate
luxury produced, distributed and consumed through the capitalist, institutionalized and globalized fashion system. When I refer to 'luxury', I am
invoking a mainstream or dominant luxury that is historically owned and
controlled by a small group of wealthy corporate or private firms and

This chapter is an Open Access publication distributed under the CC BY-NC-ND - Creative
Commons Attribution-NonCommercial-NoDerivs License. You are allowed to download
and share it with others as long as credit is given. You can not change it in any way or use it
commercially.

the study of this luxury within western academic scholarship – a philosophy of luxury in the humanist tradition, the emerging field of critical luxury studies and business management literature about the strategic use of luxury within the above system. The use of western is not without controversy: some have decried it as an essentialist oversimplification that's then mobilized to either uphold western ideals or critique imperialism (Appiah 2016). I agree that there cannot be *one* western history or identity, but in Indigenous scholarship, western is meant to differentiate *Indigenous* peoples and knowledge (Kovach 2009: 21). Western generalizes historical and ongoing systems of colonialism 'through the dynamics of opposition and resistance' and, with a 'utopian critical distance', allows us to imagine alternative futures (Tennant 1994: 10–11). In this discussion I also use 'Indigenous makers' since categories like artist and designer do not fit neatly with Indigenous forms of cultural production. Finally, I say *chi-miigwetch* ('thank you') to Jess and Nigel for initiating this discussion and for their enthusiasm in supporting Indigenous scholarship.

Situating ourselves

JESS: In initial discussions, Riley, you introduced us to the practice of locating ourselves, which is an essential means of making 'research more Indigenous and counter-colonial' (Absolon and Willett 2005: 97–8, 106–8). Why don't we begin by reflecting on location, including our relationship to our research and each other?

RILEY: Yes! The practice of locating ourselves was one of my first introductions to Indigenous research methodologies, and I return to it often. For Indigenous peoples, identifying our communal locations at the outset of any interaction is a form of accountability to our relations. Claiming a community (or having a community claim *you*) is a way of checking in. It establishes trust by addressing a natural suspicion of outsiders that Indigenous peoples use to protect ourselves and our communities. Stating that my maternal lineage is from the Desmoulins family and Bear clan of Biigtigong Nishnaabeg is therefore a form of care, but more context is needed. Locating ourselves identifies where our voice comes from and also who we do *not* speak for. I have opinions about Indigenous fashion and luxury, informed by my unique upbringing, but I don't speak for my Ojibway community, or the Anishinaabe nation, or Indigenous peoples in general. As Indigenous writer Thomas King noted, being Indigenous does not impart a 'tribal understanding of the universe' (King 1990: x). Indigenous people are expected to have the answers to any questions about our culture and history. It's assumed that we're deeply connected to the natural and spiritual worlds, bestowed with ancestral teachings, as if the deliberate attacks during more than four hundred years of colonization had no effect. The truth is I don't speak my language or know my cultural teachings. An intergenerational trauma runs through my family, triggered by European disease and assimilationist projects enacted by the Canadian state with the Residential School System, which prevented us from learning about ourselves. I grew up off-reserve, first in violently racist settler-communities where I denied my Indigeneity and then in the urban centre of Toronto. This means I'm in the bizarre position of being a cultural newcomer in my own community. It was during my graduate studies in the midst of Canada's Truth and Reconciliation Commission that I started researching and reflecting on my own Indigenous heritage. Anishinaabe thought leader Leanne Simpson (2011) introduced me to the concept of *biskaabiiyang*, or looking back, a kind of personal decolonization. I moved past the guilt and shame I associated with my Indigenous past and began focusing on the Indigenous future I was meant to have. I started imagining how my research about fashion and luxury could contribute to reconciliation or support the communities I was reconnecting with.

My location also explains how I enter into discussions of luxury and how we've come to work together. I wouldn't call myself a *consumer* of luxury. I had a middle-class upbringing that included aspirations towards standard notions of luxury – I read *Vogue* and *GQ* and was impressed by the mansions and decor on MTV's 'Cribs' – but we could never afford luxury. While studying the humanities, I worked in fashion retail, first at fast-fashion companies and then for higher-end brands. I was able to climb the corporate ladder, but to advance any further, I was told to pursue an MBA, preferably in a program with a focus on luxury. With hindsight I see the problems in this hierarchy of fashion luxury, and I see how luxury misuses Indigenous culture in ways that continue to entrench colonial structures. I was enamoured with the glamour of luxury while deeply embedded in a fashion system that's destroying the planet. I remember reading Dana Thomas's (2007) *How Luxury Lost Its Luster* and deciding I would investigate luxury for my graduate research. In a pivotal moment I left the fashion industry and began to critique it – inspired by Marxism, decolonization and the emerging field of critical luxury studies, where we met. I've come to know luxury scholarship in a very critical way because of you two, but my work is still informed by my time in the industry. My location also includes my two-spiritedness. I consider myself an *Anishinaabe-Agokwe* with the ability and responsibility to mediate relations and translate bodies of knowledge. I've always strived to combine the potentials of luxury management research, like the work of Kapferer and Bastien ([2009] 2012) in *The Luxury Strategy*, with the work of critical humanities scholars, and now I'm reconciling those two western lines of thought with Indigenous perspectives. This has been called two-eyed seeing by Mi'kmaq Elder Albert Marshall – the combination of western and Indigenous knowledges (Bartlett et al. 2012: 331), and I believe this type of hybrid looking could provide us with innovative strategies for a reconciliation in the field of luxury. So I guess I'm curious: what brings each of *you* to luxury and why?

NIGEL: Thanks, Riley, for launching our discussion with such an in-depth act of locating yourself as an individual and as a researcher. I am very interested to hear more about how you envision luxury theory and practice as a means of reconciliation in the Canadian context. But, first, I see how locating yourself is a way of maintaining a kind of ethical proximity to what we do and why we do it – as opposed to maintaining a (fictional) epistemological distance. I am, through training, a literary historian specializing in nineteenth-century French literature. I have always had a longstanding love affair with French culture, in part for its seeming authority in all things luxurious. As a teenager, I loved the idea of French high fashion, from Lagerfeld's Chanel to Lacroix and Gaultier. I was fascinated by this luxurious world that I saw as completely different from the 'ordinary life' I felt I was living. As an undergraduate, I was introduced to the poet Charles Baudelaire, whose work seemed to move from the lofty to the lowly but maintained the same refined aesthetic and gaze whether he was writing about fashionable cafés or sordid bars. Working on Baudelaire allowed me to think about an impoverished luxury – or a luxury of the impoverished – that helped me to understand luxury in a more complex way.

I'm a first-generation immigrant to Canada. I was born in Trinidad. My family moved from the working classes to the professional middle class. Our immigration was one of class aspiration. I think this history impacts my positioning as a researcher, in that I see class identity and aspiration as the engine of history. In the context of consumer culture, I think living in economic scarcity and with consumer longing is a very productive place – as a kid, I had to create my own luxurious state of being without the economic resources I imagined others had access to. Reading Baudelaire and studying the Bohème and, later, the Decadents,

I understood that this type of need can inspire great creativity. It's the same type of creativity that I later gleaned in hip hop culture. Luxury is a perception and a personal form of valuation. In our hypercapitalist and neoliberal era, certain groups seem to be detached from economic concerns, which gives them a seeming authority to determine luxury, fashion and culture. But figures like Baudelaire's dandy and the courtesan or, later, individuals like the ballroom queen, urban economically marginalized African-American women or even a middle-class gay Brown kid in Toronto create luxury through their gaze, through personal investment, through choice.

My current work in critical luxury studies focuses on ways that racialized or otherwise marginalized people, and groups use and – important for me – *misuse* or *play* with luxury, whether it's fashion, objects, speech acts or writing. These 'outsiders' to mainstream culture create luxurious selves and at the same time undermine the authority of dominant classes, groups and institutions to determine what is deemed luxurious and what is not. I guess luxury is a very personal state of being to me, one that can entail a consumer act, but I don't believe that luxury is prescribed, universal, timeless, necessarily rarefied or expensive.

JESS: I completely agree, Nigel. My approach to luxury studies is deeply rooted in the labour that undergirds it, which also undercuts any notion of luxury's timelessness or exclusivity. This doesn't necessarily reflect my personal relationship to luxury, though. I didn't think about it much growing up in a suburb of Toronto in a white, middle-class, settler family of Anglo descent. My mother is from the south of England and my father was from Newfoundland. Throughout my youth and much of my education, I didn't often reflect on luxury, just as I didn't reflect on my privilege. My move to the States to study at a private research university changed the latter. Cultural differences between the US and Canadian systems made me more conscious of power imbalances based on class, gender and race. I soon understood that there was no less inequity in the Canadian academy; it just manifested in different ways. It prompted me to more actively explore my privilege and subjective relationship to my research, which I interrogated via feminist frameworks and methodologies. I've continued on this path in the past ten years, learning from scholars, community members and my peers. There are still many things I don't know, and the more I learn, the humbler and more unknowing I feel. My main priority is to listen, acknowledging my subject position and privilege in the western academy while identifying and challenging its historical underpinnings.

I try to incorporate this awareness into my research. Since my undergraduate days, I've almost always researched historical subjects who were working- and middle-class white women of Anglo descent operating in nineteenth-century Britain. This reflected my family background and who I felt comfortable studying, despite its limitations. Now, I try to write histories of people who led, according to some, 'ordinary' lives but were in fact crucial to broader socio-cultural and economic developments. This is the roundabout way by which I came to critical luxury studies. I was writing histories of businesspeople and working-class labourers in a particular luxury industry in nineteenth-century London, starting from the 'bottom' up, if you will. This background means that my interest in luxury always comes from a desire to seek out the backstage conditions – and inequities – that underpin its creation. Structural inequities continue to define not only what is and isn't designated as luxury but also consumers' relationship to it. They also remain at the heart of many forms of luxury production, even in the case of the most sumptuous goods and services.

What is Indigenous luxury?

JESS: There have been a number of attempts to define 'luxury' as an idea, practice and experience. Could you tell us how you define luxury, particularly in relationship to your work on Indigenous luxury?

RILEY: I think 'attempts' is an apt word as I've struggled with this question for a while now. Defining luxury is notoriously difficult because it's subjective and dependent on social and historical contexts (Armitage and Roberts 2016b: 2), and defining a specifically *Indigenous* luxury is difficult because doing so requires a collaborative and ongoing process – it's being defined for itself right now by Indigenous peoples all over the world. I also hesitate because I'm not yet convinced that defining an Indigenous luxury is possible, or even appropriate. It feels like dangerous territory – using a western concept so synonymous with inequality and injustice. But part of me is convinced we can mobilize the concept of luxury for our own decolonial aims. We're in the midst of what's been called an Indigenous renaissance of art, fashion, film, photography, music and literature (Elliott 2018), and there's now a growing movement of Indigenous makers who are actively creating elevated cultural products or experiences that I feel are suited to some notions of luxury. I don't believe luxury has to be elitist and exclusively tied to wealth, and I hold onto definitions of luxury that signal quality – fine crafts-manship, high functionality, superior materials and a sustainability or timelessness that can be passed on through generations. I can envision this Indigenous renaissance producing a luxury hybrid that has these conventional qualities combined with Indigenous ethics and values.

NIGEL: Totally! Indigenous making is a luxurious production. I remember one of your talks at NeMLA when you presented Angela Demontigny's atelier and spoke about her creative process (Kucheran 2019a). I was completely taken by her method of spending time with her clients to learn about them and their hopes and then investing the pieces she makes with the hopes of the client. If I remember, when she is beading a garment for someone, the work is not only highly skilled but also extremely tailored to the wearer in that beading is also a very spiritual and generous craft. I think that this type of collaborative making can also add new depth to the idea of luxury. There is something quite sym-bolic in this gesture – although I know in this context, it is a very real act. Angela's 'weaving into' the garment the future wearers' hopes reminds me of *Phantom Thread* (2017) and Woodcock's sewing a secret embroi-dered message into the hem of a wedding dress he was making. I think that P. T. Anderson, the filmmaker, uses this gesture to evoke a kind of poetic incantatory power in the luxury object. A luxurious garment can be empowering for the wearer. All of this is to say that, without falling into the fallacy of an Indigenous 'mystical understanding of the world' that you rightfully push back against, can we talk about the personal and the spiritual aspects of Indigenous making as part of what consti-tutes its luxuriousness?

RILEY: You've put this beautifully! I think that some of the practices of Euro-pean haute couture come closest to the personal depth that Indigenous luxury provides. I figure that tailors on Savile Row might also build a life-long relationship with a client. The notion that someone could preside over a lifetime of clothing with a devoted client is very special. You're also right that Indigenous making is luxurious, but its produc-tion is *spiritual* because making passes down teachings. Our culture is continuously made and remade in communal processes accompanied by stories embedded with instructions on how to live in a harmonious way. When Angela makes something for a client, she's embodying teach-ings about the responsibility we have for one another, she's ensuring she's in a good mindset to take care of her client; it's generous, but it's also just the Indigenous way. I owe much credit here: Angela is entirely responsible for my thinking about Indigenous luxury. In the time I spent working at her Hamilton, Ontario-based boutique, I learned so much about what it means to *be* Indigenous. Angela's Cree-Métis heritage is present in all of her operations. I remember the first time I walked into her boutique I felt like I had come *home*. In a strangely familiar way it felt like I had *returned* somewhere, and upon further reflection I likened the feeling to visiting my grandmother's home when I was a child. Present there and instantly brought back from memory was a sense of comfort and warmth created with familiar scents and sounds – hide, burning sage, fresh flowers and sweetgrass, the flickering of candles and the hum of music. I was transported and lovingly welcomed by Angela with an embrace that felt like kinship. I didn't know it at first, but it was a spiritual experience. Like any luxury brand on a Canadian 'mink mile', Angela provides exceptional customer service in a luxuriously appointed boutique, filled with beautiful made-to-measure designs. The intimate setting allows clients to view and be fitted for designs made with superior quality materials and craftsmanship, either privately or at trunk shows where Angela unpacks the latest collection with Champagne and her wardrobing expertise. These are standard features of luxury retail, epitomized by large luxury brands owned by global corporations, but Angela's boutique offered something different. The store I entered on that cold day in November 2015 is routinely smudged, for example. The cleansing smoke of Indigenous medicinal plants creates sacred space by clearing the air of negative energy, which brings clarity and openness to those present. Angela's intent is not to capitalize on these sacred gifts – clarity is not for the purpose of consumption – it's a strategy to create the conditions in which meaningful and reciprocal relationships can flourish. 'Clients' are more like *collaborators* engaging in mutually beneficial exchange, and the designer acts as a mediator with a supply chain that's rooted in community. At the end of the supply chain, the retail store itself draws on Indigenous values. I likened it to a gathering space, where community could meet and share stories, participate in a workshop or just socialize. Angela also sold products of other Indigenous makers, thus supporting those who couldn't otherwise afford a physical retail platform, again, embodying Indigenous values of sharing and taking care.

I may have entered Angela's boutique looking to make a purchase and meet the designer, but instead we bonded over our shared interests and goals and spoke for hours about the history of Indigenous design, the challenges of being Indigenous in the fashion industry, the pains of cultural appropriation and our dreams for better Indigenous futures. What normally would have been a simple commercial interaction became a life-long partnership. Undoubtedly, my feeling of home created by the smudge contributed to the realization of a shared path between Angela and myself. Instead of luxury goods, I found community and purpose, and I left that day dreaming about the future of Indigenous luxury.

Luxury and Indigenous resurgence

NIGEL: It seems to me that, for each of us, luxury is a mode that exists outside of the centre. But, am I right to say that for you, Riley, the question of what is luxury focuses somewhat less on the act of personal or group legitimization and engages with a broader political concern for restructuring how luxury is produced?

RILEY: I think it's interesting that we have all taken similar roundabout paths to studying luxury, from the periphery inwards, perhaps, and I'm excited that we share a similar politics around the inequities luxury produces. My work is definitely engaged with the political concerns around luxury production, but I also see some value in that 'legitimization'. You both mentioned that you don't give credence to the notion of a true or pure luxury – that timeless, rare and expensive commodity – but I can also see how that idea could benefit Indigenous makers. What if we valued pieces of beadwork or tanned hides like a luxury? At the inception of the *Luxury* journal, Elizabeth Wilson (2014) noted that most contemporary usage of luxury simply means expensive, and at a practical level I think this is how Indigenous makers are employing the term. Luxury *branding* is a method of elevating Indigenous cultural products in the minds of consumers.

NIGEL: I see your point that luxury brand strategies can be useful for highlighting the special qualities inherent in Indigenous making. I'm always a little nervous when Kapferer and Bastien are invoked. Their perspective, for me, is really problematic in reifying luxury as a status symbol.

RILEY: I absolutely want to disrupt the notion that the central tenets of luxury – superior quality, longevity and timelessness – are reserved for wealthy social classes, while most people wear mass-manufactured and disposable clothing. Let me state unequivocally that for Indigenous peoples, access to our cultural products is a right, not a luxury. I just also think that many of the qualities of Indigenous cultural products align with those luxury tenets. To create Indigenous products, makers typically draw on certain universal Indigenous cultural values like respect and responsibility. Indigenous fashion, for example, nurtures a better relationship to land and its relations through sustainable production practices. Indigenous modes of making are also inherently communal because the process involves reciprocity and requires participation of many different kinds of knowledge holders. The 'supply chain' of Indigenous fashion consists of Elders who share stories that provide direction to hunters, hide tanners, plant dye and medicine cultivators, weavers, sewers and the designers who coordinate the process. This means that more of the community participates and shares in an economy that regenerates culture. From a business perspective, then, could we not tap into the market that buys into reified luxury? I'm also thinking about recent work around notions of craft. Richard Sennett argued for a return of craftsmanship or 'the skill of making things well' (2008: 8), which is an ideal philosophy but hard to manage under capitalism, but Adamson noted that craft actually harmed artisans because once their skills were mechanized, craft became another tool of domination (2013: xvii). Jess, this is likely more your area of expertise, but there's something in me that's holding onto these ideal notions. I'm stuck thinking 'if only we could turn back time', to when the hand of the artisan was valued so that making could be a more viable career path for Indigenous youth. Is this utopian thinking? Am I delusional?

JESS: Not at all! Historically, there were 'ideal' moments when artisanal and craft labour was, as you note, socially and economically valued in more definitive ways. But sadly, I'm not convinced this could be disentangled from broader relationships of power. I'm thinking, for example, of eighteenth-century British luxury production. As Maxine Berg shows, this was a highpoint of innovation and invention (2005; Styles 2000). But in this case, artisans' work wasn't recognized for its material or production value alone; its significance lay in its *symbolic* value to the nation and Britain's reputation on the global stage. State and public support derived in large part from these national and colonial imperatives, rather than a 'pure' appreciation for the work itself. It's just one example, but I think it's telling of the ways that historical valuations of artisanal labour were rarely only about skill.

But that doesn't mean that these broader power relations can't be marshalled in productive ways, especially for contemporary creators like Indigenous makers. Before we get to that, though, can you describe how you see the current relationship between Indigenous cultures and mainstream fashion and luxury brands?

RILEY: I actually don't think there is a real relationship between mainstream brands and Indigenous culture. Every engagement has been surface level and unsustained. One of the things I wanted to establish at the outset of this interview was that there is no singular 'Indigenous' culture. It might seem obvious to academics, but harmful generalizations happen everywhere, including the luxury sector. The beautiful diversity of Indigenous cultures is constantly conflated as one homogenized stereotype. I'm thinking about shows like Chanel's *Métier d'Art* 2013 in Dallas, Texas – a literal mash-up of 'cowboys and Indians' complete with all-white Plains-style headdresses – or Dior *Sauvage*, the perfume 'inspired by wide-open spaces' that is 'wild and noble all at once'. The campaign stars Johnny Depp, who 'reconnects with his deeper nature' (Dior 2020). These tropes draw on centuries-old stereotypes about the savage Indian versus the virtuous white settlers or the shaman more connected to spiritual and natural realms. The myth of the 'dead Indian' is a static characterization of Indigenous people that persists in popular culture (King 2013: 53). It relies on the notion that upon contact, Indigenous peoples were either non-existent (terra nullius) or that they vanished upon 'conquest' and colonization. In the vacuum left by colonialist domination, Indigenous cultures have been defined by non-Indigenous people as sinful, backwards or non-existent. We are either positioned outside of modernity or swallowed up by it. If luxury/fashion is constitutive of modernity itself, then the luxury sector has a particular responsibility to correct modernity's injustices. Mignolo and Walsh have argued that coloniality constitutes modernity, and thus 'the ultimate decolonial horizon' is the end of modernity itself (2018: 4). While my politics point in this direction, decolonization is likely too lofty a goal for luxury. Brands abandoning stereotypes would be a big win, especially given that the purveyors of luxury have the power to dictate notions of taste. If we accept that the 'trickle-down' theory has real social and economic consequences, then luxury is largely to blame for cultural appropriation. The structure of the fashion industry gives luxury the power to decide what's 'in' fashion and thus what gets emulated by less-luxurious brands. There's a direct correlation between the high-fashion headdress at Chanel and the hipster headdress at Coachella.

NIGEL: Completely! There are campaigns and products that pass through the atelier, the marketing department, through merchandising of many of the European luxury brands, and I'm astounded that there's no one who 'hits pause' and asks, 'Is this appropriate?' I think that questions of cultural appropriation and insensitivity, inclusivity and representation are really not registering with fashion and luxury brands founded in the big fashion centres. Even when some brands tout their inclusivity on the runway – I'm thinking of the beautiful Valentino Spring–Summer 2019 couture show with over forty Black models – I can't help but wonder whether it's simply a form of racial capitalism (cf. Leong 2013) at play. Are brands merely including non-white bodies to build social capital through the appearance of racial equity? I wonder if it's effective to hold these companies to task at an ethical level, like the backlash in response to the Dior *Sauvage* campaign, or to count on governments to impose fines on brands like the New York City Commission on Human Rights did with Prada in February 2020. Maybe the only pressure that might work is if, as ethical consumers, we act more critically about where we put our dollars.

RILEY: I'm never surprised when one of these fiascos happens because it's indicative of the systemic problems within dominant forms of capitalist luxury/fashion. The speed of the industry today is largely to blame – brands are constantly looking to create their next collection without ample time for proper research or engagement with the communities that 'inspire' them. But there's also the lack of diversity within luxury organizations, an issue of equity in itself, and there's an inability to voice concern because of hierarchical structures that dictate organizational culture. Importantly, the system itself was originally designed this way – it's been predicated on theft. Voyages for luxurious rarities fuelled European mercantilism; colonialism relied on the fur trade. Searches for fashion inspiration in the 'exotic other' are all connected processes. It's a sweeping generalization, but there are real patterns here, and I believe a disturbing lack of education about the real issues at hand is ultimately why *Sauvage* passed by so many people. At a foundational level there's complete ignorance. In North America the histories we learned are completely ahistorical; they mask unspeakable atrocities and unrelenting forms of oppression that continue to perpetuate injustice. In Europe, where many luxury brands are headquartered, there's even less knowledge or engagement with colonial injustices. Cultural appropriation is the logical consequence of colonialism. It's 'offensive' because it painfully reminds Indigenous people of the dispossession, the dehumanization, the genocide they endured under colonial regimes of power.

Adrienne Keene is a member of the Cherokee Nation who's been writing about cultural appropriation for a decade now. She often begins the discussion by reminding us that for centuries Indigenous peoples were prohibited by law from practicing culture; that these policies have

38

devastating legacies that are not in the distant past but present in Indigenous communities today; and that Indigenous cultures only exist because of the hard-fought battles of previous generations (2016: 56). Luxury is ignorant of this history and complicit in the ongoing process of colonialism. So to your point about ethical consumption, is history on the mind of the average consumer? We have a long way to go. Engagement is aesthetic: for consumers these purchases are seen as trendy or edgy or more 'authentic' because of their cultural affiliation, and for brands it's about sales. Everyone shares the responsibility of engaging with the past, but luxury brands have yet to do so meaningfully.

NIGEL: You're completely right, Riley. 'Authenticity' is a very slippery concept when applied to historically and culturally marginalized people and practices. Who determines what is the 'authentic' representation of an Indigenous person or of a Black woman, for example, and to what political ends? How can we overcome this hegemonic perception?

RILEY: Challenging those harmful narratives and stereotypes is a first step, but most important is that Indigenous people are defining authenticity *for themselves*. Unfortunately, the first part is difficult because the problem is so widespread, there are few legal avenues and all are largely ineffective. Patent and trademarking laws inadequately address Indigenous cultural production, and the legal costs of challenging brands are prohibitive for individual makers. There's been success when states themselves protect cultural heritage, like the Mexican government's push to protect Indigenous communities from plagiarism, most recently with Carolina Herrera, who copied traditional Saltillo shawls (Jones 2019). These are the kinds of interventions needed so that Indigenous makers can claim for themselves what is authentic and hopefully obtain the means to control if, how and when certain elements of culture are commodified. I see room for critical luxury studies to make pragmatic engagements with those in positions of power, like Kim Jenkins, a colleague at Ryerson University who has provided training for global luxury brands and industry-level organizations to set broader goals concerning diversity and inclusion, but also engagements with Indigenous makers themselves. I'm interested in supporting what Indigenous academics call 'resurgence', the everyday decolonizing acts of embodying Indigenous values. I want to see what resurgent practices create.

JESS: Given the historical – and contemporary – ties between luxury producers and colonization that you rightfully underscore, your argument that luxury brands should be at the forefront of global efforts at decolonization is particularly powerful. If you were acting as an advisor to a major luxury operation, what kind of guidance would you offer?

RILEY: I think luxury brands could be at the forefront of supporting cultural resurgence through economic development, but decolonization requires sovereignty, which is in the realm of Indigenous political and legal activists. True decolonization means the return of stolen land so that Indigenous nations can regenerate. As the land base is secured and the environmental health of land is restored, cultural resurgence can occur. So thinking *through* land might be an ambitious place to start, but I would encourage a luxury operation to think critically about the rightful owners of farm or factory land used in luxury supply chains. Can an Indigenous population benefit from luxury production? If a raw material is farmed in South America, can the infrastructure be developed to employ textile weavers, instead of bringing the material to Europe? Land includes urban places, so we need to think about how luxury-induced gentrification displaces people of colour. In my review of *Making Prestigious Places* (Kucheran 2018) I noted how luxury often has negative connotations in urban planning because of this displacement, but the power of luxury could in fact be harnessed for more social justice–orientated aims. Finally, some of the most beautiful and pristine lands left on earth are central to luxury tourism, and I speculate that the industry is not benefitting Indigenous populations as much as it could. Indigenous tourism is a burgeoning industry itself, but I worry that 'Indigenous experiences' offered by tour groups are tokenistic and reinforce harmful narratives or that they contribute to environmental degradation. That said, I can envision a community-led luxury operation in my own territory that honours Indigenous ethics, where luxury consumers experience our beautiful lands and waters, are able to learn from us and have the opportunity to purchase our cultural products. The distinction is between voyeuristic helicoptering – dropping in and quickly leaving – and sustained attempts at relationship building. If a luxury fashion brand wants to incorporate Indigenous beadwork into their haute couture collections, I'd advise them to develop a long-term strategy. Rather than a one-off commission for a collection (which happens often and can be a double-edged sword), I'd advise a brand to help open a beadwork atelier in an Indigenous community. They could consistently make orders, consult with expert beadwork artists to explore new designs, connect the community directly to clients and ensure that the working conditions were equitable. I see little difference between the elderly tailors in the Chanel ateliers and Indigenous grandmothers beading in a community circle, in terms of skill, creativity, and so on. The difference is in their status and social position, determined by colonialism and what's considered 'fashion'. When Jamie Okuma created her infamous beaded Christian Louboutin boots, the company sent her a cease-and-desist letter, but they're so beautiful! I can imagine her beadwork becoming coveted items for luxury consumers, but instead it was an incredible missed opportunity. The underlying question behind all these ideas is whether luxury can be divorced from social inequality. I'm typically pessimistic, but part of me hopes that luxury can become a force for social good. It will depend on whether luxury is willing to build authentic relationships with Indigenous peoples and make long-term investments in Indigenous communities.

NIGEL: Listening to you, Riley, it seems that the real issue isn't appropriation, as such, but is more a question of the structural imbalances in power relations that permit appropriation. You've told us of how the luxury/fashion industry is instrumental in correcting this imbalance. What about Indigenous peoples themselves? What is their role in establishing their position in the industry?

RILEY: It's unfortunate that so much energy has to be spent challenging cultural appropriation. Correcting representation is an important battle, but there are pressing issues concerning the material reality of Indigenous communities – defending land from encroaching resource extraction, environmental degradation, language preservation, ensuring safety and improving standards of living. Sometimes I feel like we don't have *time* for cultural appropriation when there's so much work needed to rebuild our nations, which is why I'm excited to see the energy of the burgeoning Indigenous fashion movement turn inwards. For the past few years I've been working with Sage Paul, founder and artistic director of Indigenous Fashion Week Toronto (IFWTO). We've spent a lot of time theorizing about Indigenous fashion, and we've both landed on the need for a real departure from the mainstream fashion industry. Sage created IFWTO because she saw the need for a platform that more accurately represented Indigenous design, which up until recently has either been tokenized or entirely absent. But given the structural problems of the industry, the model of 'fashion week' itself had to change. IFWTO grew organically *within* the Indigenous community; it wasn't introduced by the non-Indigenous old guard of fashion. This was perhaps most evident on the front row of the runways, which was saved for Indigenous Elders. I'll always remember the face of a disgruntled old-guard fashion type when she realized she'd have to sit in the back row to see the show.

FIGURE 1.1: Tania Larsson, a Gwich'in and Swedish designer based in Yellowknife, Northwest Territories, and her 2018 'Protect the Caribou' runway look. Indigenous Fashion Week Toronto 2018. Modelled by Lio Francis Keahna Warrior (White Earth Anishinaabe and Meskwaki) and photographed by Nadya Kwandibens of Red Works Photography (Kwandibens 2018). (CC BY-NC-ND - Creative Commons Attribution-NonCommercial-NoDerivs License.)

I laughed then and still smile, because it's just such an *Indigenous* thing to do – respect your Elders – so of course the front row was saved for them. There were plenty of these subtle differences throughout IFWTO. A 'marketplace' brought direct economic benefits to artisans, workshops weaved together textiles and storytelling, and there was certainly a powerful politics. With art exhibited alongside the runways and in the clothing itself, environmental protection, food sovereignty and land reclamation were all brought to the forefront of discussions. Tania Larsson was one of the designers who showed at IFWTO and her 'Protect the Caribou' look drew attention to the interconnectedness of all relations – when fracking threatens caribou habitats, Indigenous fashion is threatened because we can't have one without the other (Figure 1.1).

Ultimately IFWTO is about *holding space*, perhaps the most important factor in supporting the Indigenous fashion movement. In my own work, I lean on 'visiting', which is the nishnaabeg methodology of taking time to build reciprocal relationships and deeper understanding by physically being with someone (Simpson 2011), and when this happens, it requires theoretical frameworks founded on the place-based practices and local knowledges of the territory being visited, what Glen Coulthard calls 'grounded normativity' (2014: 53). So, for example, I've also worked with Otahpiaaki Indigenous Fashion Week in Calgary, which is produced with Blackfoot theory in mind, like the concept of *sahpahtsimah*, or 'collaborating in a good way' (Otahpiaaki Fashion Week Website 2019). Ultimately it is inside these spaces where decolonization materializes. There was once a time when, in order to quash political uprisings, Indigenous people couldn't gather in large groups, so Indigenous fashion weeks are powerful events of resistance. When carefully crafted with love and good intentions, Indigenous makers are able to gather and socialize, but also strategize and mobilize. After the inaugural IFWTO I realized that creating spaces like Indigenous fashion weeks is our best hope for challenging cultural appropriation. In addition to correcting narratives by telling our own stories, we also build entire industries, so that there comes a time when luxury comes to us, hoping to collaborate, rather than ignoring us and misusing our culture.

Indigenous luxury, critical luxury studies and capitalism

NIGEL: Broadly speaking, critical luxury studies has, since the first publications in and around 2016, focused on a western, if not Eurocentric, approach to the question of luxury. In the introduction to their edited volume *Critical Luxury Studies*, Armitage and Roberts tie the concept of luxury to 'the disciplines of art, design, and media' (2016a: 1). They also insist that the concept of luxury 'entails recognition that all human beings live in a world that is created by human beings, and in which they find meaning in sumptuous enjoyment' (2016a: 2). I think there is something very noble and correct in the premise that 'luxury' is a human phenomenon. But I think the definition of luxury is limited by the hegemonic underpinnings and the colonial history of the terms of engagement. Art, design and media are privileged areas of human activity. What has been historically deemed 'art' – by this I mean creative cultural production that has been considered aesthetically acceptable and meriting critical engagement – in the past has been tied to ideological and hegemonic conceptions in the university.

RILEY: First, I agree that luxury is a human phenomenon, but I don't think it should be. Historically, luxury has been so focused on 'sumptuous enjoyment' for humans, at the expense of our non-human relations. From an Indigenous perspective that demands respect and reciprocity when engaging with plant and animal life, luxury has been selfish, abusive even. I wonder what mainstream luxury would look like if it honoured those non-human relations at the level of Indigenous ethics. And I absolutely agree with you that defining luxury has been limited by colonial under-pinnings. Colonialism extracts resources from Indigenous land to produce luxury and fails to recognize Indigenous sovereignty, let alone recognize that Indigenous culture produces what should be upheld as luxurious. I wasn't surprised that *Critical Luxury Studies* focused on western luxury, but I feel that evoking criticality today needs to come with an interroga-tion of Eurocentrism, an acknowledgement of colonialism and a com-mitment to mobilizing social justice. Is that too much to ask? Some of the most needed kinds of *critical* knowledge production is happening out-side academia. And I know many Indigenous fashion designers who call themselves artists or fashion artists and that fashion weeks across Canada have had to define themselves as artistic or cultural festivals to qualify for grants. Both examples are connected to the historical privileging of art and marginalization of specific forms of cultural production – here fashion but also any form of Indigenous making. This divide is perhaps most stark in museum spaces, where Indigenous artefacts have been housed in ethnographic wings for centuries, and only in the last few decades has Indigenous art made its way into contemporary galleries.

NIGEL: This makes me think of the reaction to my work in hip hop and luxury. I've been asked whether hip hop can offer critical responses to capitalism or to feminist concerns. I remember a discussion I had with a nineteenth-century colleague who felt that hip hop celebrities, like Cardi B, don't express a discursive position in their manipulation of luxury fashions or in their artistic creations. I firmly disagree with this kind of perspective. I think that hip hop consciously and unconsciously expresses a use *and a misuse* of luxury signs that forces us to rethink luxury as simply a mode of exhibiting one's cultural capital or demonstrating an aspirational drive to climb the social hierarchy. Essentially, making or embodying luxury by historically, economically and racially marginalized people is a demonstration of luxury's artificial function as status symbol. And, as an artificial construct, new meanings and values can be attached to the luxury object.

RILEY: I've faced similar questions about the legitimacy of fashion as an object of Indigenous scholarship, and they can feel dismissive. Fashion is a his-torically marginalized field of study partly because the industry itself

44

has been feminized (Lipovetsky 1994: 3; Kawamura 2004), and in Indigenous studies there's a natural (and justifiable) focus on issues in education, health and self-governance. So asking if hip hop or fashion can offer criticality is an incredibly important question, especially when the stakes are so high. Can Indigenous luxury fashion truly contribute to decolonization and Indigenous resurgence, or is it doomed to participate in the capitalist economy and therefore contribute to the machine causing our imminent environmental demise? Can Indigenous fashion be emancipatory? Similar questions have been asked before – can 'political dressing' serve actually progressive aims (Parkins 2002), does 'critical fashion' lose its transgressiveness when co-opted (Geczy and Karaminas 2017: 5) and how effective is 'activist fashion' in Black and Indigenous political movements (Ford 2017; Maynard 2002)? Sadly, I think that Hoskins provides the answer that most resonates with me: that these various 'resistance fashions' do not amount to any serious challenge to capitalism (2014: 164). Of course, there's a spectrum: there's been uncritical 'critical fashion' and shallow 'activist fashion' that exist within the capitalist system and barely support its cause, and I think Indigenous fashion is strongest when it comes from community and its politics draw attention to systems of oppression and ways of moving forward. But ultimately the capacity for change – the real power – is within the movement itself (2014: 153). This is why I see Indigenous luxury as only one component of an integrated decolonizing movement. The movement has to get dressed every day, and what will we put on? In conversations with Métis fashion designer Evan Ducharme, we've theorized that '[t]he Indigenous resistance will be MAJOR [*sic*]' (Kucheran 2019b). Every community member in the decolonizing movement should be dressed in ancestral couture that regenerates our relations to land and creation. Any movement needs its fashion, its music. We just have to ensure that cultural production rejects capitalism – not attempt to reform it – and we have to rebuild our own systems.

NIGEL: This is an important question that I've struggled with. I wonder about the radical perspective that considers the only ethical position in regard to the capitalist system is that it must be dismantled. Absolutely. I agree – my perspective is fundamentally Marxist-based. But the fashion and luxury system is a capitalist system. There are creatives who subvert the system and, now, in the wake of the COVID-19 pandemic, there are designers and brands who are refusing the hegemonic fashion week cycle. I don't know if this constitutes a rejection of capitalism or a productive circumventing of the system's hegemony.

RILEY: I think we're hammering down on *the* most important question here. My biggest critique of fashion studies is that it overvalues those symbolic acts. Even within 'critical' fashion, there's always this relation to commerce and capitalism. 'Anti-fashion' (Polhemus and Procter 1978; Davis 1992) only amounted to countercultural styles whose power was subverted by the fashion system; fashion is an outlet for queer gender expression (Moore 2018) but at what cost? Even scholarship around 'the end of fashion' – Tansy Hoskins's (2014) *Stitched Up: The Anti-Capitalist Book of Fashion*, Lidewij Edelkoort's (2015) *Anti_Fashion Manifesto* and Geczy and Karaminas's (2018) *End of Fashion* – to me they advocate for minor incremental changes that fail to depart from the fashion system. Most scholars in fashion studies have yet to witness 'fashions' that are truly outside of the system, but I see it emerging in Indigenous communities. I also work for Dechinta, a land-based Indigenous university in Dene territory near Yellowknife, and there we actively model decolonization. There's less capitalism in 'the bush'. No roads, no plumbing, no electricity: we literally live off the land. It sounds dystopian from a western perspective, but it's the way Indigenous people have always lived. As we creep closer towards a time when the most disastrous effects of climate change become unavoidable, Indigenous communities are doubling their efforts to live sustainably off the land. I've always imagined a time when western fashion ends, when we can no longer physically outsource clothing production, and I've asked: will we be ready? Will we be able to clothe ourselves? I'm preparing for that future.

Indigenous methodologies

NIGEL: Our discussion has highlighted that luxury is a discursive practice, which means that luxury mirrors and counters power. Luxury materializes Bourdieu's notion of cultural capital, which, we know, is a way individuals and groups harness the symbolic power of commodities and cultural objects to assert dominance. Luxury is not just an 'idea' but a practice, an act, that can be used to situate an individual, a group or a collectivity in the social world. Do Indigenous creative practices operate in a similar discursive mode?

RILEY: I think that Indigenous makers are also interested in harnessing cultural capital and symbolic power – for Angela the idea of luxury is indeed mobilized to situate her brand in a luxury consumer's world, and it's interesting that she's been most successful in product categories most synonymous with luxury consumption like furs and fine jewellery. But yes, the motive is definitely different: dominance implies an exploitation of power for personal gain, whereas the Indigenous makers I work with are incredibly community minded. Everything they do is motivated by strong desires to help their family, their community and their people at large. Perhaps it's a different set of motivations depending on if the consumer is Indigenous or not: for non-Indigenous consumers, the goal is often education, to refute stereotypes and teach someone about our history or cultural values. For Indigenous 'consumers' I think the goal is the development of a relationship itself. I've only ever *consumed* Indigenous products after meeting the producer, coming to know them and offering my services by sharing my own cultural capital, the connections I've been able to make in the academic and business worlds.

NIGEL: For me, luxuriousness is imbued when a commodity is considered to have a surplus value, that is, some kind of value that exceeds its use value. For example, developing a relationship between producer and consumer invests surplus value in consumption. Luxury can materially and symbolically improve the lives of individuals who adopt a kind of luxurious world-view. It seems to me that Indigenous luxury operates similarly, or is luxuriousness created through different practices?

RILEY: I'm not sure! I once asked an Indigenous Elder what was luxury, and they said 'having enough fish to eat'. It was telling, informative about the material conditions of Indigenous peoples. I'm not entirely sure where I'm going with this, but conceptions of luxury change when there's been such a prolonged deficit of basic human rights, which is (I think) similar to where you're coming from.

NIGEL: That's it exactly. Luxury isn't a category or an innate quality; it is a phenomenon that practically, intellectually or spiritually betters the life of the individual and the community. Indigenous making and the ways you work with makers epitomize this form of luxurious improvement.

JESS: Practices and methods are central to Indigenous luxury makers but also to you, as a scholar of Indigenous luxury. From your work, it's clear that you devote careful attention to the relationship between method or form and your intentions as a scholar. That's why, as you describe in the opening of this chapter, we decided to organize this chapter as a discussion rather than an essay, since this form more closely aligns with your current conceptualizations of Indigenous luxury: ideas that are fluid, evolving and collaborative, as in a conversation. In your scholarship, then, what underpins your methods for studying Indigenous luxury, and how are these practices reflected in your relationships with your subjects? How can scholars move beyond 'colonial research agendas and methodologies' (Absolon and Willett 2005: 106) that continue to dominate the academy to broaden not only our definitions of luxury but also the means and forms through which we study these phenomena?

RILEY: I think the answer is in your question: relationships. Indigenous research reconfigures relationships as essential: knowledge is collaboratively generated through a relationship over a lifetime, whereas colonial research might view a relationship as a prerequisite for data collection, and even then the relationship is usually superficial and non-reciprocal; it's a means to a predetermined end. I cringe at the word 'subjects' because it reminds me of the immense imbalance of power entrenched through the anthropological research tradition: researcher and researched, expert and native. That tradition stripped Indigenous peoples of their agency and ability to tell their own stories and represent themselves. Decolonizing research attempts to correct this injustice and is underpinned by an understanding that we have responsibilities to all of our relations and that knowledge is carried in all of us. I view Indigenous designers themselves as the experts. People like Angela carry with them immense lived experience and an embodied knowledge passed on to them through generations, which manifests in the clothes they produce. I see my role primarily as a facilitator, to help bring their knowledge to wider audiences. Of course, this must be done with the utmost caution: when knowledge is disseminated, it becomes susceptible to exploitation, so there's a delicate method of translating the right knowledge to generate academic or industry collaborations. While doing this I try to share any helpful experience I've gained during my time as a scholar and fashion professional. I've been afforded privileges in life that brought me to the academy, and I'm going to spend my time sharing the advantages it brings.

NIGEL: I see the importance of reconfiguring the relationship between researcher and researched ... that there is the potential for a true sharing, a kind of generosity that has been completely eclipsed in the historically colonial approach to ethnographic research. Decolonizing the academy, then, to my eyes is introducing a more balanced relationship between epistemological subjects where the knowledge flow is reciprocal and not simply 'top-down'. Is it possible, then, for non-Indigenous scholars to adopt decolonizing methodologies in their own research?

RILEY: I think it's possible. If it's done slowly, with care and respect. It's funny, as a master's student I actually described my research as ethnographic because I didn't know otherwise, but reflecting back on my time with Angela, it more closely resembles the nishnaabeg practice of visiting that I spoke of earlier. In the Anishinaabe creation story, extensive visiting is done by the sacred being Nanabush, who travels around the world twice to recognize and build relationships with all of creation. Knowledge is first generated by observation – at one point Nanabush imitates the shape of *gitchie manameg* ('whale') and the tail of *ahmik* ('beaver') to build a canoe and paddle to cross a large body of water – but theory is generated by relations. Interactions with *mushkodayn bishikee* ('buffalo') provide lessons about survival, respect and sustainability, *odayminnug* ('heart berries' or 'strawberries') teaches Nanabush about human biology, and when Nanabush embarks on this journey the second time with a *mhiingnag* ('wolf') companion the dual perspective changes everything. For thousands of years, visiting has provided Indigenous peoples with the time and space required to share stories, take care of each other and mobilize politically. Visiting nurtures the intimate connections needed for consensus building, organizing and direct action, making it a necessary component of decolonization. Visiting mitigates the chance of power asymmetry prevalent in ethnography because it requires consent and collaboration. All of these components of visiting are present in my fieldwork, but non-Indigenous researchers can engage in visiting as well. Indigenous methodologies use methods that resemble critical feminist methods. The difference is in the political aims of Indigenous methodologies and the Indigenous theoretical paradigms they rely on, which are unique to the local Indigenous culture. A 'sharing circle' uses Indigenous protocol and takes care of participants more than a focus group. Indigenous research requires constant reflection, which makes autoethnography a suitable method. An Indigenous form of narrative enquiry could take years because the same stories are shared over a lifetime, and with each new context, they present different teachings. These methods and the methodology of visiting embody an ethics of care that is affirmed through life-long relations. If a non-Indigenous researcher is ready for the long-haul, they just have to start. I think it's more about the journey that will reveal itself than mastering a set of Indigenous methods.

NIGEL: Can we ask you about the key thinkers or writers that we can draw from to think about Indigenizing and decolonizing fashion/luxury?

RILEY: Of course! My first entry into Indigenous methodologies was Shawn Wilson's (2008) *Research Is Ceremony*, which makes it clear that Indigenous methodologies cannot be divorced from Indigenous epistemologies, ontologies and axiologies. I've worked personally with Leanne Simpson at Dechinta, where I witnessed her methodologies in action, but her body of work is highly influential in my thinking and in

Indigenous studies. *Dancing on Our Turtle's Back* (2011) and *As We Have Always Done* (2017) are great because they provide historical and theoretical contexts: there might not be a typical 'methodology' section, but the methodology is there in the stories, in the way Simpson moves in the world. In a similar way, Jeff Corntassel's (2018) edited collection *Everyday Acts of Resurgence* describes some of the daily decolonizing acts of Indigenous people: fishing, preparing traditional food, adorning oneself with clothing made by kin, recalling forgotten place names, witnessing the truth-telling of children – the 'everyday' might seem mundane, but Corntassel, following Hunt and Holmes (2015), emphasizes that these intimate and relational acts are just as important to decolonization as are the more obvious political interventions. Our friend from earlier, Kathleen Absolon, also wrote *Kaandossiwin: How We Come to Know* (2011), and the stalwarts of Indigenous methodologies are Linda Tuhiwai Smith's (1998) *Decolonizing Methodologies* and Margaret Kovach's (2009) *Indigenous Methodologies*. The latter provides the important context of 'colonizing knowledges', the history that must be understood before Indigenous knowledges can be engaged.

The future of Indigenous luxury

JESS: Much of your work, including your collaboration with Angela, explores current developments in Indigenous luxury that are dynamic, forward-facing and actively foregrounding sustainability, community and socially conscious industry practices. How do you see these developments in relation to the future of Indigenous luxury, but also luxury more generally? How do you envision the effects of Indigenous concepts, cultural values and practices on the luxury industry as well as on the field of critical luxury studies?

RILEY: When I think of decolonization as simultaneously dismantling colonial structures and rebuilding Indigenous worlds, then the work that is being accomplished by Angela, myself and the Indigenous fashion movement at large has a dual function. It supports community and has the potential to shape luxury more generally. It's my hope that these concepts and mobilizations of luxury are brought directly into Indigenous communities. I want to see rural and remote Indigenous communities engaging with their own cultural products and valuing them as luxuries. Artisans I know are aware of this already: they know their beadwork shouldn't sell for twenty dollars, but when makers don't have access to urban markets and are not online, less fair in-person sales are the only option. It's also my goal to help mobilize traditional skills already present in the community and reorientate part of the output towards luxury retail. For example, hide tanning is a beautiful act of resurgence. It's an incredibly laborious process: it's difficult and you get exhausted from scraping the animal hide over and over again until it's soft enough to work with. It also involves many community members: the hunters or trappers who harvest the animals in a respectful manner, the knowledge holders who guide the process, the workers themselves, the tailors who use the finished material – the making brings people together, and of course, the process comes with traditional stories and teachings. Some of the leather will go directly back to the community, but what if some of the leather then went to a fashion designer and was sold in a community-based store where everyone shares in the profit? This Indigenous luxury looks like practices that we have engaged in since time immemorial, and now it's about marketing those practices and creating a closed-loop system that benefits the community. Next on my research agenda is investigating alternative management structures and cooperatives: I can see a time where each Indigenous nation has its own brand, and consumers can support entire communities with their 'luxury' purchases.

Working at Angela's boutique revealed some of the unique challenges inherent in being an Indigenous luxury fashion designer, but it also opened up conversations about luxury itself. Some of her challenges would also be shared by any independent luxury producer, and addressing these problems would make for a more equitable industry. As an entrepreneur, Angela largely works solo: she was responsible for the design, production, marketing and sales of her products because she doesn't have teams of people like a larger luxury brand has. She doesn't have access to the financial capital that would be available in a larger brand or the manufacturing capability to outsource production. I guess this also means I'd like to see critical luxury studies collaborate with the business world more. Our friend Thomaï Serdari, a luxury strategist and adjunct professor at NYU Stern School of Business, once told me that her best MBA students had humanities backgrounds – that those with critical theoretical foundations were able to mobilize management tools for greater good. If Indigenous research methodologies are action orientated and require reciprocity, I want luxury scholars to work *with* independent makers to support their businesses. This is where I would encourage our efforts, but there's also room to 'Indigenize' larger corporations. To me decolonizing luxury means minimizing the harmful effects of luxury operations, which largely encompasses environmental sustainability. There's no Indigenous land-base on a dead planet.

JESS: This emphasis on longstanding practices seems a way to push back against long-held designations of what was historically deemed 'luxurious' and *not* luxurious. As you point out, the expertise and skill that goes into hide tanning aligns the practice with many other artisanal production processes deemed central to 'luxury' production. But the industry seems bound by historical designations, centuries old, through which dominant settler societies give value to certain production processes, while denying that of others, including traditional Indigenous practices. In this way, you're subverting historical categories in productive ways, revising systems that have, for too long, defined luxury. Are there other production processes among Indigenous designers that are pushing back against these dominant ideas?

RILEY: I think that's what makes the hide tanning process special, and these qualities are shared among any Indigenous craft. I'm reminded of beading circles, these often informal spaces for artisans to come together and bead. There's food, laughter, gossip, but also elements of ceremony: the act of coming together creates a sacred space that facilitates the transmission of stories. Anyone can learn how to bead from YouTube, but if you're not beading in the context of community and traditional knowledge, beading is just a technique and not a carrier of our culture. The same can be said for any land-based practice. Quillwork, hair tufting, fibre weaving. Because land-based cultural production relies on Indigenous epistemologies and values, any cultural product is going to have the same potential to heal communities, to heal our relationship to land. There are other areas of cultural production that need improvement, however. I often contrast this land-based, community-grounded, made-to-measure 'luxury fashion' with the burgeoning category of Indigenous streetwear design. There are several T-shirt companies, for example, that are using Indigenous aesthetics or political statements on garments sourced from dubious producers. While not immediately associated with luxury, these companies are doing incredibly important work. There are direct financial benefits for communities when Indigenous artists and other employees are hired; there's a critical unpacking of complex colonial histories that's done very publicly – the brand Section 35 is named for the article in the Canadian Constitution Act that recognizes Indigenous and treaty rights, and they sell a shirt that says, 'All These Treaty Rights and Still Not Treated Right'; another OXDX-brand T-shirt reads 'Native Americans Discovered Columbus'. These are powerful forms of representation that open up possibilities for engaged conversation – I've been stopped on the sidewalk and asked about the OXDX shirt – and conversations that change the narrative about Indigenous peoples is a good place to start. However, it can't be the only action: changes in representations need to be tied to transformations in material conditions, and I think that starts with production. It is my hope that utilizing a luxury strategy could elevate this streetwear to a level more akin to Indigenous design. When visiting Indigenous fashion weeks or Pow Wows, I'll tell streetwear designers to invest in their supply chain: build relations with local and organic cotton producers, find local cutters and sewers and aim for price points above $100 for T-shirts. There's much work to be done to repair consumer perceptions of T-shirt costs post fast fashion, but that relational work, if founded on reciprocity, is how luxury can move Indigenous streetwear forward. Again, it's the ethics and values of Indigenous design, like sustainability, that make Indigenous luxury so forward-facing. Those values are attainable in our everyday clothing practices.

NIGEL: Completely. Indigenous streetwear can look to hip hop culture as a model for how to 'up their luxury game'. Fashion networks like Harlem's Fashion Row and designers like Kerby Jean-Raymond of Pyer Moss are changing the American fashion scene through a similar rethinking of fashion networks. African-American creatives have borne the brunt of cultural appropriation and a surprisingly obtuse use of images that show that working within the system is not a mutually beneficial cultural model. These designers are building networks with other Black creatives and Indigenous makers to reinforce new, beneficial power structures. You are proposing a similar type of buttressing through an Indigenous creative power structure. I wonder, however, about a silo effect, where a wider conversation and exchange of ideas is foreclosed when marginalized and racialized cultural producers cut the dominant group out of the system. Do you think there is a possibility for Indigenous luxury to engage with the mainstream, maybe in subversive ways, that can lead to a change in the power dynamic?

RILEY: I'm either not sure or not yet convinced that it's possible. Why can't the independent Black creative networks remain siloed and only engage the mainstream on their own terms? I return to the question of power: who's in control? Who's dictating the narrative? Who's hiring who? I'm all for supporting wider conversations and exchange, but I'd only be comfortable if the decisions to engage are being made by Black creatives in constant dialogue with Black community members and if their engagement is on their own terms. It shouldn't be that Black or Indigenous creatives *have* to 'fall in line' to take their businesses to the next level, but then again I'm interested in destabilizing the notion that any Black or Indigenous business *needs* to be elevated to another level. Small is good, and slowness is needed now more than ever.

For Indigenous makers, how can trust be rebuilt when the dominant mainstream has been so dangerous for us? I think that decolonization would first and foremost mean a more honest form of luxury – a luxury that continues time-honoured traditions and upholds values like longevity, quality and timelessness – but also a transparent luxury. Most importantly, an honest luxury would reckon with its past. Historically speaking, luxury purveyors have reaped the benefits of colonization and global imperialism. One only needs to compare global poverty levels to the amount of capital accumulated by large luxury conglomerates – which now collectively generate over a trillion dollars in sales annually – to make the connection that luxury exists because of social inequality. So where does this leave us or leave luxury? European luxury houses especially need to examine their own histories and the roles they played in colonization, and reparations must be made. I'm not entirely sure what that looks like – I know it's not tokenizing collaborations on capsule collections, and the charitable arms of these companies are not doing enough. The COVID pandemic, still in its early stages, has shown us how quickly power dynamics can change, and post-pandemic, climate change will bring us to a similar critical nexus. I believe that Indigenous luxury provides us with a beacon to weather the coming storms, but change will depend on how well we listen.

2

Putting Canada on the Map:
A Brief History of Nation and Luxury

Jessica P. Clark

Canada's historical relationship to luxury has largely turned on its subservient position to European colonizing powers. This entailed an obscuring of what can now be understood as luxurious goods, processes and practices. From the earliest days of colonization, dominant European narratives meant that dynamic historical examples of luxury making, experiences and industry instead figured as unacknowledged contributions to global imperial pursuits. This erasure was bolstered by Canada's economic relationship to its colonizers, and especially Britain, from the early modern period. As some of the nation's earliest and leading historians, most notably Harold Innis, have shown, Canada's early economic contributions involved the procuring of beaver and other fur pelts for the benefit of the mother country as a foundational part of Canada's staple economy (Owram 1999: 156–58). Along with lumber, gold and wheat, the luxury output of fur figured as a key raw material that fueled first the mercantile and then industrializing economies of European nation states (Innis 1930: 386–408; see also Jenson 1999).

Western narratives of Canada's economic and historical development were undergirded by colonial frameworks – including the erasure of Indigenous, feminized, enslaved and immigrant labour, valuations of nature as uncivilized and therefore open to possession and the situating of Canada in a deferential economic position to its more enlightened, advanced colonizer – that shape understandings of the nation's relationship to luxury to this day. This chapter charts some of these narratives, reviewing western historical representations of Canadian fur production in the early modern period, the development of nineteenth-century nature tourism for elite patrons and the influx of Eastern European influences in twentieth-century garment production to suggest that Canada has a much longer relationship to luxury than previously acknowledged. Approaches in the nation's history via colonial lenses have obscured broad, longstanding connections to luxury making, experiential luxury and luxury craftsmanship and manufacturing. The result is that understandings of Canada's relationship to luxury remain bounded by historical definitions that excluded, diminished and marginalized colonial production, processing and experiences. More broadly, then, this chapter explores the western historical processes that, in part, designated particular productions in particular locations as 'luxurious', while other national industries were not afforded the same status.

Since its emergence, a central element of critical luxury studies (CLS) has been scholars' attempts to define luxury as a concept, both historically and in the present day, including luxury's role in the development of national economies and identities. This focus on definition has meant a number of diverse conceptualizations of luxury, especially as the term applied to particular historical locations. Maxine Berg positions luxury as a shifting category whose definitions 'were always historical, shaped by public structures of meaning and private experience' (2005: 31). In seventeenth- and eighteenth-century Britain, she argues, luxury emerged as a means of displaying national and imperial power, advancing messages of Anglo 'knowledge and civilization' (2005: 38–41) not to mention development as British producers used import substitution and product innovation to develop a robust domestic luxury market (2005: 86; see also Styles 2000). In this way, luxury goods and their production could not be parsed from broader geopolitical dynamics, contributing to processes of national identity formation (Berg 2005: x, 5, 7–8). Peter McNeil and Giorgio Riello also situate their wide-ranging history of luxury within particular temporal and geographic contexts, from the early modern 'Orient' to Edwardian London, to acknowledge contingencies of luxury based upon time and place. Luxury 'depends', they argue, 'on what a society assumes to go "beyond" the expected' (2016: 4). Yet such descriptions fail to account for circumstances regulating historically 'peripheral' locations – namely colonial dependencies – that were never expected to 'go "beyond"' as a fundamental condition of their founding (see Dosekun and Iqani 2019a). In the case of Canada, its modern geopolitical foundations – as a deferential white settler colony – means that 'the *extra*-ordinary', by definition and historical process, was not afforded to the nation's goods, products, services and inhabitants. If 'the state uses luxury as one of the tools of its façade' (McNeil and Riello 2016: 5), then the *denial* of luxury status for those ruled by imperial states also functioned as a tool to sustain power differentials between dependent colonies and their mother countries.[1] These longstanding economic and cultural conditions have significant implications for the Canadian context, where historical luxury production operated under the bounds of colonialism, which, in turn, regulated global reception of its goods and services.

Despite productive histories of luxury and its geographically specific typologies, some scholarly interpretations underplay powerful configurations of geopolitical power that, in part, helped designate what was and was not luxurious. This is especially the case in examples of colonized and formerly colonized luxury markets. Designations of luxury were not consistent across colonial holdings, however, and broader, if inaccurate, understandings of colonized cultures and people influenced reception of their goods, services and skills. In the British context, as we will see, some colonial possessions like India came to represent a type of refined, exotic 'otherness' that was not only acceptable but also desirable among middling English consumers. Meanwhile, other locations – like Canada – represented an untamed wildness in the European imaginary, which functioned as a significant justification in the claiming and possession of 'uncivilized' Indigenous peoples and their land. Disparate classifications of Britain's colonial holdings – and across its imperial project more generally – subsequently precluded attributions of 'luxury' to goods from dependent, 'unrefined' locales like Canada or the Caribbean. It was not that Canadian makers, producers and entrepreneurs did not create luxurious goods, objects and experiences; rather, political imperatives propelling British colonization of North America meant that such developments could not be defined as 'luxurious', else risk destabilizing essential narratives underpinning – and justifying – Britain's imperial presence in Canada.

This chapter revisits some of these dominant historical narratives, some of which inform the nation's global reputation to this day, to suggest new approaches to histories of Canadian luxury. It surveys existing scholarship through the lens of CLS to explore how historical ideas rooted in colonial epistemologies contributed to the erasure of a rich and complex history of luxury in this country. This included the denigration of Indigenous labour in the early modern period, the centrality of Canada's reputation as 'wild' and 'uncivilized' in the service of elite nineteenth-century tourism and the reclassification of immigrant labour from skilled to deskilled upon arrival in twentieth-century Canada. In doing so, it reasserts the centrality of Canadian actors to global histories of luxury, even if this status was denied to them at the time.

The early modern fur trade

Fur has long functioned in the Canadian imaginary as central to the founding of the nation. From the profiled beaver on the five-cent piece to enduring popular interest in Québecois *voyageurs*, the early modern fur trade occupies a central position in national mythologies, with Canada supplying fashionable beaver to satisfy an insatiable European demand for hats (Faiers 2020: 49).[2] This meant the shipping of thousands of raw beaver pelts to London and other European ports for processing by luxury producers. And yet, were fur pelts a raw material? In other words, did the production and processing of pelts in Canadian settings deserve their classification, both historically and contemporaneously, as unskilled preparation of 'raw' materials to be sent to European manufacturers for finishing as luxury goods? Rather than earn their standing as a bona fide luxury product that required skilled preparation by expert First Nations, Métis and Inuit artisans, dominant colonial narratives meant that Canadian furs figured instead as 'unfinished' materials to be refined and redistributed by skilled makers in Britain, France and other European markets.

In fact, Indigenous communities, and especially Indigenous women, undertook significant processes in pelt preparation that were absent from historical understandings of the early modern luxury fur trade and its production cycle. As Biigtigong Nishnaabeg scholar Riley Kucheran compellingly argues, Indigenous making is luxurious in its very creation, with an onus on time-honoured artisanal skills performed among communities of experts who invest their practices with attention, care and cultural value. 'What if', he asks in Chapter 1, 'we valued pieces of beadwork or tanned-hides like a luxury?' (see also 2016, 2019a). Historical implications of his argument, and specifically western devaluation of Indigenous artisanal production, can be traced back to the early modern context, when women cut, framed, scraped, dried and cleaned pelts before their transportation to Europe's leading luxury manufacturing centres (see Brown 1980; Sangster 2007; Kardulias 1990; Nadeau 2001; van Kirk 1980; Barman 2015; Podruchny and Peers 2010). The preparation of fur pelts, often by skilled female Indigenous makers, was not granted the designation of luxury in this period. However, a reframing of this historical labour in relation to alternate global markets lays bare the luxury elements of fur production in early modern North America, long before pelts' arrival in hatters' workshops across Europe.

The preparation and trading of furs had taken place thousands of years before European arrival, among Indigenous communities across the St. Lawrence basin, around the Great Lakes and northwards in Canada's sub-Arctic and Arctic regions (Heber 2011: 16–18). Yet many early histories of Canada's fur trade open in the late sixteenth century, when European demand for hats and other millinery propelled initial interest in North American furs, and particularly beaver. Beaver fur's miniscule barbs made it especially conducive to millinery processes of felting, before the implementation of industrialized carroting techniques that came to dominate in the nineteenth century (Matthews David 2015: 47–64; Faiers 2020: 45; Carlos and Lewis 2010: 16–22). Beaver pelts thus emerged, by the late sixteenth century, as the most in demand of those traded between First Nations and Inuit trappers, intermediaries and European traders, overtaking other 'fancy furs' like ermine and mink (Innis 1930).

The desirability of beaver pelts contributed to the expansion of European trade interests across North America. Initially, in the early seventeenth century, this included French traders' infiltration of regions around the St. Lawrence and Ottawa Rivers, followed by the later arrival of English and Dutch representatives (Heber 2011: 20). Major European trading centres, beginning with the French settlement at Québec (later Québec City) in 1608, turned almost solely on the trade in beaver pelts. This led to a strong French presence in the Great Lakes region and its westerly interior, but only via the labour of local Algonquin, Wendat and Innu communities, who procured furs or acted as intermediaries between the French and other Indigenous trappers and traders. By the mid-seventeenth century, competitive British interests in the lucrative beaver trade resulted in the development of new means of penetrating existing Indigenous networks that did not necessarily encroach upon French operations. From the late 1660s, this included funding efforts in the regions north of the Great Lakes, in Hudson and James Bays, which European traders had recently realized were rich in fur, as well as Indigenous partners upon whom they depended to procure, process and trade pelts with other Indigenous traders (Bird 2002: n.pag.). This led to the founding of the Hudson's Bay Company (HBC) in 1670, which gave Britain control over the trade in pelts in Rupert's Land (Heber 2011: 18; Faiers 2020: 45; Carlos and Lewis 2010: 5). The HBC represented British colonizing interests in 'New World' fur production. But it did so only via the labour and production of Indigenous hunters and traders. In this way, argues Gerald Friesen, there existed two fur trades simultaneously operating through this period: one between Europeans and Indigenous peoples and one among First Nations (1984: 45).

Despite the alleged fickleness of fashion, European demand for fur – and particularly beaver hats – only expanded through the eighteenth century. This included a dramatic growth in the British market, especially following France's defeat – and their political dislodgement from much of North America – in the Seven Years' War in 1763. Sources record 69,500 finished beaver hats being exported from England in 1700; this number increased to 500,000 hats by 1760. From the beginning of the century to 1770, some 21 million beaver and other felt hats moved from English millinery workshops (Carlos and Lewis 2010: 25; Ross 2008: 27). However, this popularity came at a cost. Demand for beaver felt hats, compounded by competition from the French, diminished some North American beaver populations through the eighteenth and nineteenth centuries. Dwindling supply, in turn, increased the demand for such hats, which resulted in higher prices for pelt procurers and producers across Canada (Carlos and Lewis 1999). This further cemented the centrality of Indigenous groups as key actors in the colonial economy, not only as traders but also through their demand, via the barter economy, for manufactured goods produced in Europe in exchange for pelts: firearms, tobacco, tools and 'other luxuries' (Carlos and Lewis 2010: 30 and 69–105).

Throughout these early modern developments, but especially as European demand intensified at the end of the seventeenth century, Indigenous communities were central to the preparation and processing of beaver pelts. To satisfy overseas markets, families and especially women undertook this labour, in addition to other work to meet the sustenance needs of local community and kin (Barman 2015; Sangster 2007: 248–55). These processes were specialized in nature, demanding significant time and skill, yet this work was not classified as part of the production of fashionable luxury items. This was despite the fact that the skill of preparation determined the grade of a pelt, a factor that had significant effects on the success of early modern French and British trading partners, not to mention final stages of processing by hat makers in European workshops (Knight 1867: 243–44).

Indeed, the preparation of peltry was, and is, a skilled process that demanded knowledge and experience, else risk damaging the fur and decreasing its value. Among First Nations, Métis and Inuit communities, practices of 'skinning, fleshing, stretching, and drying' (Bockstoce 2009: 67) were passed down through oral traditions across generations, forms that continue to underpin contemporary Indigenous methodologies (Dene Nahjo 2015; Kucheran 2016, 2019a; Smith 1999: 33; O'Brien 2016: 15, 18). By contrast, western observers, including anthropologists, produced written representations of pelt production, highlighting some variations according to geography and local specialized knowledge, but often effecting a false universalism across Indigenous groups (see, e.g., Conn 1956 cited in Sangster 2007: 252; Mason 1889 cited in Kardulias 1990: 38; Innis 1930). These modern written sources take up the Eurocentric viewpoint of an allegedly objective observer, describing pelt preparation without acknowledging the importance of culture, community and attention to the environment that undergirded these processes (Kucheran 2019a). But even as they ignore broader cultural contexts and minimize the centrality of women's labour – their 'skinning, scraping, pounding, packing' (Dumont 1996: 20) – these western texts detail skilled processes that underpinned luxury pelt preparation and determined peltry's subsequent grading for sale.[3]

Western accounts typically open their descriptions of pelt preparation with the skinning of an animal. In the case of the beaver, this could mean a straight incision from the lip to the chest and from the mid-stomach to the genitalia. Women are described as removing legs at the first joint, allowing them to pull the legs through the pelt and generate four even holes. Following the removal of the tail in some cases, preparers turned to the meticulous skinning of delicate areas around the beaver's face, a fundamental step in guaranteeing the quality of a pelt (Gibson 1876: 272; Conn 1956: 4). Authors next described the stretching of pelts, typically via hoops that increased airflow in ways that flat laying did not. It was in the binding of the pelt to the hoop that producers determined both the width and the length of the pelt; this step subsequently required great skill as yet another key determinant in overall quality. A 1956 account from *The Indian News*, a government publication from Canada's Department of Indian Affairs, depicted the craft of Cree women working in communities in Eeyou Istchee territory along the eastern coast of James Bay.[4] They used a 'large sail-maker's needle and number five baling twine', which were fashioned into expert, even stitches 'not more than one inch apart' that carefully – and evenly – pulled the pelt but prevented overstretching. This was especially important, as '[d]istorted fishtail and diamond shaped pelts [brought] a lower price on the market' (Conn 1956: 4). Having been secured to the hoops, pelts were briefly dried to prep the skin for scraping (Gibson 1876: 272).

Western accounts typically go on to describe scraping methods and follow-up processing, which again varied from location to location and according to local skilled practices. Texts describe artisans removing all flesh and fat before leaving the pelt to cure over time (Kardulias 1990: 38). In some locations, like Eeyou Istchee, this occurred in freezing temperatures as part of a frost drying method that was particular to the northern climate and produced especially fine – and desirable – pelts (Conn 1956; Sangster 2007: 252). Following that, authors noted that scraping was a meticulous process in that the pelt could be easily ruined. Skilled workers tended to use natural materials like bone as scrapers, and authors pointed out this was especially suitable for the fine-tuned nature of the work to prevent any cuts at this pivotal stage. For example, Otis Tufton Mason's *Aboriginal Skin Dressing* reported that the Naskapi Nation of Kawawachikamach in northern Québec relied on bone from the heel of a deer (Mason 1889: 566–67; see also Naskapi Nation of Kawawachikamach n.d.). The delicate nature of the process is evident in the 1956 account:

> The pelt, still laced to the hoop and still frozen, is stood on end against a support and scraped from top to bottom with long continuous strokes of a beveled scraper grasped in both hands. With each stroke of the scraper a ribbon-like strip of fat or flesh is removed and scraping is continued until the leather is reached. Great care is taken in the final stages lest the pelt be damaged by scraping too thin.
>
> (Conn 1956: 4).

Concluding steps, according to authors, included the mobilization of absorbent materials like flour or bone to soak up any remaining moisture.

In the early modern period, beaver pelt preparation also included a final – and crucial – stage, which involved the donning of pelts for extended periods of time. Indigenous craftspeople fashioned between five and eight processed beaver pelts

FIGURE 2.1: George Hunt, 'A Beaver Pelt', 1948. Courtesy of Library and Archives Canada/ National Film Board of Canada fonds/e011175745.

into a robe, which was then worn from 15 to 18 months by community members. During winter months or other cold periods, the fur was worn directly against the skin (see Lescarbot 1609: 175; Rosier 1605). While ostensibly providing warmth and comfort to community members, this was, in fact, an essential element of pelt production and particularly those of the highest quality and in greatest demand from European traders (Richardson 1829: 108). Natural oils from the wearers' bodies softened and conditioned the fur. Most significantly, it also started a process by which longer, tougher guard hairs were dislodged and fell away from the beaver felt. This left behind a layer of soft down that was the most desirable for felting processes that later took place in European workshops (Innis 1930: 10–11; Kardulias 1990: 39). These pelts, dubbed *castor gras d'hiver* by French colonizers, proved to be the most valuable of all types of beaver processed by Indigenous communities across North America. Demand from Europe's hat-making industry propelled this valuation, given *castor gras*'s particular suitability to the felting process (Faiers 2020: 45).

The centrality of pelt preparation to subsequent luxury good production suggests that the beaver pelts that fueled the colonial economy were not, in fact, raw materials but had undergone skilled processes that determined their value to and the success of European traders and manufacturers. Indeed, in her feminist history of the making of a fur coat in mid-twentieth-century Canada, Joan Sangster argues that Cree women's skills in 'creat[ing] unblemished and thus more marketable skins was so complex that in any industrialized setting, the work would have been described as artisanal and skilled' (2007: 252; Kucheran 2016, 2019a). This labour, and traditions of production, dated to the early modern period, when such processes would more accurately align beaver pelts with other luxury materials like Indian chintz, which, like furs, was processed in small, artisanal communities often bound by family and longstanding traditions. Chintz, like fur, was then transported to European markets to be refashioned into desirable luxury fashion items for European consumers (Riello 2016; Berg 2005: 52–53). And yet, chintz and other eastern luxury products received a far different classification than that of their western counterparts, both historically and in contemporary scholarship.

To begin to understand why Indigenous fur processing was not classified as part of European luxury fur production, it is useful to compare and contrast early modern rhetorics defining goods from alternate global locales. This is most notably the case in the opening up of eastern markets to European traders, which dramatically transformed the westerly movement of luxury goods from around the fifteenth century. European perceptions and reception of eastern luxuries from China and India reflected circulating discourses about the refinement and skill of eastern cultures. Berg argues that, to some British observers, Asian luxury production represented 'processes involving large-scale production, division of labour and specialization, and commercialization and adaptability to the diversity of global markets' (2005: 49). China's association with qualities like 'ethics, harmony, and virtue' appealed to British 'aspirations to human elegance and refinement' and subsequently inflected western responses to craft and luxury items (2005: 50–51). Underpinning these conceptions were circulating ideas about civilization. Europeans were drawn to Asian and especially Chinese manufactures in their desires to 'access levels of civilization beyond the market' (2005: 51). This privileging of desirable qualities of eastern luxury goods – as offering new levels of refinement and sophistication for its western buyer – in turn inflected perceptions of Asian production processes as particularly skilled and specialized.

Similar imaginaries operated in the valuation of Indigenous luxury production, albeit in an inverse manner. If the appreciation for eastern luxury goods and processes turned on consuming the refined, modern civility of 'exotic' goods, Eurocentric perceptions of the Americas precluded such estimations of specialized Indigenous labour. Instead, European interlocutors like Roger Williams, writing in the seventeenth century, asked, '[H]ow have foule hands (in smoakie houses) [been] the first handling of those Furres which are after worne upon the hands of Queens and heads of Princes?' (1643: 166). Such denigrating accounts circulated in the early modern period via western 'forms of knowledge'. From travelogues and missionaries' writings to scientific taxonomies and natural philosophies, texts often outlined alleged distinctions between Indigenous peoples and European colonizers, cementing the former's 'savagery' for metropolitan audiences as much as those in North America (Bayly 1999: 31–32; Bickham 2005). Commentators fixed on particular elements of Indigenous life to prove a lack of civilization, from some communities' rejection of Christianity to patterns of mobility that ran counter to Anglo-European privileging of settlement on private property (Bayly 1999: 30). This did not mean that western discursive representations of Indigenous peoples were stable or uniform, just as they were not always representative of actual encounters or individuals. Nonetheless, messages about Indigenous peoples, including their 'savage state', permeated eighteenth-century discourses. This increased in the aftermath of the Seven Years' War (1756–63), when Indigenous peoples in North America reportedly 'loomed larger in the eighteenth-century British imagination than any other non-Europeans', dominating British print, newspapers and literature (Bickham 2005: 3; Richardson 2018).[5]

Racist representations of Indigenous peoples figured in debates over Britain as a commercial society, as advanced by the same Scottish Enlightenment circles concurrently passing judgement on luxury and its value. Historian Troy Bickham argues that Eurocentric visions of Indigenous peoples were central to 'conjectural, stadial histories' conceived by Enlightenment figures such as Adam Smith, Adam Ferguson and John Millar (Bickham 2005: 171–209). Such stadial histories mapped out man's alleged stages of development, from his rudimentary beginnings to full political and social actualization. In some models, thinkers like Ferguson and Lord Kames also envisioned a final 'decline' stage for those 'commercial societies that had succumbed to luxury and decadence'; these functioned as 'cautionary tales for Europeans who toyed with excess luxury' (2005: 198). If European commercial societies were at the pinnacle of enlightened evolution, writers positioned Indigenous peoples in North America in 'the first stage', allegedly offering insights into Britain's previous state before the transformative advances of commerce, industry and progress (2005: 185–88). Of course, these studies, based on aforementioned 'empirical evidence' of Indigenous ways of life, primarily served to prove 'the economic, social, and technological superiority of European civilizations' (2005: 173).[6] This included the development of Enlightenment thinking on European commercial society, its relationship to its past and its potential, unbridled future. Many of these formulations turned on racist conceptualizations of an ancient savagery, perceptions that were circulated and recirculated through the broad dissemination of eighteenth-century Enlightenment writing. This, in turn, informed conceptions of Indigenous skilled labour and prevented its association with the refinement, skill and modernity bestowed upon other 'exotic' luxuries. Situated in the 'first stage' of development, Indigenous makers' skilled contributions were subsequently erased from eighteenth-century conceptualizations of fur's production cycle.

Compounding Enlightenment concepts of stadial history were dominant narratives underpinning Europe's mercantile economy in the early modern period, narratives that prevented the acknowledgement of skilled Indigenous women in the production of luxury fur. For one, beaver pelts fashioned by Indigenous women did not align with European perceptions of '[l]uxury objects produced by specialized non-local craftsmen [sic] [which] were universally desired by most societies' (Berg 2005: 61). But even when appreciating the skills of non-local craftspeople, protectionist policies by French and British governments prioritized the final production or finishing of luxury goods in the domestic setting. As part of national aims to expand domestic luxury production, mercantilist systems conceptually and practically privileged the work of French and British hatters and milliners as the true creators of luxury fur goods. In other words, mercantile patterns of production meant that it was in its 'finishing' in France or Britain that any item – including a beaver hat – became luxurious.

Nineteenth-century wilderness tourism

By the nineteenth century, political developments leading up to the Dominion of Canada's founding in 1867 shifted the economic functions of fur trading, not to mention relationships between settler interests and Indigenous providers. In this period, colonial settlements encroached upon longstanding hunting grounds as the government increasingly prioritized more intrusive forms of agricultural development over the fur trade (Rich 1967: 600–27). Internal divisions at the HBC saw conflicts over the Company's direction as a bastion of the European fur trade versus a diversified organization prioritizing 'land development and promotion schemes' (Ray 1990: 3). Treaties and land transfers ultimately meant the claiming of HBC – or more accurately Indigenous – territories for European settlement, which, in turn, altered the make-up of the national economy and especially the 'old fur trade order in Canada' (Ray 1990: 30–49; Manuel and Derrickson 2017: 62–66 and 88–93). Declining beaver stocks affected the numbers of pelts procured and processed, shifting the role of settler and Indigenous groups in a new nationalized capitalist economy predicated on free trade, state paternalism and cash transactions (Ray 1990: 40, 47–49; van Kirk 1980; Faiers 2020: 47).

It was in the wake of these broader socio-economic shifts – and the aggressive expansion of a white settler colony – that new modes of luxury came to the fore. This took the form of experiential luxury by way of transatlantic tourism targeting elite western travellers seeking to escape the demands of 'modern' life. Yet, like early modern Indigenous pelt production, these travel possibilities were not, at the time, deemed luxurious. By interrogating the boom in Canadian tourism from the early nineteenth century, however, we can see the ways that parallel tourist and settler-colonial initiatives comprised a type of luxurious experience that was obfuscated by providers and consumers alike in efforts to preserve the authentic pursuit of a 'natural' experience.

Canada's standing as a tourist destination for those desiring a return to 'the wilds' of nature emerged in the late eighteenth century before its significant expansion in the following decades. Elite European interest in seeking out unspoiled nature originated in Romantic schools of thought dominating the continent in this period. Intersections between Romanticism and nature tourism were myriad, argues Patricia Jasen, including 'the emergence of the "picturesque" and the "sublime" as major aesthetic categories; the rising importance of landscape as an element of taste; growing links between concepts of landscape, nationalism, and history; and a deepening fascination with aboriginal [sic] peoples' (1995: 7). Offering abundant imaginary possibilities in connection to each of these elements, Canada emerged as an idealized site for those seeking to satisfy their heightened sensibilities. Tourists with means flocked to the Canadian wilderness, taking up the 'Northern Tour' as an alternative to the traditional Grand Tour through Europe's principal luxury destinations (Morgan 2016: 135).[7]

European travellers' desires to seek out 'untamed' nature meant that Canada's natural wonders became some of the key destinations for a burgeoning national tourist industry. This is most evident in the case of Niagara Falls. Long before Niagara Falls developed into a site of democratized – and delightfully kitschy – mass tourism aimed at the middle classes, it remained the purview of elite European and American travellers satisfying their pursuit of unsullied and majestic wilderness (Jasen 1995: 29–54; Dubinsky 1999: 10, 19–53). The Falls itself developed into an ' "icon of the sublime" for the entire Western world' (McKinsey 1995 quoted in Jasen 1995: 29, 31), and European elites flocked to the site to experience their first view of the natural spectacle, of which 'the emotion of this moment', noted Harriet Martineau, 'was never renewed or equaled' (1838: 77). Save for a brief lull during the War of 1812, the site attracted hundreds of visitors through the early nineteenth century, rising to between 12,000 and 15,000 people by the mid-1830s (Jasen 1995: 44).

Yet, deep contradictions underpinned elite tourists' pursuit of the sublime, in the form of luxury trappings developed to satisfy their material wants and meet

FIGURE 2.2: 'Niagara Falls Fashion Plate, 1842'. Courtesy of Library and Archives Canada/ W. H. Coverdale collection of Canadiana Manoir Richelieu collection/e010947274.

standards befitting their class status. In the early days of travel, local Niagara dignitaries hosted elite travellers, but this was increasingly untenable as the volume of visitors increased. By the 1820s, a number of luxury hotels sprouted up in enviable locations along the edges of the Falls, offering European visitors unsurpassed views all while gatekeeping against more common access to these privileged natural sights. In 1822, for example, entrepreneur William Forsyth constructed the Pavilion Hotel, a three-storey balconied structure that privatized some of the most majestic views of the natural wonder. Forsyth was seemingly a master at harnessing the grandeur of the Falls for his paying clients via the design of his luxury accommodations. This included coaches specifically operated by the venue, which would ferry visitors from the local railway depot to the property. Forsyth then carefully choreographed visitors' 'first glimpse of the falls by making their way from his hotel down a dense forest path which concealed the view 'till close at the place/whereupon it burst upon them "with astonishing grandeur!"' (quoted in Jasen 1995: 37; Dubinsky 1999: 31). Forsyth harnessed the visual power of the Falls to enhance the luxurious nature of his operation, an act that simultaneously 'tamed' the wildness on display for genteel company. Other tourism entrepreneurs followed suit, and increasingly grand hotels sprung up through the 1830s, featuring 'balconies and verandas with spectacular views, as well as gardens, billiard rooms, baths, and nightly balls and parties' (Dubinsky 1999: 32).

As Forsyth's example suggests, elite tourists' desire to experience unhindered wilderness resulted in the luxury development – and eventual commercialization and commodification – of the very areas whose nature they sought to preserve. In this way, luxury wilderness tourism functioned in tandem with national processes of settler colonialism, with 'tourism before the First World War in Canada [being] closely tied to the expansionist cause' (Jasen 1995: 4). This included the development of railways as part of state nationalization projects, which expanded possibilities for elite wilderness travel as they exposed previously inaccessible natural wonders to growing cadres of European travellers with means. In some cases, such links between tourist and settler interests were explicit. For example, Alberta's Jasper National Park, founded in 1907, originated in efforts by the Grand Trunk Pacific Railway and their rival Canadian Northern to draw tourists to western Canada. Originally slated for agricultural settlement, the land was transformed instead into an elite destination, featuring a luxury hotel at the Miette Hot Springs designed by celebrated British-born architect Francis Rattenbury (Taylor 2007: 200).

This was not the only coalition between luxury hoteliers, railway companies and the federal government. The efforts at Jasper were a reaction, in part, to the establishment of Canada's first national park in 1887: Rocky Mountains (later Banff National) Park, which was similarly developed out of government and Canadian Pacific Railway initiatives (Taylor 2007: 200; Mason 2014). The Banff Springs Hotel (now the Fairmont Banff Springs) opened in 1888 as a luxury respite for elite clientele from the pressures of modern life, all while offering 'some of the continent's most opulent accommodations during the period' (Mason 2008: 223). By 1898, influential Scottish travel editor James Fullarton Muirhead declared it the second best hotel in North America, owing to its winning combination of luxury service and luxurious scenery; he lauded the 'almost absolute perfection of the [waiters]' and the 'wonderfully beautiful view from the summer-house at its northeast corner' (1898: 264–65). To bolster the success of Banff's luxury accommodations, the federal government limited the purchase of land adjacent to the park to affluent buyers, hoping to transform 'the townsite in the style of an elite European resort community' (Mason 2008: 224). Such efforts – the construction and designation of railways, national parks and luxury hotels – aligned more broadly with nineteenth-century imperial projects to forge a model white settler colony. In this way, luxury travel was central to the nineteenth-century colonial expansionist project, just as Indigenous skills were key to early modern luxury fur production. This was the case even as tourists rejected or downplayed designations of their pursuits as 'luxurious', so as to preserve the authenticity of Canada's imagined geographies.

In its ties to settler-colonial expansionist projects, nineteenth-century luxury tourism turned in large part on the presence of Indigenous peoples as proof of Canada's 'untamed' wildness. More accurately, however, the construction of a national tourist industry accelerated violent processes of dispossession, dependency and oppression that underpinned the colonization of Canada and Indigenous peoples (Manuel and Derrickson 2017: Part 1). This included the aforementioned construction of luxury hotels by powerful national railway interests. In the case of Banff, the hot springs that were allegedly 'discovered' by nineteenth-century railway workers had long been central to the lives, community and culture of the Stoney Nakoda Nations of Chiniki, Wesley and Bearspaw of the Banff-Bow Valley (Mason 2014: 50–51). By the late nineteenth century, Anglo-European tourism entrepreneurs complained of Nakoda hunting practices on 'their' land. Critics yoked their claims to conservationist arguments increasingly adopted by local and federal governments at the dawn of the twentieth century, arguing that Indigenous traditions and other 'subsistence land practices' contravened federal attempts to preserve the natural environment (Mason 2014: 55–56; Clapperton 2013: 354).

Yet these material realities and lived experiences of Indigenous peoples under nineteenth-century settler colonialism did not figure in elite tourism, which instead turned on longstanding tropes of Indigenous peoples' relationship to nature – and thus their exclusion from modernity. In this period, many European travellers' ideas of 'savagery' among Indigenous peoples directly linked to circulating anxieties over industrializing society and their relationship to narratives of progress. Indeed, concerns over modern civilization animated the Romantic turn to nature as a reaction against the encroachment of modernity in the forms of industry, urbanization and their attendant anomie; wilderness travel functioned as a means to escape such stresses, serving as a 'purifying and restorative tonic for many of the ills of the city' (Dubinsky 1999: 25). But if Canadian travel functioned as an antidote to modern life, this was owing to its perceived *lack* of civilization and also that of its original inhabitants. As Jasen observes, European travellers defined themselves – and their civilization – against circulating notions of the 'Other', including Indigenous peoples who they encountered in their travels to Canada. In terms invoking early modern stadial histories of development, when 'urban life became steadily more complicated, people naturally wondered what might have been lost through the processes of civilization'. This curiosity was allegedly satisfied by European travellers' interactions with Indigenous communities. 'If the wild man stood for savagery', Jasen argues, 'he also stood for freedom' (1995: 13; see also Richardson 2018: 8, 103–04). But witnessing a society that had, in European eyes, not yet undergone the transition to modernity also functioned as a means to reify their own superiority. Conditions in Canada did not merely satisfy European demand for experiences of untamed nature but also suggested 'degeneration' across 'the rest of the world' for disdainful western observers who were mollified, in their own estimations, by their comparative progress (Jasen 1995: 16; Dubinsky 1999: 62).

Demands of elite travellers to experience the 'uncivilized' world first-hand subsequently resulted in orchestrated events across the country, in which some Indigenous people interacted with European visitors in an attempt to satisfy these desires. In the case of Banff, despite the government and tourist industry taking action against them – including banning them from the park and townsite – some Nakoda people from the Morley reserve were later recruited to take part in a local festival to enhance tourists' luxury experiences. 'Banff Indian Days' launched between 1887 and 1897 when an overflowing Bow River prevented elite hotel guests' departure by rail (Clapperton 2013: 352; Mason 2014: 77–106; Drees 1993: 8). The event included a parade of Indigenous participants, some donning headdresses and buckskin fashions, as well as sporting events like bow and arrow competitions (Drees 1993: 12). Laurie Meijer Drees argues that the event presented an opportunity for cross-cultural assertion, where Indigenous participants could emphasize the 'differentiation of Indian [sic] from White [sic] culture at a time when these distinctions were beginning to disappear' (1993: 20). But elite white visitors were not necessarily interested in understanding or appreciating elements of Nakoda culture through these displays, a position that Indigenous participants clearly understood in their later efforts, through the 1920s, to 'show themselves as complex people, despite the attempts by outsiders to essentialize them and preserve them *as* nature' (Clapperton 2013: 369; original emphasis). In the nineteenth century, however, power ultimately lay in the hands of white tourism entrepreneurs, who emphasized 'pre-colonial representations of Aboriginal people', which 'did not portray the current lived realities of local Indigenous communities' (Mason 2008: 227). This spectacle of 'otherness' helped substantiate Canada's proximity to 'wilderness' for elite, foreign visitors via a carefully calibrated performance of 'pre-modern man' for luxury clientele (see Clapperton 2013). The desires of these same elite constituencies – for wilderness, for encounters with the 'Other', for authenticity – all the while meant obscuring luxurious elements of their travels, in the service of maintaining the illusion of a retreat from 'civilization'.

However, European visitors were not always satisfied with these performances of nature or otherness, periodically expressing disappointment at either the lack of majesty of natural wonders like Niagara Falls or the alleged failure of local Indigenous peoples to live up to dominant expectations of 'the noble savage' (Dubinsky 1999: 62–66). In an example of the latter from 1865, famed commentator George Augustus Sala described an unnamed Indigenous man at Niagara's Suspension

Bridge as possessing 'facial angles of his countenance [that] would not have been amiss on a medal representing one of the Twelve Caesars […] but there his classicality stopped'. He then descended into a racist cataloging of the man's 'very ragged' appearance (1865: 182 cited in Dubinsky 1999: 65). Sala concluded by noting the incongruity of the Indigenous man in the context of the area's expanding tourist economy. 'Niagara was wanted for tourists and excursionists, for hotel-keepers and guide-book sellers', he remarked. The Indigenous man 'was an anomaly and an anachronism here' (1865: 183). Such contradictory assessments aligned with other nineteenth-century travel accounts, in which Indigenous peoples figured as 'too ferocious or too tame, romantic figures or pathetic drunkards, uncivilized and unchristian, or boring (or ridiculous) in their attempts to mimic white lifestyles'. Some European writers, argues Karen Dubinsky, subsequently 'felt cheated by their visits to the contact zone' (1999: 63). Such 'disappointments' were the effect of dominant western fictions defining civilization, wilderness and Indigeneity, untruths that tourism entrepreneurs perpetuated through their careful obfuscation of the material realities of tourists' luxury travels. Stubbornly circulated by European interlocutors and based on dominant settler-colonial mythologies, many of these falsehoods were destabilized upon people's arrival and interaction with the lived environment and some of the First Nations actors who inhabited it. In response, some elite travellers criticized both natural phenomena and Indigenous individuals and groups for insufficiently meeting European expectations of an imagined 'Other' rather than accept the material realities of a nation in the midst of violent processes of settler colonial expansion and dispossession. This disappointment functioned alongside broader fictions at play, including the denial of the luxury accommodations and services that undergirded many early excursions to Canada.

Twentieth-century garment production

Long-circulating narratives about Indigenous peoples' alleged lack of civilization were a central feature in fictions of 'naturalness' that drew elite, white Europeans to Canada. Pursuit of 'wilderness escape' also meant denying the luxury amenities that characterized Europeans' travel, just as early modern western commentators denied the labour of Indigenous women in the fur trade for two hundred years before that. Yet, fictions that obscured the nation's relationship to luxury did not always derive from extra-Canadian sources like Europe. This is evident in the case of Canada's garment-manufacturing industry of the early twentieth century, in which luxury artisans from Eastern Europe found themselves – and their skills – subsumed under dominant discourses about Canada's role as a paternalist provider to global networks of immigrants in need. This included nativist gatekeeping among established Anglo-Canadian settlers, which limited new immigrants' mobilization of their extant luxury skills in the Canadian fashion industry.

If Canada represented the opportunity to reconnect with 'the wild' and escape the travails of modern industrial life, for thousands of other, less-affluent Europeans, the nation was a chance to secure economic and familial security via immigration. Beginning in the late nineteenth but especially in the early twentieth century, this included an influx of Jewish immigrants from Eastern Europe, who propelled, in part, the expansion of Canada's modern garment industry (Dillon and Godley 2012; Godley 1997). As in other industrialized western centres, the nation's garment industry underwent dramatic shifts from the late nineteenth century. This was primarily fueled by the growing popularity of ready-to-wear men's clothing, followed thereafter by expansions in ladies' ready-to-wear apparel. Urbanization, new technologies like the sewing machine and the rise of contracting made for faster, more efficient and cheaper production. While some bespoke tailoring outfits continued to great success (Cariou 2004), Canada's garment industry increasingly turned on the mass production of ready-to-wear items (see, e.g., Frager 2008; Steedman 1997; Poutanen 1985; Payette-Daoust 1986).

An influx of immigrants beginning in the 1880s, and particularly those from Eastern Europe, accelerated these shifts in garment production. Between 1896 and 1914, the Canadian state pursued an aggressive recruiting campaign for potential immigrants, including those from Eastern European holdings (Vigod 1984: 8; Hiebert 1993: 248, 252). This proved especially ideal for Jewish populations who, from the late nineteenth century, lived under anti-Semitic rule in Czarist Russia. This included violent pogroms in and around the Pale of Settlement, the almost 1 million square kilometre territory in present-day Russia, Poland, Ukraine and Lithuania to which many Jews were relegated (Berson 2010: xxi; Vigod 1984). This persecution, coupled with political and economic instability, drove some 2 million Eastern European Jews to settle around the world, including in major urban centres like Montréal, Toronto and Winnipeg (Hiebert 1993: 249; Frager 1992b: 10–34). Between 1881 and 1921, Canada's Jewish population expanded from less than 3000 to more than 125,000 people through the immigration of primarily Yiddish-speaking Ashkenazi Jews from Russia and Poland (Vigod 1984: 3–4). By 1931, Canada's Jewish population was 156,726, with some 27,373 individuals – still primarily from Russia and Poland – categorized as 'Foreign Nationals' (Rosenberg [1939] 1993: 392). In Canadian cities, these new immigrants lived and worked alongside longer-established Jewish communities who had emigrated from Britain and Germany earlier in the nineteenth century (Hiebert 1993: 249).[8] There was, however, initially limited integration between the groups due to differences in religious orthodoxy, language and class, with many Eastern European immigrants clustered in dire socio-economic conditions in urban 'slums', such as the Ward in central Toronto (King 1897; Vigod 1984: 7; Hiebert 1993; Frager 1992b: 14).

Upon arrival, many East European Jewish immigrants gravitated to work in Canada's expanding garment trades, further engendering the sector's shift to ready-made wares. Jewish immigrants' concentration in the garment trades occurred for a number of reasons. Geographer Daniel Hiebert and others note patterns of ethnic sectoral concentration when established Jewish employers came to depend on Eastern European Jewish immigrants to staff their small- and mid-sized garment operations (1993: 247; Dillon and Godley 2012: 48). But there were also other, skill-based factors existing before immigrants' arrival to Canada that predicated their movement into the garment industry. For instance, discriminatory ordinances in mid-nineteenth-century Russia codified some Eastern European Jews' sectoral concentration as guild-registered artisans and craftspeople and resulted in considerable numbers of the community becoming skilled tailors, needleworkers or seamstresses (Hiebert 1993: 249; Lowenstein 1984; 306–07; Vigod 1984: 10). Some immigrants subsequently arrived in Canada equipped with extensive artisanal skill and experience; examining comparable statistics in the United States between 1881 and 1910, Hiebert found that 'a large proportion of East European Jewish immigrants were either semiskilled or skilled workers', and in total, '[s]ome 33 percent had acquired sewing skills before leaving Eastern Europe' (1993: 249; Frager 1992b: 16).

Upon arrival in urban Canadian markets, however, skilled positions for artisans were not always open to Jewish workers, despite their premigration experience or training. In the early twentieth century, Anglo-Canadian garment workers maintained a monopoly on the most skilled – and powerful – positions in the industry, namely as cutters (Steedman 1997: 24; Berson 2010: 63; Frager 1992b: 83). Anti-Semitism and discriminatory hiring practices meant that the skills of Eastern European immigrants in creating desirable – and luxurious – goods were often devalued, as employers relegated them to low-paying, low-skilled jobs reflective of their ethnic and social class rather than their skilled knowledge (Frager 2008: 144). Bound by conditions in which 'many Jewish immigrants were experienced tailors when they arrived, and that they desperately needed work' (Hiebert 1993: 255), Jewish immigrants were ultimately 'victims of deskilling' and marginalized by Anglo-Canadian tailors as a threat to existing trade hierarchies (Frager 1992b: 81; Frager 2008: 144).

The subsequent flooding of the Canadian market with skilled but underpaid and undervalued labourers perpetuated systems of sweating in a range of occupational settings, from small contract workshops to large-scale manufactories (McIntosh 1993: 111–12; Dillon and Godley 2012: 48; Steedman 1997: 30). A steady stream of government-sanctioned Eastern European immigration until

1914 sustained these exploitative labour systems. In fact, argues Ruth Frager, 'early twentieth-century Canadian immigration policy had been strongly shaped by key Canadian entrepreneurs whose insistence on the open-door policy stemmed partly from their plans to benefit from an ethnically diverse labour force' (2008: 150). Among deskilled immigrant workers, anyone who complained of unfair conditions was promptly replaced by more recent, often desperate arrivals (Frager 1992b: 23–24). This was especially evident in the 1912 strike against T. Eaton & Co., the major national retailing outfit analysed by Nigel Lezama in this volume. Many of their products were 'Made in Canada' by Jewish workers of Eastern European descent, and over one thousand of them marched off the job in February of that year. The action garnered significant union support from the International Ladies' Garment Workers' Union (ILGWU) and the United Garment Workers (UGW) (Frager 1992a: 191). However, Anglo-Canadian co-workers did not support the job action, Eaton's held strong against labourers' demands and the strike was soon crushed. In response, 'for a very long time' in the aftermath of the unsuccessful strike, a union official recalled, 'the T. Eaton Company would not hire any Jews' (quoted in Frager 1992a: 204).

In Canada's burgeoning garment industry, then, ethnocentrism periodically pre-vented the integration of Jewish labourers' artisanal skills as a means to expand a national luxury market; rather, these abilities were exploited, as workers were fun-neled into low-paying, low-skilled jobs. One exception to this trend was arguably Canada's modern fur industry which, in the early twentieth century, transformed upon the arrival of Eastern European artisans. Rather than find themselves shunted to low-paying, low-skilled work, some fur artisans propelled a small but lucra-tive wholesale industry for urban Canadian markets (Vigod 1984: 12). Fur and fur goods subsequently emerged as the 'second largest occupational group among Jews in Canada' by 1931. According to that year's census, Jewish workers made up '32.9% of all persons of all origins engaged in this branch of manufacture in Canada' (Rosenberg [1939] 1993: 178–79). Joined by Greek manufacturers after the Second World War, Canada's urban centres of fur garment production emerged in Toronto, Winnipeg and Montréal (Sangster 2007: 256; Rantisi 2014; Nadeau 2001: 151; Colpitts 2013: 140–41). The industry was not free from ethnocentric gatekeeping, dangerous working conditions and significant labour conflicts, espe-cially by the midcentury (see Frager 1992b; 2008: 148; Sangster 2007: 257–62). Communities of small-scale family-owned workshops nonetheless developed a reputation among consumers for their artisanal skills of production.

The influx of European fur cutters, dressers and sewers enhanced the skilled workforce of Canadian furriers and buoyed the popularity of the nation's fur industry through the interwar period. Growing demand and the relative democra-tization of consumption meant that, in this moment, 'Canadian furriers produced

FIGURE 2.3: Interior view of Alter Furs, Yonge Street, Toronto, *c.*1927. Courtesy of Ontario Jewish Archives, Blankenstein Family Heritage Centre, item 1282.

an astounding 1.3 million fur coats for women and an equally expansive stock of fur for women's fashion accessories and clothing trim' (Colpitts 2013: 134). This boom derived in part from demand but also from 'technical, industrial, and chemical innovations' originating in small workshops located in Montréal and Toronto (Colpitts 2013: 136). These new techniques facilitated the production of mock varieties of fur that imitated traditional luxury pelts for a fraction of the price. As George Colpitts shows, some seventy-four varieties of fake fur were available by 1923, circulating in a variety of forms. 'Offenders included "Adelaide chinchilla," really the Australian opossum, the "Alaska bear" (a darkly dyed raccoon), and the skunk posing as "black marten"' (2013: 140). While imitation furs prompted derision from some industry observers, they were, in fact, reflective of creative innovations coming out of a localized Canadian scene. Colpitts highlights the dubious French accents of these successful furriers, but demographer Louis Rosenberg's findings in 1939 suggest that Canada's fur wholesalers and retailers owed much of their successes to skilled Jewish workers who dominated trade labour ([1939]

1993). Jewish artisans dressed, dyed and trimmed fur, before overseeing cutting and seamstressing into desirable luxury and mid-market creations. These were meticulous practices, controlled by men, who undertook 'techniques of sorting, wetting and stretching, blocking, then cutting the skins'. This preceded later mid-century processes, described by Sangster, that 'involved the cutter knowing how to select, cut and recut skins countless times, so that they could be sewn together to form an elongated, almost seamless coat' (2007: 256).

Notably, many Jewish furriers would have brought these luxury skills to Canada from their countries of origin and were able to apply this pre-immigration experience to the Canadian context. Writing in 1939, Rosenberg confirmed that '[t]he majority learned their craft in European countries from which they came'. Maintaining western historical designations of 'raw' peltry, as discussed above, he emphasized the centrality of skilled Jewish workers to the development of Canada's twentieth-century fur industry.

> It is the immigrant Jewish population which has converted Canada from a country which was a producer of raw furs for export to other countries, into a country which dresses, dyes and makes up all the furs it requires for its own use, besides exporting its surplus of raw and dressed furs to other countries.
>
> ([1939] 1993: 179)

To this day, small workshops run by manufacturers of European descent dominate Canadian production, positioning themselves as a traditional craft industry despite their relatively recent history in Canada (Rantisi 2014: 227). '[N]early 80% of Canadian fur manufacturing, valued at over 150 million dollars' derives from such ventures in Montréal, with Canada ranking within the top seven global suppliers of fur commodities (2014: 229).

Despite these historical inroads, Canada's luxury fur industry remains a relatively marginal sector that is dominated by small-scale artisans of European descent based in urban settings. The dominance of these same operations – with their own histories of subjugation to nativist, Anglo-centric attitudes that attempted to limit their industry success – has arguably come at the cost of a new generation of Canadian designers who seek to modernize the nation's fur trade. The sector continues as a 'traditional craft industry', argues Norma Rantisi, due to its artisanal modes of production but also the fact that 'aesthetic innovation (or "creativity") is secondary' (2014: 224). The sidelining of design innovation in these small, often family-run businesses runs the risk of stagnating the industry in the face of digital advances, global outsourcing and animal rights advocacy (see Nadeau 2001). It is here, argues Rantisi, that the influence of Indigenous providers and other designers, and especially women, represents a potential shift 'from craft production to a more design-intensive form associated with the fashion industry' (2014: 229; see also Nadeau 2001: 167–94). This movement towards product differentiation is, according to some, the best means of forging Canadian success in a luxury fur market that increasingly depends on places like Greece and East Asia for manufacturing (Skov 2005: 26). However, Indigenous and/or female designers face challenges breaking into these established industry systems. It is perhaps ironic that these contemporary trade hierarchies, originally built in resistance to historical privileging of Anglo-Canadian supremacy, are now challenging the luxury contributions of new actors based on their gender and Indigeneity (Kucheran 2016).

Conclusions

If, as Berg argues, national 'identities were […] made in trade and empire, in facing the "otherness" of different civilizations and cultures' (2005: 8), such perceptions of otherness were not equally extended to groups around the world, and especially in the defining of what was and was not luxurious. Whereas 'exotic' eastern luxury productions communicated 'civility, taste, and moderation' (2005: 20) in the early modern period, semi-finished luxury products from the 'New World' allegedly did not. In the case of early modern pelts, they were not associated with modernity, unlike eastern objects, nor were they appreciated for their adaptability. Instead, the deeply skilled, feminized process of pelt preparation was not only undervalued as a key element of luxury production but also erased. By the nineteenth century, luxury status was further denied when elite western tourists framed their descent into the Canadian 'wilds' as a flight from modern capitalist life rather than the experiential luxury that it was. The disavowal of their material amenities was central to the fictions that underpinned their pursuits, as acknowledging the existence of a luxury tourist industry would negate any illusions of escape. Rather, elite tourists sought out 'authentic' interactions with nature and Indigenous peoples, only to find themselves disappointed by the lived realities – and contradictions – that undergirded settler-colonial state building. By the twentieth century, luxury was actively deskilled when immigrant artisans found themselves subsumed under inequitable Anglo-Canadian industry hierarchies, which perceived their potential contributions to Canada's luxury trades as a threat rather than an asset. With the exception of some trades, Canadian nativism and anti-Semitism affected the integration of skilled immigrant labour into a luxury economy, initially precluding opportunities to advance the nation's reputation on the global luxury scene. Similar trends persist in today's fur industry via new modes of exclusion against design initiatives from women and Indigenous innovators.

Historically, argues Berg, 'luxury was [...] about cultural displays of power' (2005: 38). Examples across Canadian history that erased, denied or actively deskilled instances of luxury making, experiences and artisanship are subsequently telling. For one, they reflect the nation's standing, in the settler-colonial imaginary, as an outlier in relation to Britain and Europe more generally, which meant an inability to assert what was and was not luxurious in relation to Canadian subjectivities, productions and processes. Historical examples further reveal how these discourses were eventually integrated into a nativist Canadian ethos, which, by the twentieth century, replicated gatekeeping practices around conceptualizations of luxury by denying power to skilled artisanal providers, in large part because of their 'foreignness'. And yet, attention to historical examples such as beaver pelts, wilderness tourism and immigrant fur production shows that there were, in fact, luxurious elements underpinning Canadian historical development, even if they were not classified as such. It is now up to current and future makers, thinkers and luxury providers to determine how luxury will be conceptualized among Canadians in years to come. This includes the conditions of power – and the dangers of erasure, denial and inequality – that will continue to figure in Canada's relationship to luxury in the twenty-first century.

NOTES

1. Scholars of fashion, art and space have addressed problematic distinctions between European contexts and extra-European settings in designations like 'art' versus 'artifacts' or 'luxury' versus 'craft'. See, for example, Gaugele and Titton (2019), Gilbert (2013), Haehnel (2019), Kucheran (2019a) and Scholze (2015).
2. For an important alternative to settler-colonial narratives of the beaver, see Simpson (2020).
3. On challenges and shortcomings of relying on western sources to write about Indigenous historical actors, see, for example, essays in Podruchny and Peers (2010), Brown (2003) and Brown and Vibert (1996).
4. It is unclear what community Conn visited. It could include the First Nations of Eastmain, Waskaganish, Wemindji, Chisasibi or Whapmagoostui, among others in the territory of Eeyou Istchee (see Cree Nation Government n.d.).
5. Richardson (2018) advances a more nuanced understanding of 'the Indian's' role in eighteenth-century British culture, arguing that the figure operated as a mirror for western processes of modern self-making. He does so via attention to literary depictions of cultural hybridity.
6. In conceptualizing stages of man's civilization, Bickham notes, 'the Scots philosophers generally operated under the assumption that the commercial society in which they lived was the outcome of a social evolutionary process that had substantially altered European government and manners' (2005: 178).

7. This was especially the case during the Napoleonic Wars (1803–15), when many European travel plans were dashed by the disruptions of war (Jasen 1995: 32).

8. Many German Jews were in '[t]he textile business and retail dry goods trade [which] meant that they also dealt in imports and knew about sophisticated luxury goods such as trimmings and ribbons as well as fabrics'. They brought this expertise to North America upon immigrating (Dillon and Godley 2012: 42).

3

From Unvalued to Surplus Value: 'Made-in-Canada' Luxury at Eaton's in the 1920s

Nigel Lezama

This chapter investigates the 'lowly luxuries' of the working and rural classes in Canada in the 1920s. How does luxurious value emerge from domestically produced basic commodities? What refinements are necessary for a Canadian mass retailer to become a purveyor of luxuries? In the first decades of the twentieth century, domestic manufacturing was at the heart of Canada's economic and foreign affairs policy: how to protect nascent industries and spur on consumption of Canadian-made goods. It is this second ambition to promote 'Made-in-Canada' goods that inspires the following analysis of 'Canada's Department Store', the T. Eaton Company Limited. Founded in 1869 as a small dry goods store in Toronto, Canada, by Timothy Eaton, an Irish immigrant, Eaton's became one of the key players in the Made-in-Canada movement. The store pioneered a number of new retail practices that enabled its remarkable growth and eventual domination of the market. 'Cash only' and fixed pricing policies, while new to the Toronto retail scene, were established innovations in British and European markets. These new practices helped Eaton's both prosper and expand, growing into a department store in 1890 and, by 1940, becoming the eighth largest retailer in the world with forty-seven stores and one hundred mail order offices across the country (Belisle 2011). Eaton's mail order business started in 1884 and continued with major Fall–Winter and Spring–Summer catalogues sent to homes across Canada until 1976, when both retail and mail order profits began to steadily drop. By the end of the century, Eaton's market share had plummeted and the company filed for bankruptcy protection in 1997. After a failed restructuring, the former Canadian giant shuttered in 1999.

This chapter focuses on Eaton's Made-in-Canada campaign of the 1920s during which the economic and political conditions in the country significantly shifted and the campaign converged two distinct motivations: to build economic capital and assert a national cultural identity. Studying three aspects of Eaton's strategies, namely the promotion of 'Eaton-Made' commodities over foreign fineries, the catalogue's discourse surrounding Canadian-made fashions and, lastly, the company's project to build a prestigious all-Canadian outpost in Toronto, facilitates the exploration and definition of a distinctly Canadian luxury, based on civic ideals rather than social distinction. This Made-in-Canada luxury challenges current thinking on luxury by privileging humble and ordinary goods manufactured outside of traditional centres of luxury production as the source of a re-centred prestige.

Creating 'Canadian-made' surplus value

In a speech given by R. Y. Eaton to the Imperial Order Daughters of the Empire (IODE), reported in Toronto daily *The Globe* on February 8, 1927, the third president of the Timothy Eaton Company Limited explained the department store's foreign importing practices to the assembled group of elite Toronto women. 'At the present time the T. Eaton Company is importing only 20 per cent. of its merchandise' (*The Globe* 1927), announced R. Y. Eaton. Throughout the post-war decade, Eaton's elaborated a campaign through newspaper advertising, its iconic mail order catalogue and sales events featuring Canadian-made fashions, furnishings and home wares, highlighting the department store's importance to the domestic economy and for the country's working classes. Pertinently, the *Globe* article reported that Eaton's president contrasted the company's Canadian-made merchandise with foreign-sourced 'luxuries'. The reporter insisted that the volume of domestically manufactured merchandise is significant 'even when taking into account such luxuries as Oriental rugs, chinaware, linens, French fashion goods, tapestries, perfumery, books, art goods and rare pictures' also on offer in Eaton's stores. Surprisingly for a company with buying offices in Tokyo, Manchester, Leicester, Belfast, Zurich and New York by the end of the First World War (cf. Belisle 2011: 35), the department store's president apparently wished to distinguish between a negligible volume of foreign-made, *non-essential* goods and a substantially important volume of Canadian-made merchandise offered through the company's nation-wide stores and mail order catalogues.

This distinction between foreign luxuries and domestic essentials echoes imperialist and long-established discourses that still hold currency in today's world markets. Luxurious, elite goods come from metropolitan centres of cultural and fashionable production: Paris, London, Antwerp, Milan and Geneva in Europe; Tokyo and Kyoto in Asia; New York and Los Angeles in North America. Specialized and exotic goods come from 'far-flung' regions, like the Middle East and China. In

R. Y. Eaton's time, expensive foreign goods and fashions that circulated in markets across the world, but were sourced in these fashion capitals or exotic regions, functioned (and still do) as cultural capital[1] – a means of expressing social and economic standing – for the purveyor of these goods, as well as for well-to-do or middle-class consumers. In peripheral regions and second-tier cities, these foreign goods demonstrated cultural and economic capital for worldly and in-the-know consumers who could afford to accumulate expensive foreign commodities. To this day, domestic goods in peripheral markets generally do not emit a message of exclusivity, as these commodities are neither rare nor necessarily expensive.

Conversely, during the 1920s for the T. Eaton Company Limited, Canadian-made commodities captured the attention of the company's numerically more important lower-middle- and upper-working classes as well as rural spenders (cf. Belisle 2011: 27). However, Eaton's Canadian-made products also focused a *surplus value* necessary in a productionist model of national wealth-building that transformed seemingly ordinary commodities into luxuries. In the interwar period, this Canadian department store introduced and actively featured 'Eaton-made' and 'Canadian-made' commodities as a way to promote a distinctly *Canadian* means of supporting Canadian industrial manufacturing and smaller-scale handcraft, as well as Canadian workers and families. Most of the commodities promoted by the company were presented as notable for their lower price point and therefore more apt to entice the department store's key customer base. These products do not, at first blush, read as luxurious. However, Eaton's promotion, advertising and catalogues couched consumption of these domestically manufactured commodities in nationalist terms that gave them a surplus value. For example, the aforementioned *Globe* article reported:

> Mr. Eaton commended the quality of work being done in the men's clothing industry in Canada, stating that in style it compared favorably with the American output. In this department, he said, 98 per cent. of the sales of his company are of Canadian manufacture.
>
> (*The Globe* 1927)

The president's encomium is tempered despite the promotional purposes of his speech. Yet, the comparison is significant in that American fashions – from the established fashion capital New York – were a source of both real and symbolic capital for the department store, equal in status to Paris fashions. Accordingly, R. Y. Eaton's distinction of domestic production versus imported luxuries, while hegemonic in ideology, did not entirely reflect the store's use of the Canadian-made label to promote a sense of national duty and unity. Further, Eaton's Canadian-made commodities represented a broad range of products, from fashions to home

FIGURE 3.1: An advertisement from *The Globe* newspaper, dated 28 January 1922, that announces the 'Made-in-Canada' sale. Note the message from Eaton's then president, John C. Eaton (1876–1922), promoting the surplus value of 'Keep[ing] Canadians Busy' imbued in Made-in-Canada goods. Image in public domain.

appliances to sundries to literature. Given the department store's primarily modest and rural clientele, this reasonably priced domestic merchandise was equally a source of improvement for the standard of living of Canadian families outside of urban centres and of poorer working-class families by equalizing access to formerly luxurious wares that became affordable necessities through domestic manufacture. At the same time, Eaton's Canadian-made goods were indeed Canadian luxuries that inspired consumption based on 'Canadianness' over any objective value inherent in the commodity itself.

The Made-in-Canada campaign was not, in fact, the T. Eaton Company's invention. Launched by the Canadian Manufacturers' Association (CMA) in 1911, the campaign was tied to the political and economic turbulence of the pre-war period. As part of a response to growing US economic hegemony in North America, the movement to promote Canadian manufacturing formed one strategy for supporting national economic development. Historians Andre Siegel and James Hull (2014) cogently analyse the evolution of this movement, arguing that the Canadian-made campaign demonstrated that Canadian businesses adopted means beyond import tariffs to protect domestic manufacturing. Both before and after the war, foreign trade was a fraught issue for Canadian economic policy. During the 1911 federal election, the governing Liberal Party sought re-election on a platform focused on a negotiated free-trade agreement with the United States. However, manufacturing and business interests preferred protectionist, tariff-based policies, which had been the foundation of the Conservative Party's economic policy since the late nineteenth century (cf. Johnston 2005). Unsurprisingly, through the concerted efforts of these interests, the Conservative Party won the election and overturned the Liberal-negotiated Canada–United States free-trade agreement. Despite the entrenchment of tariff-based protectionism, industry and government continued to seek further ways to promote domestic economic productivity. In the wake of the election, this included the Made-in-Canada campaign, which emerged as a viable means of supporting domestic manufacturing.

The CMA came up with the idea of a 'Made-in-Canada train' that, in partnership with the Canadian Pacific Railway, would transport the finest Canadian-manufactured goods from coast to coast during the spring of 1912, introducing Canadians to Canadian merchandise that could rival imported goods in quality.

> Items on display included rubber products, pianos, bicycles, motors, pumps, kitchen appliances, a two-ton safe, beds, paints (including a miniature display of a paint manufacturing plant), farm supplies (including a miniature model of an automatic grain weighing machine and a kerosene power plant for lighting farm residences and barns), a completely furnished home, and many more.
>
> (Siegel and Hull 2014: 7)

While this first effort in the battle for Canadian-made goods was successful, the Great War forestalled further transcontinental voyages of the Made-in-Canada train. After the outbreak, the CMA sustained the campaign through its organ, *Industrial Canada*.

Up to, during and in the immediate wake of the Great War, the CMA's Made-in-Canada campaign focused on capitalist-based growth for the country's nascent industries. Conversely, in the 1920s, Canada's elite classes entered the fray, wishing to counter the commercial concerns promoted by the CMA. In her fascinating book *Buying Happiness: The Emergence of Consumer Consciousness in English Canada* (2018), historian Bettina Liverant explores the tensions that emerged as the professional, artistic and academic classes sought to build and promote a national *cultural* identity. The idea of Canadian-made for these cultural producers was to be placed in stark contrast to commercial goods and production, such as popular novels and mass-market magazines, the burgeoning film industry or saleable souvenirs, which were cast as a baser form of production that pandered to an uninitiated public and merely supported economic gain. In her analysis of the nationalist campaign coming from the field of high cultural production, Liverant insists on the *perceived* differences in value separating high from mass cultural production in the eyes of elite players.

> Profits made in cultural industries aimed at mass audiences increased with the numbers sold. Profits in elite cultural production depended on judgements of value by recognized experts. Affordability was seen as a threat to high standards. Works produced in limited quantities were deemed rare and valuable – in contrast to mass-produced items, which were considered vulgar and common – and could command higher prices.
>
> (2018: 64)

Focusing on high cultural discourses, Liverant is careful to point out that while producers of elite culture were quick to dismiss any form of production tied to commercial interests, these seemingly economically disinterested forms of production existed on a continuum with mass-produced commodities. Despite a desire by the elite classes of Canadian society to bracket off high culture from economic determinations – what French sociologist Pierre Bourdieu calls *euphemization* in his important text 'The forms of capital' ([1983] 1986) – both mass and high culture operate in a capitalist system for which all forms of capital can be reduced to the economic form.

What is the value of Canadian luxury?

The Made-in-Canada campaign was spearheaded in a pre-war moment for commercial reasons. The CMA harnessed patriotic sentiment at a moment when Canadians were beginning to assert a newfound status as a nation state that required civic duty equivalent to that which bound subjects to the British Empire. At the outset of the war in 1914, many Canadian industrialists saw the Made-in-Canada promotion as a means to grow profitability, but couched corporate desires in nationalist and protectionist terms.

Industrial Canada warned that shortages of workers, with men away at the front, might idle factories and allow predatory American producers to seize Canadian markets which would be difficult to wrest back after the war. The necessary counter to this was 'the Canadian who is determined to buy only the manufactured products of his own country during the war'.

(Siegel and Hull 2014: 8–9)

Siegel and Hull point out that patriotic sentiment became the main fodder for journalists.

The *Toronto Globe* editorially excoriated those who would try to evade trading restrictions to obtain German goods. A columnist in the same newspaper declared his own determination to buy only Canadian cloth and apples, and urged Toronto's men's clubs to stock cigars made in Canada from Canadian tobacco.

(Siegel and Hull 2014: 9)

There is an isomorphic form of Bourdieusian *euphemization* at play in the creation of a surplus value for Canadian-made goods as that which high-cultural producers harnessed to downplay the economic stakes that underpinned elite cultural production. Both manufacturers and cultural producers made use of the surplus value of Canadian patriotic sentiment to construct a commodity that was composed of more than its use value. Value in the Canadian-made lay beyond any inherent or material qualities of the saleable commodity. Indeed, some cast aspersion on the quality of Canadian-made products during the height of the wartime campaign.

The *Journal of Commerce* took the CMA to task for not ensuring that their members manufactured their 'Made in Canada' goods to proper standards, thus bringing the slogan into disrepute. They mentioned most particularly shoddy 'Made in Canada' footwear supplied to Canadian soldiers.

(Siegel and Hull 2014: 11)

For Liverant, during the post-war period the dominant classes faced a similar challenge of building an elite cultural production that was up to the task of demonstrating quality equivalent to the cultural production of more established metropoles. Artists, poets and academics (all agents of the cultural economy) determined that 'judgements of literary value, particularly of nationally important work, would be made by members of the professoriate and a small circle of influential friends and colleagues and not the book-buying public' (2018: 72). Quality control for a Made-in-Canada culture was ensured by the seemingly economically disinterested professional caste of critics who actively 'favoured narratives that supported the idea of Canada as an autonomous nation' (2018: 76). Importantly, both high culture and lowly commodities were imbued with a surplus value that was meant to increase the stature of the young country in which these divergent forms of capital were produced.

Luxury in the context of the Made-in-Canada campaign demonstrates a place-specific deploying of value, different from the luxuriousness imbued in exotic and imported commodities or the 'Made in …' labels denoting the fashion capital provenance of a given commodity and connoting a luxurious heritage of specialized craft. The 1920s in Canada was a period of economic transition, particularly for department stores. The decade started in a recession. Price levels and nominal wage rates in Canadian cities had only begun to equalize at the outset of the Great War, yet throughout the decade, real incomes – the spending power of skilled and unskilled workers – were not leveling out across the country.[2] Cities in the west of the country benefited from a lower cost of living than those in the east, and Toronto emerged as the city with the highest cost of living. Further, post-war inflation raised prices in department stores, while the advent and introduction of a number of American and Canadian chain stores, such as Loblaws and Woolworth's, created a competitive environment that brought lower prices to consumers. In her foundational study of Canadian department stores and the growth of consumer culture, *Retail Nation: Department Stores and the Making of Modern Canada*, Donica Belisle explains:

> By 1925 chains were earning the same percentage of the Canadian market as were department stores, and in 1930 they surpassed department stores' sales, bringing in $210 million net more, excluding $77 million net earned by catalogue operators, including those earned by department stores.
>
> (2011: 37–38)

Further, increased automobile sales and demographic shifts changed the way that Canadians shopped in the 1920s. 'As rural and semi-urban North Americans acquired more cars, customers travelled to downtown department stores less often, preferring instead to drive to stores located closer to their homes (Belisle 2011: 38). In this context, Eaton's Made-in-Canada campaign could be deemed more a means of spurring profit growth than the way to build a domestic luxury market.

However, the Made-in-Canada campaign, particularly for Eaton's, flourished at a moment when advertising was moving towards more 'scientific' methods of deployment.

> Daily newspapers then enjoyed the highest circulation figures they had ever seen. National consumer magazines were enjoying their first taste of success. So too were

national advertisers, many of whom had begun using national advertising for the first time in the 1910s.

(Johnston 2005: 251)

Advertising in the 1920s became more focused through the development of market research and the decline in political affiliation that had traditionally linked advertisers and media outlets. Advertising agencies, now acting as intermediaries between advertisers and newspapers, determined the best publications in which to advertise based on cost and statistical data, rather than on traditional political allegiance. In response to declining partisanship-based advertising and the challenging conditions of wider competition for reduced buying power, Eaton's Made-in-Canada promotions could trumpet a national consciousness that superseded political affiliation and instrumentalized consumption as a new mode of creating social identity for consumers concerned with value and cost. Commodities promoted as Made-in-Canada were imbued with a value that collapsed class differences and political affiliation to the benefit of a broader national identity.

What is democratized luxury?

Throughout the 1920s, the T. Eaton Company featured Canadian-made commodities in newspaper advertising and in their seasonal cross-country catalogue, promoted both as a means of supporting economic prosperity and as easier access to fashionable and modern goods for lower income consumers. This double focus on macro- and micro-level support for Canadian progress expressed what Belisle characterizes as 'the notion that mass retail democratized luxury' (2011: 58). The question remains, however, of what happens to luxury when it is democratized. The idea of democratized luxury and progress has roots in the rise of consumer society in the political economy of the eighteenth century. Maxine Berg and Elizabeth Eger (2002) argue that growing trade and access to foreign and exotic goods elicited much reflection on the definition of luxury and what were the moral implications of increased consumer access to luxurious commodities.

Contemporary perceptions of the category of 'luxury object' changed over the course of the eighteenth century. Mandeville referred to buildings, furniture, equipages and clothes. Melon mentioned foodstuffs and raw materials – sugar, coffee, tobacco and silk – but also wrote elsewhere of rich stuffs, works of gold and silver and foreign laces, and diamonds. It seems that it was not until Adam Smith that we see luxury goods distinguished in analytical terms – ornamental building, furniture, collections of books, pictures, frivolous jewels and baubles –and separated from expenditures on retainers, a fine table, horses and dogs.

(Berg and Eger 2002: 13)

Throughout the eighteenth century, the definition of luxury expanded so that neither 'foreignness' nor expense, in the absolute sense, were essential qualities for this category of commodity. Luxury came to include civic and class-based charac- teristics. 'Luxury was thus not just about goods, but about social behavior' (Berg and Eger 2002: 13). Edward Hundert further suggests that eighteenth-century pol- itical thought tied commerce to social practice and progress so that luxury could potentially represent a mode of civic participation. Paraphrasing Mandeville, he explains that '[l]uxury consumption, first of all, enriches a nation through the pro- motion of avarice, the particular vice which has as its unintended consequence encouragement for the manufacture and circulation of goods' (2003: 32). For the Anglo-Dutch political economist, luxurious tastes multiply wants at all levels of society, the satisfaction of which propels the nation's civilizing process.

In much the same way, Eaton's Made-in-Canada campaign of the 1920s used social behaviour as a motivation to promote national identity through consump- tion. R. Y. Eaton's speech to the IODE distinguished foreign luxuries from Can- adian commodities. However, through the discourse of its famous catalogue and the focus on the working and rural classes, Eaton's promoted a new model of *lowly luxuries* for the penny-wise whose consumption of low-cost, Canadian-made fash- ions, furnishings and appliances was touted as encouraging progress and increasing prosperity for both workers and the nation as a whole. The discursive detachment of foreign luxuries – non-essential wants – from Canadian-made commonplace goods – fundamental needs – was merely a rhetorical strategy; these domestic prod- ucts were indeed national luxuries 'supplying home needs and creating a demand for Canadian products abroad', as R. Y. Eaton asserted in his speech (*The Globe* 1927). This conception of luxury – that includes goods that fall outside of the categories of rarity and expense and considers consumer desire originating from more modest social strata – diverges from contemporary critical analysis of luxury as a fundamentally socioeconomic marker of distinction, a conception grounded in Bourdieu's theorization from his influential opus *Distinction: A Social Critique of the Judgement of Taste* ([1979] 1984). Nevertheless, unbinding luxury from elite or aspirational consumption follows Christopher Berry, who asserts at the outset of his study *The Idea of Luxury: A Conceptual and Historical Investiga- tion* that 'it is the factor of extensiveness or general desirability that enables us to identify the range of goods to which, in contemporary society, the term "luxury" is standardly applied' (1994: 5). In fact, luxury is neither restricted by cost nor the exclusive domain of the wealthy; to wit, 'luxury goods do not constitute a discrete, separate category, [...] such as "necessities"' (Berry 1994: 6). Further, Berry's refusal to isolate 'luxury' as a category opposing 'needs' prevents prioritization (moral or otherwise) of one category of goods over the other. Jonathan Faiers concurs that luxury 'has of late undergone a conceptual shift more akin to the eighteenth-century understanding of the consumption of luxuries as a necessary display of good citizenship' (2014: 8). However, Faiers seems to betray a belief in the reduced status of the luxury commodity that follows in the wake of a return to a more civic luxury: 'today, the term itself can just as easily be applied to margarine, toilet tissue and tinned dog food, as to luggage, watches and spa treatments' (2014: 8). For Faiers, luxury consumption in the name of good citizenship trivializes the luxury commodity so that high- and low-status goods are now to be found in the same formerly exclusive category. Eaton's promotion of the Canadian-made in opposition to foreign luxuries risks this recategorization of the lowly national luxury into the same class of exclusive foreign goods.

However, what R. Y. Eaton's speech to the IODE accomplished was to build the desirability of the company's Canadian-made goods. 'Suitable raw products, competent workmen and good factories combine to make possible a splendid production of furniture in this country and in the business of the T. Eaton Company, only 6 per cent. of the furniture sold is imported' (*The Globe* 1927), the journalist paraphrased. Underlying Eaton's promotion to this group of elite Toronto consumers is the inherent desirability of domestically manufactured goods as well as encouragement to support a worthy manufacturing sector. The article closes by reporting on a brief intervention by Mrs C. E. Burden, regent of the Toronto chapter of the IODE and daughter of Timothy Eaton, during which she 'urged the necessity for women encouraging and supporting home manufactured goods. She stated that Canada imports from the United States at the rate of $74 per person, whereas the United States purchases in Canada only at the rate of $4 per capita' (*The Globe* 1927), echoing a Mandevillian perspective of consumption as essential to commercial expansion and consumer society (cf. Berg and Eger 2002: 10). While this 80 per cent of Eaton's domestic goods was marketed as economical, practical and decidedly *un*luxurious (as compared to the 20 per cent of the store's imported fineries), these 'home manufactured goods' functioned as national luxuries for the department store by adding a surplus value that superseded their basic use value.

Refinement and the civic luxury

To speak of 'national luxuries' in the context of Eaton-made fashionable goods also adds a new perspective to discussions of high fashion and luxury (often bound together in the epistemological process) in Canada. Alexandra Palmer's foundational study *Fashion: A Canadian Perspective* takes inspiration from Canada's seeming and self-conscious secondary status to delve into a fruitful investigation of the history of Canadian fashion production. 'The non-Canadianness of Canadian designers and fashion, and why they are not recognized as such, raises complex issues of internationalism and the globalization of fashion and Canada's role within this matrix' (Palmer 2004b: 4), asserts the fashion historian and curator in the introduction to the collection. Palmer's perspective echoes the concerns and motivations of R. Y. Eaton and the Canadian Daughters of Empire at their gathering almost 80 years prior. Much like the department store's promotional strategy, the essays in Palmer's collection evoke the cultural capital of the Canadian fashion scene, from couturiers to consumption to journalistic and advertising practices. What Palmer's volume demonstrates is 'that there was and is such a thing as Canadian fashion, and that only by examining this history in its complexity can we begin to assess its significance and impact today and for the future' (Palmer 2004b: 11). *Fashion: A Canadian Perspective* offers engaged histories of Canadian fashion. By shifting the focus to a discussion of luxury and Eaton's 1920s campaign of Canadian-made goods, the engagement becomes expressly political by analysing the ideological tools through which (inter)national stature is ratcheted up. Berg and Eger highlight the power of luxury for the imperialist nation as the definition of luxury evolved in the eighteenth century.

> The philosophers of the Scottish Enlightenment were particularly keen to establish new definitions of luxury as a progressive social force. David Hume and Adam Smith associated luxury almost entirely with commerce, convenience and consumption. [...] Adam Smith was similarly proud of national industry, arguing that the wealth of a nation lay in its ability to increase the quantity of 'necessaries and conveniences' which its labour could produce or exchange relative to its population.
>
> (2002: 11–12)

Production of commodities that fulfill or inspire consumer desires is a luxury production with the potential to increase a nation's standing. Palmer's unarticulated goal in looking at Canadian fashion and Berg and Eger's focus on the philosophical evolution of luxury highlight the 'soft power' that a nation wields through its production of widely desirable commodities. The focus on Eaton-made commodities challenges the current perceptions of luxury by harking back to Enlightenment conceptions that, first, allow for luxury consumption at all levels of society, independent of rarity and exclusivity of the goods themselves and, secondly, engage with macro-level commercial and political concerns.

Eaton's, while seeking to position itself as a champion of Canadian international standing, needed to consider the young country's status as a member of the British Commonwealth and the long history of imperialist dominion. Belisle (2011) argues that, in the first half of the twentieth century, Canadian department stores buttressed nationalist fervour in their advertising campaigns by calling attention to the role of Canadian department store commerce in the functioning of the British Empire. Eaton's promotion of Canadianness was tempered by a persistent link to a specifically British-centred nationalism. Belisle proposes that

> [i]t also helped keep Canadian attachments to Britannia alive and well. By broadcasting messages of empire to Canada's inhabitants both rural and urban, department stores implied throughout the period of 1870 to 1940 that it was normal and desirable to embrace England as Canada's mother country.
>
> (2011: 57–58)

This double focus is evident in the IODE event reported in *The Globe*. Mrs Burden closed the event with an entreaty to support both Canadian enterprise and the mother country. 'I think it would help very materially if we would pledge ourselves to buy only Made-in-Canada goods for this one week as far as possible', said Mrs Burden. 'And again, in Empire week, we might pledge ourselves to purchase nothing but British goods' (*The Globe* 1927). Consumption remains at the heart of the civic gesture in the discourse of the department store and those marshalled to promote it.

It is by tying the notion of civic duty to these 'ordinary' commodities that they become bona fide luxuries. In Canada, the link joining consumption to citizenship had already been established during the Great War, although in an inverse mode. In her most recent book *Purchasing Power: Women and the Rise of Canadian Consumer Culture*, Belisle (2020) documents the Canadian government's attempt to promote the idea of thrift, particularly in food consumption, as a female civic responsibility. Affluent Canadian women responded by organizing and proselytizing in less affluent neighbourhoods.

> In casting themselves as an army of savers, Canadian women activists attempted to demonstrate their value to the war effort and legitimate their importance within the Dominion. In doing so, they also presented a specific iteration of femininity premised on a patriotic form of homemaking.
>
> (Belisle 2020: 65)

Belisle (2020) determines that throughout the war, Canadian women's organizations used guilt and surveillance as a means of controlling consumption. In the post-war period, however, civic duty no longer needed to be expressed in austerity, but from a euphemized form of consumption. Mrs Burden's entreaty to buy Canadian as a means of demonstrating civic responsibility created com-modities that would be valued for more than their use value. In his 1913 classic treatise *Luxury and Capitalism*, Werner Sombart proposes that the surplus value required of a luxury good comes from its refinement, which is to say from an external value placed upon the good that exceeds its basic use value. ' "Refine-ment" is any treatment of a product, over and above that which is needed to make it ordinarily useful' ([1913] 1967: 59–60). It is Eaton's promotion of consump-tion of its Canadian-made goods that transforms these ordinary commodities into luxuries. The civic responsibility to 'buy only Made-in-Canada goods', as Mrs Burden entreated her fellow Daughters of Empire, is a moral value added to the basic use value of the commodities on offer at her father's department store. By virtue of this moral surplus value, the status of these goods exceeds – at least for the week of the Made-in-Canada sale – that of the 20 per cent of foreign luxuries regularly on offer in the department store. Eaton's circulation of domestic goods, with their surplus of *civic* value for the consumer and the potential to support a developing yet worthy Canadian manufacturing industry, created a luxury good that became a tool of 'soft power' for the nation.

Cataloguing the luxury of modernity

The most effective tool in the T. Eaton Company's campaign to bind corporate identity to the idea of *Canadianness* was its famous mail order catalogue. Launched in 1884, the Eaton's catalogue served Canada's largely rural population[3] bringing both domestic- and foreign-sourced goods to less-serviced regions of the country. At a basic level, the Eaton's catalogue, along with the other main national depart-ment store catalogue of the period from the Robert Simpson's Company, was the means of equalizing access to consumer goods and levelling out price and quality nationwide (cf. Belisle 2011: 26). In the late nineteenth century, the Eaton's mail order catalogue announced its namesake company as 'Canada's Greatest Store'. The catalogue supported this view by emphasizing the progress represented by the store's technological and personnel growth as well as the expansion of the company's reach through its harnessing of modern infrastructure and technologies.

The Fall–Winter 1896–97 catalogue copy starts with a comparison to one of the most modern and accessible technologies of the time: 'Catalogue No. 36 goes direct to families all over Canada, and is intended as a kodak of the store to those who live too far away to visit it very often' (The T. Eaton Company Limited 1896: 1). Like the store, which the first pages present in its full progress of growth and technology, the catalogue itself is an expression of the very same modernity – a photograph, a faithful reproduction of the store's commodities brought to the homes of Canadians from one coast to the other. 'There's nothing in this entire establishment that you can't have precisely as if you stood in person before any counter – and exactly the same price' (1896: 3). The mail order catalogue, in this sense, is the store made ambulant.

> Canada's increasingly complex railway network supported the store by enabling both people and goods to travel great distances. Not only did rail enable shoppers to travel to Eaton's downtown Toronto store, but it also carried manufactured goods from distant markets to Eaton's warehouses and transported commodities from Eaton's warehouses to customers across the dominion.
>
> (Belisle 2011: 27)

Interesting, in this stage of Eaton's development, is the absence of tension regarding domestic- and foreign-made goods on offer by the store. In fact, the catalogue uses the company's importing practices as another means of expressing its modernity.

> We were audacious enough to send buyers over to Europe and establish a name for ourselves in the leading markets of the world. [...] Heads of departments cross the ocean at regular intervals in search of new goods, as well as bargains, and a special trans-Atlantic express service greatly facilitates all shipments.
>
> (The T. Eaton Company Limited 1896: 4)

In this period before the Canadian political economy initiated a concerted effort on practices of protectionism,[4] foreign-sourced goods could be promoted as a sign of both progress and distinction for a Canadian department store and its clientele.[5]

For evident reasons of market share, in the catalogue, Eaton's insisted that shopping for these foreign fineries (and bargains) would not create class-based or urban–rural differences in service. 'Rich and poor are treated with uniform courtesy, out-of-town customers are reached with the long arm of the post-office and telegraph, and every consideration of honest quality and right methods create the promise of a steadily increasing success' (1896: 3). The levelling of the social playing field becomes another factor in the modernity and progress represented by the department store, so that in the emerging Canadian consumer culture, shopping was one means for the individual to participate in the modern mass culture promoted by Eaton's and other contemporary department stores. Eaton's catalogue demonstrates that in the Canadian context, the department store was not a staunchly middle-class institution, as historians of consumer culture such as Erika Rappaport (2000) find in the continental context. The Eaton's catalogue called both the 'rich and poor' to consume the store's goods, the impact of which would create a mass culture based on consumption. In fact, '[a] growing propensity to consume among populations that had previously lived at or near subsistence levels was a final spur to the late-nineteenth-century rise of Eaton's and other mass retailers' (Belisle 2011: 28). Belisle further notes that the potential for household spending increased among the working classes by the end of the century, as homeownership became a more viable option, allowing working class homeowners to 'spend money on goods and services [...] that would otherwise have been spent on rent' (2011: 29).

Made-in-Canada cultural capital

In the 1920s, 'Canada' became a more potent symbol in the images and copy of the catalogue. It is interesting to recall that by this time, the CMA's Made-in-Canada campaign had waned, whereas the high cultural Made-in-Canada movement was gaining traction among the country's elite. This cultural mode of patriotism stratified the market, making cost and profitability suspect to the benefit of perceived aesthetic value. Liverant (2018) determines that elite players used the nascent mass market as a counter value so that cultural commodities deemed worthy of canonization would not appear beholden to economic motivations. However, the historian is not misled by this process of mystification: high cultural production requires patrons and an audience, which are 'also an aspect of corporate capitalism' (2018: 64). For Eaton's to enter into the Made-in-Canada fray, its fashions and wares would require a surplus value to elevate their status to a form of luxury commodity that could 'erase the stain' of the mass-produced.

> Citizen and consumer are often understood as opposites; however, in interwar Canada, the consumption of the right sort of cultural goods and experiences became associated with patriotism and good citizenship. A new generation of aspiring cultural providers (including artists, authors, critics, gallery owners, and publishers) formulated and diffused their vision of a new national culture. Among the primary virtues of this culture was its rejection of commercial values and mass-produced culture associated with Americanization.
>
> (Liverant 2018: 65)

The value of 'Canadianness' attached to Eaton's commodities formed a concerted response by 'Canada's Greatest Store' to elevate mass-produced commodities to the status of luxurious Canadian symbols.

The Spring–Summer 1921 catalogue, entitled 'Canada's Progress', uses a laden cover image presenting, for the first time, an imagined history of domestic exchange and consumption that positions Eaton's as the *natural* conclusion to a long tradition of Made-in-Canada trade.[6] Two composite scenes occupy the foreground of the image. In the bottom-left corner, a stereotypical representation of an Indigenous Elder wearing a long brown-and-black cloak sits holding up a rope of sparkling and coloured glass beads or semiprecious gems. He looks at the strand admiringly. Behind him sits an open wooden chest overflowing with sundry European goods: a (perhaps Chinese) blue-and-white jar rests in the chest while a lacquered jewellery box is set atop a stack of silver trays resting in the chest's domed cover. Behind, another connected scene of colonial trade fills the upper left quadrant of the cover image. An Indigenous man, bare chested, adorned with a feather in his hair, necklace and a white wrist cuff, holds up a pelt and is engaged in discussion with an explorer, dressed and groomed in early seventeenth-century French fashion. The European looks intently at his Indigenous interlocutor, holding up two fingers on one hand while pointing to the pelt with the other, as if in the midst of negotiating a price for two skins. A superimposed blue banner with antiquated script provides the title of and the key to reading this vignette: 'The First Sale'. The two superimposed images represent the two component elements of idealized colonial trade where both European consumer and Indigenous seller leave the interaction satisfied. Cutting across the midplane of the image is a large river – perhaps the St. Lawrence – where a small group of people stand on the near shore beside a large seventeenth-century sailing ship, anchored close to the shore. On the far side of the river, as a symbol of progress, large buildings with rows of symmetrical windows rise up, some with smokestacks spewing the smoke of industrial modernity into the air.

Belisle (2011) argues that Canadian department stores used the rhetoric of progress to suggest that patronizing these establishments promoted a Eurocentric form of Canadianness that erased Indigenous and non-white people from modernity. The historian points to the 1905 building of an Eaton's store in Winnipeg as an example of the colonial discourse that privileged the image of white settler society.

> Located away from the downtown area, the Eaton's store lured Winnipeg's 'retail traffic' away from historic Fort Garry, which used to be the starting point of the 'old Indian trail to the far West.' The location of Eaton's in Winnipeg thus symbolized the birth of modern white civilization in the region. An early window display played up this theme. It took the 'form of a Pageant of Western Progress, showing Indians, trappers, pioneer settlers, etc., etc., in their respective relations to the growth of the Prairie provinces'.
>
> (2011: 66)

For Belisle, displays of this sort typified department store marketing and privileged a European settler-based idea of progress. She determines that 'this window pageant implied that First Nations belonged in the past and white modern commerce, especially retail, was the newest stage of evolution' (ibid.). The cover image of Eaton's Spring–Summer 1921 catalogue can be read in the same vein. Colonial trade belongs to a mystified past that has been superseded by a modern, industrial and Eurocentric consumer culture. However, it is important to note that in the context of Canadian luxury, this cover art both discursively and figuratively accords a fundamental importance to First Nations trade and appreciation of luxury commerce. This is not to obfuscate or rewrite the historical reality of asymmetrical relations of imperialism and settler colonialism. What the Spring–Summer 1921 cover does is bind Indigenous trade to Eaton's contemporary commercial modernity, which would not be possible without 'The First Sale'. The roles of buyer and seller have existed since before the arrival of Europeans on Indigenous lands. The goods displayed – the porcelain jar, the lacquered box and the pelt – all represent modern luxuries, which circulated precisely from imperialist trade in the seventeenth and eighteenth centuries. Trade with First Nations people, along with China, Japan and India, for example, brought exotic commodities to Europe and spawned a new form of luxury consumption that eschewed the older, nobiliary and sumptuary modes. In the eighteenth century, 'new forms of luxury goods appeared that were aimed not at achieving grandeur or magnificence, but at satisfying the needs for novelty and delectation of a much wider number of consumers' (McNeil and Riello 2016: 99–100). Eaton's Spring–Summer 1921 catalogue casts the two First Nations men on the cover image as sellers. Not necessarily avatars of the past, the two men's activity represents the roles inherent to a Canadian commercial luxury system and, significantly, prefigures the role that the T. Eaton Company would play two hundred years later. The European figure, along with his ship, symbolizes the commerce that brought new luxuries back to Europe and initiated the changes in consumption that opened the luxury market to classes formerly excluded. However, in the context of Eaton's catalogue, this early luxury circulation is transformed into 'Canada's Progress', a specifically Canadian context that does not occult the important foundational role played by First Nations people. In fact, while idealized, the catalogue cover image links this early global luxury trade to Eaton's contemporary Made-in-Canada luxuries.[7]

Using a romanticized Canadian past to promote Eaton's modern commercial activity is particularly poignant in this period of the Made-in-Canada campaign during which Canada's cultural elite also harnessed a similar symbology to build the country's cultural capital. Liverant explains that for Canada's cultural class, '[t]he Québécois peasant, like the Maritime folk, the Indigenous artisan, and the wilderness landscape, were approached as cultural resources: sources of material and inspiration for the development of cultural goods and the tourism industry' (2018: 82). Canadian elite classes used these seemingly less-developed people and places as symbols of an authenticity that they deemed lacking from the burgeoning mass and commercial culture. 'When aspiring intellectual and cultural leaders self-consciously took up the project of culturing Canada, they found the essence of the nation in the wilderness landscape and in the experiences of those they perceived as living closest to nature' (2018: 74). Eaton's use of Indigenous trade on the cover of the Spring–Summer 1921 catalogue creates a surplus value for the Eaton brand by linking its commercial activity to an imagined 'authentic' history of trade. 'The First Sale' suggests that Eaton's modern commercial practices are *authentically* Canadian and, accordingly, the company's goods are imbued with a surplus value of Canadianness.

It was, in fact, during this period that Eaton's catalogues began to systematically highlight Canadianness as an added value to their commodities. The last page of the Spring–Summer 1921 catalogue explains three key symbols found throughout: 'Eaton Made', 'E Special Bargain' and 'Canadian Made' (The T. Eaton Company Limited 1921: 374). While in the pre-war and war years, Eaton's catalogue guarantee regularly proposed that they brought goods from the world's finest cities, as of 1921 catalogues focused more on the Canadian-made label and the impact on Canadians of buying Eaton's Made-in-Canada fashions and wares. 'All Canada Will Profit When You Buy Goods Made-in-Canada' (1921: 374) proclaims the headline for the Canadian-made symbol, a maple leaf. The copy further explains the benefits of buying Canadian-made goods. 'Buying goods "Made-in-Canada" will indirectly benefit you. Every dollar you spend on "Canadian made" goods helps to keep some fellow citizen employed and the benefit eventually works back to you in the general prosperity of the country' (1921: 374). By Spring–Summer 1923, the catalogue moved this page to the inside front cover and further refined Eaton's commodities by insisting on their civic impact. The first panel explains the Canadian-made symbol with the headline 'Buying Canadian Products Keeps Canadians at Work' (The T. Eaton Company Limited 1923: n.pag.). Just underneath, the second panel for the 'Eaton-Made' symbol doubles the value of the brand by announcing in the headline ' "Eaton-Made" Means Also "Canadian-Made"–What Better Buying Opportunity Could You Have?' (1923: n.pag.). The back side of the front cover of the Fall–Winter 1924–25 catalogue expands on the theme of Eaton's Canadianness with its headline 'The Eaton Organization Is Growing with Canada' (The T. Eaton Company Limited 1924: 2). The copy on this page links the department store to a modern and growing Canadian society. Further still, Eaton's connects the country to global markets so that Canadians can benefit from consumer culture as much as citizens of older nations do. 'Under its roof are goods from practically every corner of the earth, gathered there so that our own Canadian People may have as broad a choice as the people of other lands and as good value' (1924: 2). However, in keeping with the Canada-centric theme, this advertising page also reminds consumers that Eaton's factories produce a great deal of the commodities and that 'EATON Factories are Canadian Factories' explaining that '[t]hey keep Canadians busy making things for Canadians and everything they make is sold through the EATON Store or Mail Order Catalogue' (1924: 2). Much like R. Y. Eaton's speech to the IODE in February 1927, Eaton's catalogues of the 1920s concertedly portray the department store's merchandise as Canadian merchandise whose value lies not only in cost savings or practicality but also in a symbolic value of supporting Canadian workers and the economy. Buying an Eaton-made dress or suit, for example, becomes a Canadian luxury purchase because, by the 1920s, the company created a brand whose symbolic civic value exceeded the use value of its goods.

Building Canadian luxury

Luxury goods are imbued with a surplus value that refines their basic use value. For the Eaton's consumer in the interwar period, this surplus value was based on the perception of the Canadianness of the goods on offer. The T. Eaton Company had participated in the CMA's Made-in-Canada campaign launched after the 1911 federal election. The Canadian department store continued and elaborated on the campaign in the 1920s, using its own image of Canadianness as a means to create surplus value in the consumption act. However, because of the commonplace nature of much of the Made-in-Canada goods on offer, their use value could run the risk of overshadowing any luxuriousness that the Made-in-Canada label was meant to emit. As Paris and Fang suggest in the introduction to the compelling volume *Making Prestigious Places: How Luxury Influences the Transformation of Cities*, contemporary luxury brands can use the 'power of place' (2017: 6) to buttress other traditional markers of luxuriousness. For these urban studies specialists, the relationship between luxury and place moves unidirectionally, with the luxury offering creating the prestige of the place where it is situated. 'Luxury is a catalyst generating several opportunities (visibility, events, new heritage and shared spaces, etc.) and not only parasitizing its historical and urban values' (2017: 6–7). From the perspective of urban studies, luxury functions as a change agent for the space where it is situated. Paris and Fang's analysis privileges the creative power of the luxury commodity or service to build prestige in the various spaces it inhabits in the urban setting. They seek to 'analyse the potential of luxury to create specific stimuli for places, and if they can – and how – convert a space into a "prestigious place"' (2017: 11). This approach, while fruitful in the context of urban studies, does not sufficiently problematize the source of luxury's power of mystification. In the context of the T. Eaton Company, it was through a discourse of civic duty that the company's goods acquired a luxurious status, emitting a power that could only be expressed in the buying act. However, in the war years the discursive impact of 'buying Made-in-Canada goods', it seemed, would not be sufficient alone for domestic goods and wares to acquire a fashionable stature equivalent to the foreign luxuries and fineries imported by the mass retailer.

In November 1916, *The Globe* published an investigative article entitled 'Big Departmental to Be All-Canadian', speculating on a proposal submitted to the Toronto City Council to erect a department store building at the corner of Yonge and College Streets (*The Globe* 1916). The article's subtitle suggested the prospective owner: 'Persistent Rumor Connects T. Eaton Co. With It'. The article had a double focus: on the one hand, shedding light on the speculation surrounding the corporate entity behind the proposal; on the other, foregrounding the importance that Canadian building materials would occupy in the proposed building. The opening paragraph laid out the key information. 'An all-Canadian affair: built of Quebec granite, Ontario bricks, and Canadian steel, with all-Canadian capital invested in it' (*The Globe* 1916). The unnamed journalist interviewed Mr H. H. Williams, an active Toronto real estate agent at the turn of the century, closely affiliated with Sir John C. Eaton (Timothy Eaton's son and president of the company from 1907 until his untimely death in 1922), and who would eventually assume the role of chairman of Toronto's Town Planning Commission. Williams, refusing to reveal the name of the future proprietor, confirmed the importance of the all-Canadian materials that would be used for the commercial edifice. 'I will say this though: the store will be erected of all-Canadian materials, with Canadian capital, which proves it is not an American concern coming here' (*The Globe* 1916).

In the protectionist period after the 1911 election, this proposed all-Canadian edifice echoed the contemporary CMA movement to promote and safeguard the Canadian manufacturing industry. It would take twelve years to break ground on Eaton's original vision of an uptown store. In that time, the discourse about the edifice changed considerably. In 1916, the message focused on the prospective building's stature as a representation of Canadianness and a potential prestige site for the city. Williams explained that building materials were being prepared for this new shopping district north of the traditional commercial centre of the city. He further stated that they were

> ready to give the City Council choice of two designs for the building. We will spend $10,000,000 on an ordinary structure that will be sufficient for store purposes, or

add another $5,000,000 to that and erect a thing of beauty and a joy forever. We will beautify this district and make it a real businesses section.

(The Globe 1916)

Collectively, the promotion of a Canadian-made edifice for a Canadian store with the proposed desire to 'erect a thing of beauty and a joy forever', in the words of Williams, expresses the desire to add prestige to the Made-in-Canada movement. In 'Prestige and luxury: Places of urbanity in paramount locations', Lineu Castello (2017) argues that prestige and luxury are connected by a causal relationship in which the prestige of the urban place aids in the agglomeration and perception of luxurious goods or the luxuriousness of the place instils it with a sense of prestige. For Castello, there is a symbiotic relationship

between luxury places and prestigious locations; the occurrence of a luxury place positioned at the interface of a prestigious location; and when a luxury place can be considered responsible for determining the perception of prestige extending over an entire area of the city.

(2017: 98–99)

Eaton's 1916 project to build a new and prestigious outpost, while circumstantially delayed for fourteen years, demonstrates the importance of prestige for creating a Canadian-made luxury. The proposed edifice, as described by Williams, harmonized the goals of the Made-in-Canada campaign, launched four years earlier, with commercial interest in building a prestigious place. Castello asserts:

A sense of prestige is felt when seeing one's home finely decorated with exclusive *objets d'art*; or appreciating the precious trend-setting fashion of an *haute-couture* item from a super-exclusive *maison* in one's wardrobe; or yet again, enjoying the delicate *gourmandise* of exceptional food served by a refined *chef de cuisine*, certainly a *connoisseur*.

(2017: 106, original emphasis)

Eaton's intention to 'erect a thing of beauty and a joy forever' (*The Globe* 1916) plainly situates the company's desire to introduce a prestigious location to Toronto's geography. 'We will beautify this district', announced Williams, 'and make it a real business section' (2017: 106). Castello (2017) uses the example of Los Angeles's architectural renaissance in the 1980s and 1990s to demonstrate how prestigious place-making and the establishment of luxurious enclaves help increase stature to urban spaces. Similarly, in 1916 Eaton's proposed to use a new site and building to transform the public space and add to the store's prestige.

Cynthia Wright explains that 'the architecture of the [Eaton's] College Street premises was planned with a view to "the transformation of the store's image"' (1992: 248).

Building a prestigious new consumer enclave with 'all-Canadian materials' would have increased the refinement of the Made-in-Canada fashions and particularly the home furnishings that would have been displayed in the new shopping emporium. However, the war thwarted the T. Eaton Company's plan to expand

FIGURE 3.2: An advertisement from *The Globe* newspaper, dated 28 October 1930, that announces the imminent opening of the Eaton's College Street store. Note the use of perspective in the image that foregrounds the grandeur of the new building and the ad copy that emphasizes the modernity of the space and its offerings as opposed to any specific qualities of 'Canadianness'. Image in public domain.

to this northern satellite, which was not revived until the end of the 1920s, at the height of Canadian department stores' economic and cultural domination. Interestingly, when the new building was finally announced in 1928, the discourse had shifted from Canadian exclusivity to one of international modernism. 'Great Eaton Store Will Be Last Word in Modern Building', heralded *The Globe* on July 14, 1928. Later that year in the same newspaper, the headline 'Eaton's Huge Store to Tower 670 Feet Above Street Level' (*The Globe* 1928) expressed the grandeur expected of the modern era. In the article, Eaton's proposed new building (as construction had not yet commenced) was trumpeted as 'a stupendous building program' that would 'result in the construction of the first unit of one of the most magnificent buildings in the world' (*The Globe* 1928). The reporter closes the article explaining that 'contracts [have been] awarded for excavation, foundations up to street level, and for steel for the entire structure' (*The Globe* 1928). Pertinently, no mention is made of Canadian sourcing for the building materials. This change in focus can be explained by the department store's own stature by the beginning of the 1930s. 'By the dawn of the Great Depression, Eaton's was not only the key player in the nation's consumer market but it had also emerged as a major Canadian institution and was one of the biggest retailers in the world' (Belisle 2011: 39).

Wright notes that the College Street store was inspired by the *Exposition Internationale des Arts Décoratifs et Industriels Modernes* held in Paris in 1925.

> For the first time, 'the domestic interior was the subject of an international exhibition of this size' and all 'the latest ideas in furniture and interior decoration' were on display. Eaton's College Street, when it opened five years later, enthusiastically embraced the modernist movement.
>
> (1992: 245)

With its dominant position in the Canadian market, building and promoting the surplus value of its Canadian-made commodities was no longer necessary. However, a store of Eaton's stature could now assert a wider dominance through an adoption of international, modernist cultural capital to underscore the brand's status as an arbiter of dominant taste. Canadian women's magazines, such as *Châtelaine* and *Canadian Homes and Gardens*, 'identified Eaton's College Street as *the* site of taste in furniture and interior decoration, the link between Canada and the Paris-based modernist movement in design' (Wright 1992: 246, original emphasis). Eaton's no longer needed to build the luxury status of Made-in-Canada goods, as its dominant position in the market allowed its merchandise to share in the store's aura of modernity, refinement and international flair.

Conclusion

In the decade leading up to Eaton's dominance of the Canadian retail market, Made-in-Canada was an important marker of refinement, so much so that the key feature of the earlier envisioned building of 1916 was its Canadianness, as opposed to any external qualities of aesthetics or expense. This difference in conception highlights the socially arbitrary nature of luxury, as well as the political underpinnings of the surplus value ascribed to consumer goods. Berry (1994), Berg and Eger (2002), and Armitage and Roberts (2016b, 2016c) have all pointed to luxury's demoralization during the Enlightenment and the advent of consumer culture. However, for these luxury historians and theorists, luxury remains firmly beyond the reach of definite categorization. To the question 'What is luxury?', Armitage and Roberts categorically assert that, because luxury is fundamentally relational and circumstance-dependent, 'we cannot introduce a set definition of luxury into any and every context and expect it to make sense' (2016b: 3). Faiers, in light of the contemporary world's stark distribution of wealth and impoverishment, questions whether 'true luxury can be recognized at all today' (2016a: 10). For Featherstone, luxuries are no longer restrained to their materiality, but are 'signs that stand for something else more inchoate, that might at some point suddenly emerge and flood us with happiness' (2014: 60).

The T. Eaton Company's use of Made-in-Canada fashions and wares, however, most closely aligns with Faiers's (2016b) proposal of luxury in his insightful ' "In a galaxy far, far away ...": C-3PO, mink, and the promise of disruptive luxury'. Looking to the Centre for Studies on Sustainable Luxury, Faiers finds in the centre's idealized luxury consumer, 'who has both the means and the motivation to ensure that other people improve their quality of life' (2016b: 87) a mode in which luxury transforms consumption; this mode 'brings us closer to an understanding of deep or disruptive luxury that, in its very consumption, can have a beneficial or philanthropic intention, one that disrupts luxury's traditionally understood purpose of bringing pleasure to the few rather than the masses' (2016b: 87). Eaton's Made-in-Canada fashions and wares offered the potential of a consumption that was conceived of as valuable for a new and growing nation. Eaton's in the 1920s (along with the manufacturers who, at the behest of the CMA, initiated the campaign earlier in 1911) used the Made-in-Canada label to set its merchandise on equal footing with the goods imported from the United States or the foreign fineries imported from more exotic global locales. While the protectionist fervour of the first decades of the twentieth century that inspired the Made-in-Canada movement betrays the capitalist underpinnings of consumption, Eaton's Made-in-Canada discourse made for a very different kind of luxury, one that was based on a surplus value that was not exclusive but ideologically disruptive, a Canadian luxury 'for rich and poor'.

This investigation has demonstrated that luxury is a construction that does not depend on exclusivity of price or rarity, but is both culturally and spatially relative. The hegemonic conception of luxury goods coming out of the older or more established capitals is one mode of circulation. However, secondary and peripheral spaces can create and promote goods that become luxuries within local markets. Eaton's Made-in-Canada goods as well as the brand itself concentrated a message of national identity, which added a surplus value to its rather ordinary and commonplace offerings so that they became more than simple commodities. Luxury is a refinement, as Sombart asserted in 1913. This refinement, however, does not need to come from specialized handcrafting or rarified materials. Refinement is an idea that adds value beyond usefulness to the luxury good. In this, each and all have access and a right to luxury.

For Eaton's in the 1920s the campaign to bind consumption to civic duty, while perhaps commercially motivated, created the potential for consumers to consider their purchases as more than simply 'stocking up'. Beyond the mere consumption of necessities, these Canadian-made fashions and wares became a means for Canadian consumers to acquire luxuries without the air of danger that surrounded foreign fineries. Moreover, these domestically produced goods were discursively positioned in a way that their circulation in Canadian society built the idea of civic identity and responsibility. While perhaps not the sole goal (if indeed it was a goal at all) of the T. Eaton Company Limited to build the nation's 'soft power' along with its own market share, the promotion of Canadian-made goods opened up the potential for Canadians to purchase domestic fashions and wares and experience the luxuriousness of not just buying for necessity but also acquiring goods imbued with surplus value. The example of Eaton's Canadian-made campaign in the 1920s demonstrates a strategy for manufacturers in peripheral states to imbue their products with an aura of luxury for the domestic market that can compete against the luxurious imports of globalized conglomerates whose manufacture is both diffuse and obfuscated.

NOTES

1. Pierre Bourdieu ([1983] 1986) defines cultural capital as one of the forms of value that socially situate individuals. Cultural capital is an embodied form of knowledge that is inculcated through family investment and educational institutions that individuals express through their manipulation of material culture.

2. For a detailed analysis of the cost of living and wages during the first half of the twentieth century in Canada, see Emery and Levitt (2002).

3. Belisle explains that during the 1890s 'the country remained overwhelmingly rural, with 3.3 million inhabitants living in rural areas compared to 1.5 million in cities and large towns' (2011: 22).

4. Belisle points to the lack of government intervention in the final decade of the nineteenth century in the growing hegemony of the department store:

> Dominion, provincial, and municipal governments of this period were loath to interfere with the machinations of capital, preferring to let what was known as the invisible hand of the market drive the economy. Thus, although independent shopkeepers in the 1890s formed such organizations as the Retail Grocers' Association to lobby against what they perceived as unfair competition represented by mass retail, governments tended to avoid implementing any laws that would seriously curtail the emerging monopoly of Eaton's and, to a lesser extent, that of Simpson's, Morgan's, Woodward's, and the HBC.
>
> (2011: 27–28)

5. Nevertheless, Canada's first prime minister had instituted the National Policy, a programme of tariffs on imported goods, in 1879 (cf. Belisle 2011: 29).

6. Prior to this issue, catalogue covers were generally one-dimensional representations of Eaton's Toronto store and buildings or *mise en abyme* of the catalogue in home settings. Occasionally, in the early years of the century, the covers featured urban scenes of fashionable living, such as an elegant couple on a velocipede ride in Queen's Park in Toronto or an elegant family on a stroll. In the 1920s, covers became less tied to brand promotion and, occasionally, featured women wearing contemporary high fashions or elegant fashions available in the catalogue. Other covers of this period show still-life images of flowers or a young girl in a field of flowers, for example, images that reflect the season of the catalogue.

7. See Jessica P. Clark's insightful re-evaluation of the Canadian fur trade, titled 'Putting Canada on the Map: A Brief History of Nation and Luxury', in this volume. The first part of the chapter re-centres the role Indigenous labour played in establishing national and international trade networks since European arrival in North America.

PART 2

SPACE AND PLACE

Recent studies have shown that conceptions of luxury and luxury markets are often deeply connected to identity, space and place. This can happen on a broad scale, in relation to the nation state or other geopolitical configurations. But luxury also unfolds on more intimate scales, in retail spaces, workshops and other sites of experiential luxury. To date, many studies of luxury spaces and places privilege the development and transformation of retail and urban locations into new sites of luxury consumption, leisure and pleasure. This line of enquiry often focuses on sites typically linked to western understandings of luxury, namely global fashion capitals such as Paris, Milan and New York. Despite this focus, thinkers and developers continue to seek out new ways to enhance the luxuriousness of given spaces around the world, including Canadian cities like Toronto and Vancouver.

Attempts to create or co-opt luxury spaces – to imbue sites with spatial and cultural capital – are not without ruptures and frequently raise issues of gentrification, inclusion and equity in the neoliberal, capitalist context. As the chapters in this section demonstrate, the forging ahead with luxury projects can ignore or obfuscate existing social dynamics, histories, demographics and constituents, overlaying or appropriating these existing realities in the pursuit of new luxury experiences and markets. This is not without resistance, as the following essays confirm, whether via historical legacies of given neighbourhoods that complicate new luxurious labels imposed by multinational firms or from artists whose work is co-opted by gentrifying forces. Attempts at forging luxury spaces also periodically lead to failures for the luxury venture, local residents or both. This section foregrounds tensions that underpin some endeavours to develop luxury events and space, some of which are never fully resolved.

In Chapter 4, Kathryn Franklin and Rebecca Halliday examine the on-again-off-again Toronto Fashion Week (TFW) as a space permeated with the tensions of local and national identity politics. This comparative study highlights the significant discursive differences of hosting a highly symbolic, high-fashion event in a smaller market. The protean movement from a public (read: civic) space to a commercial venue foregrounds the challenges of discursively situating fashion production in Canada. As opposed to Paris or London Fashion Weeks, which are able to harmoniously express both local and national identity, TFW has difficulty reconciling its status as a 'Toronto' event and a national forum for Canadian fashion talent. Transformations in TFW, including its 2017 move from a central downtown location to the elite Yorkville Village, betray the challenges in balancing the needs of a localized fashion market while reaching global constituencies of observers, luxury brands and financiers. Franklin and Halliday conclude that, by tapping into Yorkville's historical luxuriousness, glamour and bohemian pedigree – characterized by its 'spectacle of performance' – organizers attempt to harness the location's storied past in service of an international, global-reaching future.

In Chapter 5, Julia Polyck-O'Neill focuses on two public art commissions in Vancouver to shift the discussion to public luxuries and their role in gentrification. In Canada's most expensive city, in terms of real estate and housing, Vancouver's monuments materialize the city's spatial, cultural and economic capital. This chapter examines the tensions coming out of the contradictions inherent in *public luxuries*. Focusing on Douglas Coupland's *Digital Orca* (2009) and Ken Lum's *Monument for East Vancouver* (2010), Polyck-O'Neill illuminates the concomitant development of public art and urban space in a period of rapid transformation, commercialization and gentrification. The two pieces transformed the public spaces in which they were installed, resulting in a 'purpose-built and replicable aura of cultural capital and luxury'. But these same processes heightened the risks of exclusion and subsequent alienation for those frequenting these spaces, processes that threatened the intent and purpose of at least one of the artists in the conceptualization of their work. As Polyck-O'Neill concludes, public artworks as a form of spatial luxury cannot be divorced from broader elements of power at play in their creation. These processes are not limited to Canada and extend to multiple urban centres seeking to become players in global luxury markets. In this way, Part 2 questions the role of space and place in second-tier cities' mounting of glamorous events and public luxuries in the model of more cosmopolitan and established luxury capitals. What strategies do these phenomena marshal to reconcile the necessary excessive symbolic capital with the realities of a secondary cultural capital market?

4

Runway off the Mink Mile: Toronto Fashion Week and the Glamour and Luxury of Yorkville

Kathryn Franklin and Rebecca Halliday

In recent years, Toronto's midtown Yorkville area has developed (and been developed) into a monied and luxurious retail and residential hub that draws from Toronto's storied countercultural and fashionable past, fusing these resonances with more contemporary global sensibilities. Yorkville's residents are a well-to-do set whose average household income level in 2011 was CAD 138,660, and 47 per cent of residents live in condominiums as either owners or renters (Canadian Urban Institute 2016: 29–30). Yorkville's focal attraction is the 'Mink Mile', the stretch of storefronts that line Bloor Street, between Avenue Road to the west and Yonge Street to the east, which forms the southern border of the neighbourhood (Figure 4.1). The Mink Mile was established in part with the arrival of Canada's Holt Renfrew luxury department flagship store at 50 Bloor Street in 1979, but its consumer draws have expanded to international luxury retailers of the likes of Louis Vuitton, Hermès, Gucci, Prada, Burberry, Chanel and Cartier interspersed with mid-level brands such as J. Crew, Calvin Klein, Banana Republic, Brooks Brothers and (formerly Canadian-owned) Club Monaco.[1] It is considered Canada's premier retail mecca and 'one of the most luxurious shopping streets in North America' (Traikos cited in Johnston 2017: n.pag.). As of 2017 the Mink Mile ranked sixth in the Americas and 25th in the world in terms of property rental rates at USD 231 per square foot per year (Cushman and Wakefield 2017). Meanwhile, independent fashion retailers, such as famed Canadian brand Pink Tartan, are situated in the quieter and more affordable but no less upscale blocks north of the Mink Mile, where walk-up storefronts have been annexed by condominium developments.[2] Menswear boutique Uncle Otis relocated from Bellair Street to Chinatown in 2018 (Mok 2018). The upscale denim mecca Over the Rainbow, situated at 101 Yorkville

Avenue since 1982, closed in 2017, when its building was sold to developers to build a contemporary luxury retail complex, and reopened in 2019 in the Manulife Centre at Bay and Bloor underneath Toronto's new Eataly location (Grant 2019).

Toronto Fashion Week (TFW) was founded in 1999 and, as we outline below, has run in several locations around town. As part of a structural overhaul, the event relocated in 2017 to Yorkville, and specifically to the Yorkville Village shopping complex, the former Hazelton Lanes. This move can be read as a transition away from the sense of internationalism represented in the event's former ownership by the International Management Group (IMG) and a return to a sense of Toronto's former clout as a destination known for pushing aesthetic envelopes. While the

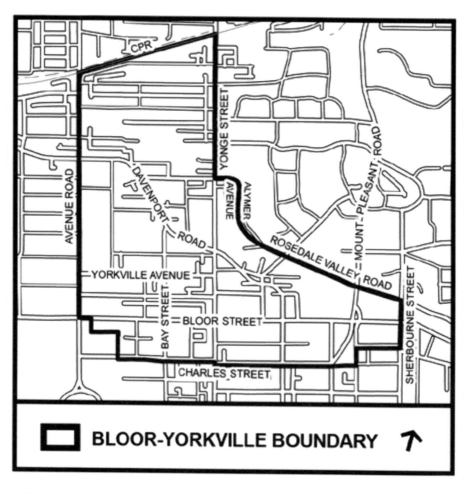

FIGURE 4.1: Map of Bloor-Yorkville Boundary. Courtesy of City of Toronto.

event's actual site is still a short distance north of the Mink Mile, Yorkville Village remains off the beaten path in an area more devoted to Canada's independent luxury designers and is situated in the midst of increasing condominium development. This location positions the event in a Toronto-centric milieu in which its urban semiotics – architectural structures, environments and municipal discourses – are those of Yorkville as a residential area where one's comforts and recreational and aspirational pursuits are possible within a short stroll. The Mink Mile, within the small, tony neighbourhood of Yorkville, has been a crucial space for the enactment of glamour and luxury in and for Toronto.

The twin pillars of glamour and luxury are concepts that paint a portrait of desire, beauty and riches. However, glamour and luxury not only possess a distinct language but also a lengthy history. In their exhaustive exploration into the history of glamour, Buckley and Gundle assert that 'glamour is a visual language of the enticing that seduces through the deployment of images of theatricality, luxury, sexuality, and notoriety' (2000: 346–47). Meanwhile in *Luxury: A Rich History*, McNeil and Riello acknowledge that glamour is an important concept that 'until recently [was] left unexplored and unconnected to luxury' (2016: 313n1). Glamour's etymology traces back to the old word 'grammarye': an alteration of the word 'grammar', which has connotations pertaining to learning as well as having the ability to charm. The word's introduction into the English language is believed to be from the eighteenth-century Scottish poet Sir Walter Scott in his 1805 poem 'The Lay of the Last Minstrel' where the speaker remarks that a magic spell 'had much of glamour might'. Glamour, in this instance, was a reference to the conjurer's ability to change the appearance of an object from ordinary to extraordinary, a sleight of hand that often characterizes glamour's allure to this day. Luxury's origins date even further back. The *Oxford English Dictionary* notes that the earliest current sense of the word was used in the mid-seventeenth century, although Roman lawmakers debated laws on luxury between 182 BCE and 18 BCE in an attempt to regulate banquet expenditures (Dari-Mattiacci and Plisecka 2010: 2). Theories of glamour and luxury are equally fluid. Buckley and Gundle are quick to point out that 'there are no theories of glamour' (2000: 334), while McNeil and Riello observe that luxury is a heuristic method that has continued to underpin key sociological, philosophical and historical theories (2016: 7).

Much like the concepts of glamour and luxury, so too does Yorkville have a unique and fluid history separate from its current affiliation with gentrification and wealth. Long before Yorkville was metonymical for high-end luxury, the neighbourhood, in the 1960s, was considered Canada's 'Haight-Ashbury' (the San Francisco birthplace of 1960s hippie counterculture) and was internationally recognized for its lavish display of bohemian glamour. In considering the case of TFW's decision to move its runways to Yorkville, the concepts of glamour and luxury offer an epistemological inquiry into the dynamic relationship between fashion and cities.

This chapter applies the cultural and industrial functions of fashion weeks and fashion cities to TFW as a Canadian case study in the cultural semiotics and associations of fashion weeks in urban, national and international contexts. To this end, we focus on a recent, critical moment in the event's timeline: the sale and relaunch of the series and its relocation from a set of tents in David Pecaut Square in Toronto's downtown cultural, tourist and nightlife district to the upper-class Yorkville Village. While TFW aims to provide a platform for Canadian fashion and to recruit presenters from across the nation, its recent re-establishment within Yorkville, one of Toronto's most monied retail and residential districts, situates it within a particular, elite urban context. We first offer a history of TFW's social and locational positioning as Canada's premier trade and cultural showcase for fashion leading up to its 2016 cancellation. We then chronicle the rise of the Yorkville fashion scene and the performance of a particular glamour, luxury and entrepreneurialism in the neighbourhood starting with 1960s counterculture to the influx of more internationalized fashion retailers in the past two decades. Finally, we read the revival of TFW (with an emphasis on Toronto) in the 'heart' of Yorkville as a calculated move that addresses the neighbourhood's fashionable history while ensuring its future for an internationalized fashion market.

Laying down the runway: Toronto Fashion Week's beginnings

The fashion show is a one-off performance during which a fashion line presents its upcoming seasonal collection to an audience of insiders that includes editors, retail buyers, bloggers, celebrities, and invited and exclusive clientele. Fashion week series are scheduled industry affairs that combine fashion shows from known and up-and-coming designers in one urban location in addition to trade shows, buyer appointments, and networking and social events. The 'Big Four' Fashion Week circuit is a biannual presentation series held in New York, London, Milan and Paris; however, additional fashion weeks in cities around the world have earned increased industry and academic attention in the past two decades.[3]

Fashion scholars such as David Gilbert (2006, 2013) and Jennifer Craik (2013) observe that fashion weeks indicate new and established design talent as well as a set of fashionable looks or aesthetics specific to host cities. Fashion weeks work in tandem with retail establishments, advertisements and cultural discourses to enhance cities' status as cosmopolitan fashion capitals, tourist destinations and centres of manufacture. At the same time, cities that hold fashion weeks often come to stand in as a metonymic referent for a national fashion market, as has historically been the case in New York, London and Paris and to a lesser extent Milan, which sees competition from Florence as Italy's fashion centre (see White 2000). Joanne Entwistle and Agnès Rocamora (2006, 2011), writing on London Fashion Week, draw from French sociologist Pierre Bourdieu to observe that fashion weeks manifest fashion as a cultural field in which admission indicates membership and attendees perform their member status via dress, comportment and prescribed social enactments. The authors use Bourdieu's term *habitus*, referring to aesthetic orientations based on class, education and cultural exposure, to describe attendees' *fashion capital*, that is, social, intellectual and embodied forms of capital.

Toronto launched its fashion week in 1999 under the banner of the newly established Fashion Design Council of Canada (FDCC) and its president, the auspicious retailer and designer Robin Kay, in partnership with designer Pat McDonagh, one of the pre-eminent figures in the early Yorkville fashion scene (see Georgijevic 2016). Since its inception, TFW has been held in several locations both classic and more conceptual: first at the Windsor Arms Hotel, then in tents at Nathan Phillips Square, at a car lot in Liberty Village and at Exhibition Place. While press and popular discourses have tended to refer to these events in a familiar shorthand as 'Toronto Fashion Week', these events have had numerous titles based on the FDCC's recruitment of premier sponsors. In 2002 the event was sponsored by Beauty by L'Oréal Paris and dubbed L'Oréal Fashion Week, and in 2008 it was renamed LG Fashion Week (for Life's Good Electronics) even though it remained sponsored under L'Oréal (Elliott 2013: 1). In 2012, international event management firm IMG purchased TFW from the FDCC for an undisclosed sum; World MasterCard came on board as the title sponsor, and the rebranded event was launched, still under Kay's leadership as both president of the FDCC and fashion week executive director (see Elliott 2013). IMG's takeover constituted both a corporate vote of confidence and an act of financial rescue for TFW, while the FDCC boasted that its involvement could enhance the market reach and media profiles of Canadian fashion companies on an international scale. In fact, IMG had been involved with TFW from the outset as Kay had consulted with them on event coordination and in 2010 offered IMG the reins in 'production, marketing, communications, operations, and sponsorship sales' (Elliott 2013: 1). The decision to sell TFW to IMG reflects a condition that sociologist Frédéric Godart (2012) terms the *imperialization* of fashion: when corporations have assumed control of fashion houses and brands, and even fashion weeks, creating a sense that lines are more 'international' and blurring the locational and social distinctions between fashion cities.[4] As of 2016, IMG's fashion week portfolio also included mainstays in New York, London and Milan as well as fashion weeks in Berlin, Istanbul,

Mumbai, Miami, Moscow, Sydney, Tokyo and Zurich.[5] IMG's takeover of TFW fits with the event's aspirations to compete in the international fashion market but also lets the multinational firm further its 'imperialist' agenda in fashion event ownership and promotion.

To reflect TFW's international aspirations, IMG moved the event to a temporary, seasonal tent complex erected in David Pecaut Square, a multi-use urban outdoor cultural hub. David Pecaut Square is tied to Toronto's municipal heritage: formerly Metro Square, the site was renamed in 2011 for the late civic planner who 'wanted to continue to build Toronto's cultural significance' (Elliott 2013: 3). This relocation was perceived as an attempt on the part of TFW to model itself after New York Fashion Week, its closest locational competitor on the international fashion week calendar (also under IMG's control). From 1993 until 2010, New York Fashion Week ran shows out of tents in Bryant Park to critical approval before the event made a controversial move, under IMG, to the Lincoln Center (Elliott 2013: 3–4). However, it remained impossible for TFW to match the scale or profile of New York Fashion Week since, as of Spring 2013, the Canadian event hosted 27 shows in total, compared to New York Fashion Week's 148 shows, while the tent capacities of '800 people in the Runway Room and 120 in the Studio' were miniscule compared to those of Bryant Park even in the first seasons of the 1990s and nowhere close to the Lincoln Center's capacity to 'house 3,550 people throughout four venues' (2013: 4). Another crucial difference between TFW and higher-profile series is that members of the public can purchase tickets to almost all of the shows at TFW, a move that renders the event more accessible but diminishes the exclusive allure that characterizes invitation-only fashion weeks in cities such as New York, London, Milan and Paris. Indeed, the fashion shows in these cities and other higher-profile fashion capitals are hot tickets in part because the international press is interested in the collections. *FASHION* editor-in-chief Bernadette Morra explained to the Canadian Broadcasting Corporation upon the 2012 sale to IMG that the difference is one of scope and status: 'In a city like Paris, people are coming from all over the world – China, Russia, retailers and media. [...] A show in Paris can pack a huge tent, so there's no room for outsiders' (cited in Walji 2012: n.pag.). In other words, TFW needed to be open to the public to drum up local support for domestic creative talent.

Both the decision to sell TFW to an international corporate firm and to relocate to David Pecaut Square reflected continued, inherent tensions as to the event's status as a celebration of local creative talent and its aspired national and international visibility. In this sense, the event exposed Canadian fashion's own cultural and market insecurities. Indeed, the Canadian fashion scene had attempted to produce a cohesive showcase since the post-war period:

> The strategy for showcasing Canadian apparel has been evolving for decades. The Association of Canadian Couturiers [founded in Montréal] held presentations in Montréal as early as 1954, and in 1956 the Garment Salesmen Ontario Market held their inaugural two-day, biannual show at the Royal York Hotel in Toronto. The event, a mix of designer booths and live presentations, was the leading showcase of Canadian fashion, especially after the Montréal organization folded in 1968.
>
> (Georgijevic 2016: n.pag.)

Toronto-based curator Alexandra Palmer situates the efforts of the Association of Canadian Couturiers as the first promotion of Canadian fashion as 'fine art' on an international front, which included a touring presentation in New York in 1954 and a tour of 'Milan, Paris, and Brussels' in 1955 (2004a: 91–94). It was not, however, until these international tours happened that Canadian fashion publications were willing to feature Canadian designs in their pages, and, even then, press attention was not consistent (Palmer 2004a: 95, 103). The association's dissolution resulted from a lack of federal support for Canadian couture, insurmountable tensions between the spectre of an articulable 'Canadian' aesthetic and a monolithic European (here Parisian) influence, and the eventual demise of couture as the predominant fashion model in the 1960s (Palmer 2004a: 103). These are the same conditions that have continued to characterize the Canadian fashion industry into the current millennium, with, as Palmer describes, design talent such as Dean and Dan Caten leaving Canada to launch careers abroad and retail success stories such as Club Monaco and MAC Cosmetics assuming American ownership (Palmer 2004b: 3). In 1985, the Festival of Canadian Fashion was launched in Toronto with '24 shows over four days' under the sponsorship of the Eaton's and Holt Renfrew department stores; this event, however, lasted just five years at a loss of $400,000 (Georgijevic 2016: n.pag.). A later fashion showcase under the Matinée Foundation (of Matinée Cigarettes) started in 1992 and overlapped with TFW for a time: 'After providing $50-million in business development funding and marketing support over 11 years, it ended in 2003, around the time a ban on tobacco sponsorship was introduced by the government' (2016: n.pag.).

While TFW is intended as the main fashion showcase event in Canada, it is not the sole one of its kind: Vancouver Fashion Week has operated since 2001, Western Canada Fashion Week has run in Edmonton since 2005, Atlantic Fashion Week has been held in Halifax since 2012 and 'Sask' Fashion Week was launched in Regina in 2015. Montréal Fashion Week was cancelled in 2013 but has since been incorporated into the annual Festival Mode and Design. Indigenous design communities in Vancouver and Toronto have established Vancouver Indigenous Fashion Week, launched in 2017, and Indigenous Fashion Week Toronto, launched in 2018. This multiplicity of events demonstrates a richness in Canadian talent but has also frustrated attempts to promote a unified national fashion identity on an international front. Still, TFW publicized itself to potential exhibitors and audience members as *the* prime showcase for Canadian fashion at home and abroad. Rocamora (2009) uses the term *fashion media discourse* to describe how media texts position certain cities as fashionable (or as fashion capitals in a double meaning), and the term is applicable here in considering TFW's attempt to brand itself as at once local, national and international. Press discourses following IMG's acquisition of TFW reveal a discordance as to whether the event should be considered a launching pad for Canadian talent – or whether the industry should accept its more miniaturized 'regional' status (Morra cited in Walji 2012: n.pag.) or what urban studies scholars would term its *second-tier* status among fashion cities (Rantisi 2011). In a *Globe and Mail* editorial, Jeanne Beker, former host of Canada's iconic *FashionTelevision* (1985–2012), lamented that TFW was insufficient to ensure the success of Canadian designers, itemizing the difficulties of forming a stable fashion brand in Canada. Beker called on consumers and retailers to 'recognize the value of what's intrinsically Canadian, and how supporting these brands is vital to our national identity and, ultimately, our sense of ourselves' (2014: n.pag.). It was perhaps ironic that Beker would call for reflection on distinct characteristics of Canadianness as critics have argued that *FashionTelevision*'s focus on international trends undermined the market for domestic lines (see Fulsang 2004). The rebranded World MasterCard Fashion Week emphasized that its exhibitors were from Canada in social media content, press materials and even neon signs outside the tents; nonetheless, its situatedness within Toronto's downtown tourist environs spoke to a need to assert Canadianness to an *international* rather than domestic audience.

The erection of the TFW tents in David Pecaut Square became part and parcel of Toronto's exhibition of its own corporatized internationalism. Adam Jaworski and Crispin Thurlow define *semiotic landscapes* as 'any (public) space with visible inscription made through deliberate human intervention and meaning making' as well as the itemization and interrelation of textual and visual signifiers – for example, architecture, directional signage and advertisements or posters – within such spaces (2010: 2).[6] Processes of reading semiotic landscapes are enmeshed within social and media discourses and informed via local and international sociocultural influences (2010: 11–12). Fashion weeks impress a specific set of luxurious signifiers onto urban environments, through the mass arrivals of editors, retailers and celebrities in fashionable clothes – often with attendant photographers – the placement of signage and distribution of promotional materials and, in certain cases, the erection of tents. The ephemeral nature of tents in tandem with the international sensibilities of fashion weeks can lend these structures a sense of placelessness or dislocatedness even within specific urban locations (Gilbert 2006; Craik 2013). The FDCC proclaimed that David Pecaut Square offered TFW a 'highly visible location' to showcase Toronto's 'state-of-the-art fashion epicentre' (Fashion Design Council of Canada 2012: n.pag.). The arrival of personnel, local fashionistas, national celebrities and photographers to the site enhanced (and was enhanced by) the cachet of performance venues and tourist attractions such as the Mirvish theatres; the Roy Thomson Hall concert and symphony venue; the Toronto International Film Festival (TIFF) Bell Lightbox cinema and restaurant complex; the Ritz-Carlton and other hotels; and restaurants and nightclubs in the immediate area, all of which combined to produce associations of Toronto as cosmopolitan. While Craik's (2013) concept of *fashion tourism* articulates a reciprocal relationship between fashion shows and historical or tourist attractions in cementing the fashionable quotient of cities such as New York, London, Milan and Paris, TFW depended on its architectural environs for its cultural legitimacy. David Pecaut Square continues to be used as a red-carpet venue for the Toronto International Film Festival, the world-renowned annual event that has seen international film celebrities descend on Toronto since 1976, and as an outdoor free concert space for the Luminato Festival, an upscale and eclectic summertime arts and culture festival, launched in 2007, which features Canadian and international artists and has benefitted from similar sponsors under the banner of L'Oréal Canada. Situated in David Pecaut Square, TFW, like other cultural events on that site, thus operated as what theatre scholar Ric Knowles, writing on international theatre festivals, terms governmental or corporate 'showplaces' that function as an 'international market for cultural and other "industries"' and are 'postmodern marketplaces for the exchange, not so much of culture as of cultural *capital*' (2004: 181, original emphasis). Further, the adjacent stretch of King Street is also Canada's Walk of Fame, which features the names of several celebrities who have achieved fame outside of our national borders. This location therefore did not reflect a Torontonian culture per se but reinforced the fact that a substantial portion of Toronto's cultural clout resides in its role as an arbiter of and market for international content and tourism; rather, the tents invoked a semiotics of cultural tourism and demonstrated that Canadian fashion still mingled at the peripheries of an international cultural scene.

Within its municipal context, however, World MasterCard Fashion Week failed to find a substantial cultural foothold. This can be attributed in part to a lack of retailer and even press interest (Georgijevic 2016: n.pag.) and to the existence of alternative opportunities for designers to showcase at more local, competing fashion weeks or to build a customer base through e-commerce or social media. Geographers Taylor Brydges and Brian Hracs find that transportation and media affordances have allowed Canadian designers to market their lines without having to move to urban centres such as Toronto, Montréal or Vancouver and observed that Canada still lacks a 'dominant "fashion capital"' to anchor itself in a global market (2019: 9), much as the coordinators of TFW would wish to consider Toronto as such. On 7 July 2016, the press reported that IMG had relinquished its control of TFW and, as a result, the upcoming iteration scheduled for October would be cancelled. The Canadian fashion scene received the news as a shock despite ominous indications four months earlier when World MasterCard had pulled out as the title sponsor (Georgijevic 2016: n.pag.). IMG's decision to drop TFW from its international roster precipitated considerable introspection within the Torontonian and Canadian fashion scenes, from post-mortems on the cultural tensions and market inefficiencies that plagued the event to calls for a re-evaluation of governance structures for Canadian fashion and a new showcase event that better met creative and commercial imperatives (Parker 2016a, 2016b). What happened instead was that various corporate and non-profit enterprises stepped in to fill the void. Two new series titled Toronto Women's Fashion Week and Toronto Men's Fashion Week debuted in 2016 in the southern Harbourfront district near Lake Ontario, in addition to a plethora of events and pop-up installations launched around town that have included RE/SET in the Queen West district; FAT, Toronto's Alternative Fashion Week at the Daniels Spectrum cultural centre in Regent Park; Yorkdale Mall's FashionCAN showcase; Indigenous Fashion Week Toronto at the Harbourfront Centre; and African Fashion Week at the Globe and Mail Centre in the Front Street East area (see Delap 2017). While all of these events can be considered competitors to TFW, no one had claimed the rights to the event that IMG left behind until a purchase from IMG by an 'ownership group consisting of Canada's top real estate, media, and finance executives' formed under real estate impresario Peter Freed of Freed Developments (Freed 2019: n.pag.). In September 2017, Freed relaunched TFW as a smaller-scale three-day affair prior to TIFF. While the Freed website bills the new format as 'a diverse program that celebrates the Canadian fashion and design community', the site mentions Yorkville twice as 'Toronto's preeminent luxury retail and brand destination' (Freed 2019: n.pag.). To illuminate the discursive and semiotic implications of TFW's relocation to Yorkville, it is important to consider the historical dress and countercultural transformations in the latter half of the twentieth century that gave rise to the district's attraction not simply as a fashion hub for Torontonians but later as an ideal market for international high-end luxury retailers.

Tracing the geographies of luxury and glamour in 1960s Yorkville

Certain urban spaces and eras are forever marked by glamour's indelible touch. New York City's Greenwich Village evokes the glamour of the 1950s beatniks, while Paris's Montmartre recalls the glamour of the Bohemians of the Belle

Époque. Similarly, Carnaby Street conjures up images of 'Swinging London' and its youth decked out in tailored mod suits and Mary Quant miniskirts seduced by the glamour of youthful independence. Decades before Yorkville was synonymous with luxury condominiums and upscale boutiques, 'The Village', as it was most commonly referred to throughout the 1960s, aligned itself alongside other popular urban cultural centres as an adopted space for white, middle-class youth enchanted by the promise of a new bohemia 'shrouded in counter-cultural glamour' (Bain 2006: 423).

Of course, Yorkville was not Toronto's original bohemian epicentre. Gerrard Village, which was located on and around Gerrard Street, between Elizabeth and Bay Streets, was an area that prompted notable Canadian journalist Pierre Berton to declare the space 'our ghetto, our Bowery, our Chinatown, our East Side' (Berton cited in Baute 2008). For a certain period in the early twentieth century, Gerrard Village was a veritable who's who of Canadian literary and artistic talent. Most famously, the Group of Seven's Lawren Harris did many of his early sketches in the area, including his 'Houses on Gerrard Street' (1918). Another well-known Toronto-based artist, Albert Franck, rented a shop in the village and sold his work showcasing Toronto's wintry cityscape and the houses and stores that dotted the village scene. It was also in the village that the legendary relationship between Ernest Hemingway and Morley Callaghan was cemented while Hemingway was working at the *Toronto Daily Star*; the two of them were found frequenting the bars and cafés (although, according to Toronto lore, it was mainly the bars) in the 1930s. By the 1960s, the village grew and encouraged a growing beat culture that saw scores of Toronto's literati, actors and musicians spending countless nights in coffee shops, in particular the famed Bohemian Embassy, which was located on St. Nicholas, a street halfway between Gerrard Street and Yorkville. The Bohemian Embassy, replete with an entrance above which hung a flag bearing the Coat of Arms of Bohemia, acted as a nexus between the two bohemian poles until Gerrard Village's position as the first bohemian mecca was razed to make way for the construction of the Toronto General Hospital. According to Stuart Henderson:

> When it opened on St Nicholas St in 1960, the Bohemian Embassy seemed like a bridge between the gloaming Gerrard St scene and embryonic Yorkville. Famous for its wildly eclectic entertainment, the Embassy promoted local talent of all kinds, from folksingers to comedians, writers to painters. Toronto's strong stable of poets were encouraged to use the Embassy's stage to try out new material, and Margaret Atwood, Milton Acorn, Earle Birney, and Gwendolyn MacEwen all made that heady scene.
>
> (2011: 49)

The Embassy was not only a frequent annoyance for the Toronto Police Department, which fielded calls from nervous parents about the goings-on of their children, but was also a headache for the Bell Telephone Company that had listed the Embassy in their yellow pages under 'Consulates and Other Foreign Government Representatives', causing confusion for residents that would call the coffee shop to learn from 'your colorful country' (Elliott 1966: 45). Incidentally, the Embassy handed out 25-cent citizenship cards that, as owner Don Cullen promised, would be 'in aid of the lost causes of: Culture in Toronto, Intelligent Conversation, Informality, Inter-Galactic friendship, and General Subversion' (Cullen cited in Mount 2017: 100).

The tales of debauchery and the discoveries of famous literary and musical talents that have come out of the Bohemian Embassy point towards a particular performance of glamour imbued by the myth of the bohemian. As Elizabeth Wilson (2000) notes in *Bohemians: Glamorous Outcasts*, bohemian culture relied on collectivity, as artistic identity was built upon proximity to like-minded peers. In the spirit of collectivity and finding a space of their own, young Torontonians were performing and revelling in glamorous subversion, as was mandated on their Bohemian citizenship cards. While the beatnik aesthetic of the early 1960s and the growing counterculture ideology were heavily influenced by the mid-1950s beat culture of the United States (Henderson 2011: 47) – creating a trickle-down effect that on the surface may have appeared as though Toronto's hip culture was only an imitation – the revelry in bohemian glamour was indeed distinct to the city. Toronto-based fashion designer Marilyn Brooks, whose popular store The Unicorn was first established on Gerrard Street, recalls her first time at the Embassy:

> I'm from Detroit, Michigan – it was like *woooooah*, this is hot! You walked up the steps and you got stamped and then you sat there and you got your coffee – I mean, it wasn't a bottle of white wine, it was coffee after coffee. And somebody would read poetry against St Nicholas Street [...] and I thought, wow, this is *it*, you know?
> (Brooks cited in Henderson 2011: 50, original emphasis)

In finding *it*, that indefinable phenomenon that Joseph Roach notes very few possess 'but almost everyone wants' (2007: 4), Toronto's youth culture saw the possibility for glamorous production and the creation of a particular bohemian luxury that coffeehouses such as the Bohemian Embassy could provide in retailing 'high-end' coffee such as espresso and cappuccino. The legacy of Gerrard Village as a bohemian enclave was realized on a grander scale in the Yorkville scene which demonstrated the area's profound influence on the youth culture. Indeed, Berton's assessment of Gerrard Village as an 'intriguing island in the heart of downtown

Toronto, whose doom has been predicted (wrongly) for so many years' (Berton cited in Baute 2008) was correct, as its heart continued to beat in Yorkville.

At the height of Yorkville's popularity in 1967, sociologists Reginald Smart and David Jackson conducted an in-depth analysis of Yorkville's burgeoning subculture and concluded that 'Yorkville is to Toronto what the village is to New York and Chelsea is to London' (1969: 109). Smart and Jackson continue with their cosmopolitan comparisons by noting that ' "Yorkville," like "Hollywood," creates an image of particular, eccentric styles of life. It could be seen as a kind of non-alcoholic skid row for young people – where youthful social drop-outs congregate for shared drug experiences' (1969: 110). For Smart and Jackson, Yorkville was less a space of glamorous bohemian exploration and more of a meeting spot for lurid encounters. Through their study they identified four groups that populated the village environs: hippies; weekenders; motorcycle gangs, which saw themselves as the 'defenders of the village'; and Greasers, a classist and racially charged epithet that was used because, as one villager put it, 'they put grease in their hair and grease in their food' (Jackson and Smart 1969: 117). Of the four groups, the weekenders and hippies were predominantly from middle-class white families, while the greasers and motorcycle gangs were from mainly lower-class backgrounds. Smart and Jackson paid particular attention to the 'weekender', hip youth that brought 'charm, colour, and money to Yorkville' (1969: 115); nevertheless, they were considered interlopers by resentful local villagers who referred to these weekend tourists as 'Plastic Hippies' (1969: 116).

The phrase 'plastic hippie' was not unique to the hippies of Toronto's Yorkville Village. In 'The Flowering of the Hippie Movement' published in 1969, the sociologist John Robert Howard studied the rise of the hippie phenomenon in San Francisco's Haight-Ashbury area and, like Smart and Jackson, focused on four categories of hippies: the visionaries, the freaks and heads, the midnight hippies and the plastic hippies, and analysed their impact on the larger society. Howard concluded that plastic hippies were 'young people who wear the paraphernalia of hippies (baubles, bangles, and beads) as a kind of costume. They have entered into it as a fad, and have only the most superficial understanding of the ideology' (1969: 43). The tension between the *plastic* and *authentic* hippies reflects the paradox of the myth of the bohemian. While the glamour of the artist bohemian resides in their commitment to the tenets of art, beauty and love, often the reality of this lifestyle is less idealistic with many devotees falling prey to degradation, drug addiction and sickness. Meanwhile, the 'plastic' bohemian has the luxury to revel and relish in the glamour of the iconic hippie image – often without consequences such as homelessness or poverty. In this, the use of the word 'plastic' is instructive. Plastic, as Judith Brown notes when describing the glamour of cellophane in *Glamour in Six Dimensions*, 'is mere idea' and 'connotes a kind of luxurious royalty' (2009: 169) as its lustre reflects the fleeting ephemerality of desire. Indeed, '[weekenders] are in a state of transition; eventually they will either become committed to a village group or they will leave, having satisfied their curiosity' (Jackson and Smart 1969: 116). Plasticity, according to Brown, has historically been causally linked with glamour as a corollary of modernity. She cites an article in *Fortune* magazine from the 1930s that enthusiastically declares: 'the synthetic plastic [...] is a glamorous substance and a tribute to the powers of man' (2009: 150). Hippies, of course, are not interested in the powers of man but rather the power of community and collectivity. The myth of the glamorous hippie, with her 'romantic, druggy, murky and floaty' (Wilson 2000: 173) fashions and expression of being, was just that: a myth. As a matter of course, Yorkville was complicit in the performance of this mythology.

Yorkville's performance of glamour and luxury

Through their study, Jackson and Smart concluded that '[p]eople from Toronto who enter the village as permanent residents generally begin as weekenders' (1969: 116), which implicated the instrumental role that the plastic hippies played in performing Yorkville's bohemian glamour. Henderson similarly addresses the role that the plastic hippies had in shaping the wider Yorkville myth:

> In Yorkville, tourists came to see Toronto's Haight-Ashbury, Canada's 'hippie ghetto' – the district becoming famous as a 'foreign country'. And although the signs they were looking for – drug use, free love, outlandish clothing, bohemian artistry, heavy bikers, long-haired boys, and barefooted girls – were often being performed by people who were themselves tourists in the scene, come to the Village on their days off school to dress up as Villagers and play the part, it didn't matter.
>
> (2011: 118)

Indeed, to walk down the narrow corridors of Yorkville's winding neighbourhood streets in the 1960s was an effective performance of conspicuous glamour informed by Yorkville's mythological status in the urban imaginary. Henderson suggests that the various performances of identity through the totems of glamour such as fashion, luxury and celebrity were at the root of the Yorkville scene. He recorded the observations of one resident who commented upon the seduction of this public spectacle:

> God, you know, they were *watching* you [...] there's all these people coming to watch ... *us*. [...] There was all kinds of back and forth performativity, I'm sure.

The people in the cars are performing for the people outside the cars, who are performing for the people inside the cars, who are also boys looking for girls, girls
looking for boys, people looking for dope, whatever.

(Henderson 2011: 117, original emphasis)

Yorkville, therefore, operated for many as a visual experience. In the years after
1964 as the village became more popular with the migration from Gerrard Village,
Yorkville saw scores of people from across the province, and even the country,
come to the area to bask in the spectacle of performance of the hippies. Many
youths who descended upon Yorkville did not subscribe to the hippie ethos, but
simply aspired to the fashion of the scene. These scenesters often sported long
wigs and dyed their clothes in what one of the villagers said was an effort 'to look
cool' (Henderson 2011: 117–18). John Berger claims that '[t]his state of being
envied is what constitutes glamour, and publicity is the process of manufacturing
glamour' (1972: 125). For middle-class suburban Canadian youth, the Yorkville
scene allowed them to showcase a lifestyle that was antithetical to their parents',
and that embraced a particular glamour and a luxury that was steeped in the values
of the counterculture. While these plastic hippies may not have fully digested the
implications of the hippie ethos as Howard argues, their aesthetic choices reflected
a conscious and willing desire to publicly showcase their commitment to a specifically Toronto bohemian glamour.

Reading the language and grammar of glamour and luxury into Yorkville's
history is a revelation of the urban imaginary's protean nature and the capricious-
ness of aesthetic economies, that is, the way in which aesthetic values and economic calculations are intertwined with fluctuating cultural concerns (Entwistle
2009). Wilson expresses how changing aesthetics in fashion often correlate with
shifting perceptions of glamour; a similar argument may be made for the concept
of luxury as she argues that

[d]ress did not simply indicate power in the obvious sense of a uniform; nor was it
about mere wealth. More subtly, it brought the combination of person and clothing
to a pitch at which that person created glamour by means of daring departures from
the conventionally well dressed, combined with an aura of defiance.

(2007: 98)

Indeed, the variants of glamour and luxury speak to the flux of fashion, and certainly by the height of its popularity, Yorkville was a space that recognized its glamorous allure and promoted luxuriating in what the locale had to offer. Yorkville,
with help from its denizens, was actively promoting itself as Canada's hippie
destination in the same vein as San Francisco's Haight-Ashbury and New York

City's Greenwich Village. Specifically, the fashion that was exhibited on Yorkville's streets was a major attraction (Figure 4.2). In an article in the *Toronto Star* from 1968, the headline in bold letters proclaims 'Beautiful Girls of Yorkville' alongside photographs of chic young women parading along the village's winding streets followed by a detailed description of the various looks that one may come across on the Yorkville scene:

> Although Toronto's Yorkville district most often makes headlines as a local trouble spot, it's got a definite double nature. It's also a major fashion centre, especially for the young set who want to keep up to date on what's happening in design. [...] Swinging youngsters gravitate to the area, not to hang around or look for trouble, but to find out what's the latest groove in hip young fashion. As a high percentage of the fashion-conscious crowd are attractive young women, all this activity makes the area a real paradise for girl-watching enthusiasts. And whether they're dressed up for an evening at the theatre or for window shopping, the beautiful girls of Yorkville provide a rich contrast in styles. In one short evening's survey you're likely to see everything from the briefest of minis to trim pantsuits and flowing Indian saris. Office girls in neat suits and hats, university students in casual slacks and sweaters and hippies in 'antique clothes' resurrected from grandma's attic are among the young women who turn out to Yorkville to see and to be seen.
>
> (Mason 1968: 39)

Many young women during this period were making their way to stores such as The Unicorn, which had at this point moved to Yorkville's Cumberland Street. In an interview with the *Toronto Daily Star* in September 1968, the owner Marilyn Brooks gushed that 'Toronto is the hottest boutique centre on the continent', and she went on to exclaim that it 'beats San Francisco, Chicago and New York' as 'the designers in Toronto boutiques are making their own creations [...] but in other cities the boutiques that made it big five years ago have gone super big and are selling manufactured items' (Brooks cited in Evasuk 1968: 35). The rise of the boutique in Yorkville, and with it the hordes of young women who came to the village to scour the latest fashionable finds, which ranged from 'brief tunic dresses and glamorous evening pants to Eskimo art dresses and evening gowns that look as if they stepped out of the Victorian era' (Evasuk 1968: 35), contradicts Henderson's assertion that 'overt male fashion is the only performance mentioned [in the media], as though women couldn't make the cut, had no real purchase over this aspect of the scene' (2011: 111). For Henderson, the dominant image of the long-haired bearded hippie became a shorthand for Yorkville, and therefore, he concludes that the scene was read as male. Certainly, the village scene was steeped in misogyny and sexism, and of course, the media was quick to print

FIGURE 4.2: Donna Mason, 'Beautiful Girls of Yorkville', *Toronto Daily Star*, 29 July 1968. From *Toronto Star*. ©1968 Toronto Star Newspapers Limited. All rights reserved. Used under license.

stories involving the sexual exploitation and corruption of young white women. Nevertheless, while the media, and scholars such as Henderson, favoured the public vision of the archetypical villager who tended towards the bearded and beaded, less focus has been on the women who participated in fashioning much of this hip Toronto scene.

Of particular note were the fashions from designer Pat McDonagh, who had just come back from London after designing costumes for Diana Rigg's Emma Peel in *The Avengers*. McDonagh was credited for bringing the mod look to Canada (Ferrier Mackay 2014), and this 'swinging 60s' London style influenced the Royal Ontario Museum's (ROM) major exhibition of 1967, titled *Modesty to Mod: Dress and Underdress in Canada, 1780–1967*, which was opened by Princess Alexandra, who shrouded the event in a patina of glamour and luxury as befit her royal highness. McDonagh went on to become the designer of choice in Toronto and opened a store in Yorkville called The Establishment and then another store on Yonge Street called Re-Establishment. McDonagh, alongside other fashion designers and boutique owners such as Marilyn Brooks of The Unicorn, Rohaise Nicholls of The Bizarre, and Suzy, the 'swinging owner' of Poupée Rouge (Moreau 1967: 61), fashioned many of the aesthetic identities of hip Toronto youth in the 1960s. McDonagh in particular was singled out in a *Toronto Daily Star* article for her designs that created 'glamorous moments at home, for the theatre, for cocktail parties' (Stapleton 1969: 59). Dyhouse points out that 'glamour stayed somewhat out of fashion from the 1950s through to the 1970s: the word itself was much less frequently used by fashion editors and in women's magazines. There was less need for coded sexuality in a world of free love' (2010: 3). Nevertheless, for young Torontonians, whose aesthetic tastes were often behind the times of their 'groovier' urban counterparts in London and New York, glamour became a sensual expression of the scene, and these glamorous moments were often created through fashion. McDonagh recalls an event in Toronto from 1967: 'I did a show for my store on Bloor Street, up on the rooftop above Bellair. The models – three black girls, three Swedish blondes and three fiery redheads – had searchlights on them and iron balls chained to their feet. Traffic backed up down to Yonge Street' (1997: C12). The clothes were from her *Avenger* collection of that season which contained primarily vinyl minidresses. The audience, among them the famous model at the time, Twiggy, stood in a parking lot across the street. According to an article in the *Globe and Mail*, this was the hippest night Toronto had seen, until the police arrived and charged the audience members with drinking outdoors without a license. Their champagne glasses were confiscated (McDonagh 1997: C12).

Ironically, to stroll along the streets in and around present-day Yorkville is to hear the clinking of many glasses of expensive champagne delicately held by well-heeled imbibers at chic restaurants that often host Toronto's socialites and

Hollywood celebrities. When famed cyber punk writer William Gibson went to revisit the Yorkville of his youth, he was disappointed to discover that '[i]t's as though they tore down St. Mark's Place and built the Trump Tower' and lamented 'my Bohemia is gone' (Gibson cited in Bunch 2013: n.pag.). While Yorkville no longer sports the bohemian glamour of its past with its hip boutiques and coffee shops overflowing with long-haired youth and artists, its modern incarnation as an affluent and respectable neighbourhood for Toronto's wealthiest reveals an altogether different glamour, one that is steeped in modern luxury and elitism. Alison Bain argues that 'the counter-cultural glamour that was played up in the media was soon exploited by land speculators, developers, realtors and ultimately the upper-middle class' (2006: 423), and for this Yorkville has become a symbol of gentrification in Toronto, or, as Joni Mitchell sang of the changing neighbour-hood, in her renowned song 'Big Yellow Taxi' (1970), 'They paved paradise and put up a parking lot'. The irony therefore was palpable when, in 2007, Toronto's Luminato Festival paid homage to the 40th anniversary of the Summer of Love with a tribute to Yorkville's hip history. According to the *Toronto Star*,

> [t]he sight was slightly surreal as local 1960s- and 1970s-era bands rocked out on a stage in front of a towering Williams-Sonoma sign. Meanwhile, a handful of hip-pies in their 50s smoked pot next to curious passersby who clutched cellphones, Holt Renfrew shopping bags and specialty coffees.
>
> (Sorensen 2007: A8)

Indeed, as of 2017, the Williams-Sonoma location at 100 Bloor West on the Mink Mile had closed and was replaced by a 12,000 square-foot expansion of the Hermès store formerly located at 130 Bloor West, another material demonstration of international (in this case French) fashion's *imperial* expansion (Godart 2012).

Toronto Fashion Week in Yorkville

Like TFW, Yorkville Village has also undergone an overhaul, rebranded from its former incarnation in honour of its environs into a 'shopping, dining, and life-style experience' and a 'hub for movers and shakers […] host to some of the city's most notable top-tiered art, fashion and cultural events' centred around fashion, including magazine launches, fashion and costume exhibitions, and the revamped TFW (Kirsch 2018: n.pag.). TFW's latest incarnation presents fewer shows but includes panel discussions; the RE\SET showroom, a trade show environment; and Style Plate, a partnership series in which local restaurants create and serve dishes inspired by the works of specific Canadian designers during the run, allowing patrons to venture further into Yorkville and sample the neighbourhood's culinary flavour.

For the first iteration of TFW in Yorkville, the three main TFW spaces consisted of the RE\SET trade showroom, which was open to the public; a runway environment for which the event team took over the complex's parkade; and an enclosed runway tent that stretched 426 feet along Yorkville Avenue from Old York Lane to Bellair Street (Regal Tents & Structures 2020: n.pag.). These set-ups utilized the architecture of the existing retail and urban environments as a luxurious set, while at the same time avoiding too-specific associations with individual stores. Several of the stores inside Yorkville Village are independent but with a broader North American or European flavour, in addition to US corporate imports of the exclusive fitness centre SoulCycle and the pricey organic grocery store Whole Foods. The RE\SET showroom was situated in a lower-level promenade accessible from the main level via escalator or elevator and visible from above over glass railings. Event organizers branded or decorated various architectural elements such as the escalator sides and the outside of the railings overhead, creating the feel of entering an exclusive and contained environment. Most of the mall storefronts were sectioned off and rendered absent via the imposition of sheer white curtains which indicated that the event team preferred to invoke the modern, streamlined sense of a retail complex in the heart of Yorkville while selecting which businesses to visually or professionally associate itself with, in other words, emphasizing a sense of urban locatedness rather than a specific architectural venue. If one read this aesthetic calculation as a distinction between urban space and a particular place, the mall architecture as space thus functioned not for itself but rather to incarnate Yorkville as a luxurious *place* (see de las Rivas Sanz 2017). The parkade lent the feel of a sparse urban studio or warehouse environment that could be converted into a runway with minimal intervention. The third complex was a velvet (black) carpet and tent combination used for fashion shows and for taping panel discussions for the *FashionTalks* podcast in partnership with the Canadian Arts and Fashion Awards. This windowed structure was superimposed on Yorkville Avenue and intersected the Old York Lane patio walk that provides a shortcut and shopping promenade linking Yorkville Avenue with Cumberland Street and the Mink Mile to the south. This street-level runway tent – exclusive but still visible to the public – was two blocks removed from, rather than on, the Mink Mile, positioning its branded semiotics squarely within the Yorkville scene. The effect of this relocation off the Mink Mile (while still in proximity to it) is that TFW maintained a more exclusive and niche feel, visible to shoppers or area residents but no longer visible to tourists per se to the same degree as the tents in David Pecaut Square, even as Toronto's fashion elite could still exhibit their fashion capital across Yorkville's outdoor spaces. The event's expansion for Fall–Winter 2019 to hold certain shows at the ROM could be said to have taken the event closer to the Mink Mile and to reinvoke the confluences linking cultural and curatorial institutions, in particular the museum as Bourdieu's bastion of cultural capital and habitus. For its latest incarnation for Spring 2020, TFW held its public trade show in the Yorkville Village parkade accessible to shoppers directly from Yorkville Avenue (Figure 4.3). While TFW continued to use the ROM as a presentation venue, it also appropriated the two-storey 80 Yorkville Avenue storefront at the north end of Bellair Street, rendered vacant when international mid-level retailer Anthropologie closed out its Yorkville location the previous summer (Figure 4.4).

In its juxtaposition of whitewashed studio and warehouse spaces with upscale retail destinations, one can make comparisons between the urban aesthetics of Toronto and New York as the closest geographical international fashion capital and a feasible destination for Canadian designers to showcase in the US fashion market. Each fashion week has its own attendant associations informed by its city's cultural and architectural histories and the specific locations at which organizers and/or designers elect to present their shows. Nonetheless, there exist striking parallels between TFW's presence in Yorkville and its utilization of the available architecture and New York Fashion Week's current occupation of studio and retail locations while still under the control of the corporate behemoth Endeavor WME | IMG. New York Fashion Week's main venues are also multipurpose studio structures – including the Spring Studios and Industria complexes in Chelsea – that

FIGURE 4.3: A street view of the RE/SET showroom in Yorkville Village during Toronto Fashion Week, Fall 2019. Courtesy of Rebecca Halliday.

FIGURE 4.4: The street outside the former Anthropologie store during Toronto Fashion Week, Fall 2019. Courtesy of Rebecca Halliday.

purport to cater to all manner of fashion content and event production for high-profile international luxury brands and whose fashion presentations rely more on views of the architectural landscape than on interior décor (Halliday 2020). Press rumours have abounded in recent seasons that the event will partner in future seasons with the brand new multi-million-dollar Hudson Yards luxury retail mecca, but plans to move the event to this location have been complicated after several companies refused to show in the space in the face of developer Stephen Ross's fundraising efforts for Donald Trump's re-election. These similarities in fact suggest that despite TFW's return to Yorkville and its specific historical and cultural connections to Toronto, the event still exhibits a more international flair and *imperialized*, ambiguous sense of location rooted in financial and fashion capital rather than in countercultural or subversive fashion experimentation.

While TFW bills itself as a platform for Canadian fashion and has featured more resistant and experimental brands, such as the popular line Hayley Elsaesser, its Yorkville location in the present is indebted to Yorkville's countercultural and subcultural histories yet oriented to a more monied and whitewashed scene. The shifting semiotics of the Yorkville location and its sense of performative glamour is evidenced by a recent editorial from Elsaesser (2019: n.pag.), known for her separates in eclectic prints and fashion shows for a youthful customer base that feature a diverse cast of unconventional models. Elsaesser (2019: n.pag.) critiqued

TFW for its failure to properly promote diverse identities and perspectives in fashion, placing blame on the event's indebtedness to international capital and behemoth brands. It is notable too that Elsaesser's brick-and-mortar retail storefront is located on Queen Street West in an area west of Spadina Avenue, considered a more affordable and amenable alternative to Yorkville showrooms and a centre of indie fashion more reminiscent of Yorkville's initial period of glamorous, creative production.[7]

Conclusion

To set up the next incarnation of TFW in Yorkville as a precursor to TIFF cements a certain image of the city as a historical site of glamour as the runways and red carpets recall the village's spectacle of performance. To reiterate the argument that the presence of a fashion week offers a place-specific aesthetic within cities (Gilbert 2006, 2013; Craik 2013), we seek to underscore Yorkville's role in supporting Toronto's ontology; Yorkville's compelling history is foundational to Toronto's essence. As urban columnist Shawn Micallef rightly points out, 'When the subway pulls into Bay station, the fine print underneath the word "Bay" says "Yorkville," a reminder that Yorkville is an important enough location to warrant mention, an honour the TTC hasn't given to any other Toronto neighbourhood' (2010: 76). In this regard the geographies of glamour and luxury play an important role in city branding efforts. As Elizabeth Currid-Halkett and Allen J. Scott attest, 'Cities that offer a great diversity of social and cultural attractions illuminated by the auratic light of celebrity and glamour are obviously well-positioned as contestants in [the] global race' (2013: 8). TFW's move to Yorkville is in a sense a return to its fashion roots. Of course, Yorkville today is associated with a different type of fashion. The glamour and luxury that radiates from the neighbourhood's affluence is what Judith Brown would refer to as glamour's 'sheen of indifference' (2009: 37) that comes from a luxury that few can afford. Nevertheless, as previously argued, the concepts of glamour and luxury remain slippery. McNeil and Riello's history of luxury opens by asking, 'What is your luxury?' to acknowledge that one person's idea of luxury may be another's person's banality, but the question also recalls Toronto urban development guru Richard Florida's oft-quoted call of 'Who's your city?' Relocating, or rather, resurrecting TFW in Yorkville ahead of TIFF is certainly an answer to both questions. It is perhaps a declaration that Toronto – at the cusp of an international luxury marketplace – is serious about establishing itself as a viable fashion space, tourist destination and a world-class city, yet like the concepts of glamour and luxury for which Yorkville has come to inhabit, this, too, remains fluid.[8]

NOTES

1. At the time that this manuscript went to production, ten months into the COVID-19 pandemic in Toronto, the J.Crew, Calvin Klein Underwear and Banana Republic stores had closed down, and the Brooks Brothers and Club Monaco locations were under threat of closure.

2. In December 2020 this location also closed. Indeed, the impact of the pandemic in the Yorkville retail scene has been felt disproportionately by mid-level chain retailers and independent business owners rather than the international luxury retailers.

3. The 2015 exhibition *Global Fashion Capitals* at the Museum at the Fashion Institute of Technology in New York listed 23 fashion capitals, in addition to the 'Big Four', in order of when their fashion weeks were founded: Madrid, Tokyo, Melbourne, São Paulo, Rio de Janeiro, Sydney, Beijing, Johannesburg, Mexico City, Moscow, New Delhi, Seoul, Shanghai, Rome, Copenhagen, Kiev, Stockholm, Mumbai, Berlin, Barcelona, Istanbul, St. Petersburg and Lagos (Museum at FIT 2015).

4. Imperialization runs parallel to a phenomenon that Valerie Steele termed fashion's *internationalization* in which designers with marked ties to home nations have chosen to establish their careers in disparate locations or showcase at fashion weeks that offer higher prestige than those in their domestic markets (2000: 16–17). Internationalization can be used to describe Canadian-born or Canadian-educated designers that have moved to the United States or Europe to launch their lines. Examples include Rad Hourani, Erdem Moralioglu, Jason Wu, and Dean and Dan Caten of Dsquared2.

5. In 2014, IMG was acquired by the talent firm William Morris Endeavor to become WME I IMG, and in 2017 this multinational operation was renamed Endeavor.

6. Julia Polyck-O'Neill's chapter in this volume, entitled 'Vancouver's monuments to capital: Public art, spatial capital and luxury', offers an excellent analysis of the semiotics of public space and the dynamics of power that underpin commissioned public art works.

7. Elsaesser closed her brick-and-mortar location in February 2020, albeit with an aim to move her operations more online, before the COVID-19 pandemic and resultant shutdown impacted independent and chain retailers across Toronto, with a particular concentration of closures in the Queen West area.

8. In yet another development, on 14 January 2020, TFW organizers announced their 'decision to pause production' of the event's Yorkville incarnation to re-evaluate the efficacies of a fashion week and to consult with stakeholders (Toronto Fashion Week 2020). Whether this decision was made for financial or creative reasons remains undisclosed, but the event's most recent cancellation (at least for now) indicates a continued exigence to critically assess the ambiguous situation of TFW both as an institution within its urban environs and within nationwide cultural fabrics.

5

Vancouver's Monuments to Capital: Public Art, Spatial Capital and Luxury

Julia Polyck-O'Neill

In this chapter, I perform material analyses of Douglas Coupland's *Digital Orca* (2009) and Ken Lum's *Monument for East Vancouver* (2010), two public art-works that emerged out of funding initiatives related to Vancouver's successful bid to host the 2010 Winter Olympic and Paralympic Games. Given that public artworks have a unique relationship to their viewership, and as such necessitate a different interpretive perspective and framework than other forms of art, I closely consider the spatial and historical contexts for the artworks' commissions and explore how they have contributed to the construction of space during a dramatic period of commerce-led development that transformed the city. Public art com-missions and narratives around them interact with urban space according to a co-constructive dynamic: each shaping the other. This intentional shaping, varyingly performed by stakeholders, artists and community members, takes place around and within the production context of these artworks, revealing how place-based[1] economic networks synthesize to develop a purpose-built and replicable aura of cultural capital and luxury, contributing to the process of 'place-making', and, perhaps conversely, gentrification.

Mario Paris and Li Fang consider how the synthesis of place-making and the development of place-based luxury are premised in how 'luxury takes advan-tage of urban qualities of power' (2017: 8) and the contradictory intermeshing of the 'emblematic power' of rarity and exclusivity with mass marketing (2017: 7). Citing Edward Relph's sense of ' "places" as the fusions of human and natural order' and that '[places] are the significant centres of our immediate experiences of the world' (2017: 10), Paris and Fang argue that 'working on prestigious places means avoiding the repetition of ready-made formats and interacting with local contexts' (2017: 11). They explain:

Operators, each from its own point of view – often related to scale and financial power – seek to create vibrancy and variety for those spaces. Luxury, with its specific rituals and seasonalities, sometimes becomes a driver for the insertion of alternative rhythms and living practices in consolidated territories, so that they become fragments of urban tissue which contain multiple spatialities and are able to re-activate parts of metropolitan landscapes.

(2017: 11–12)

Following Paris and Fang's argument, luxury is a driving consideration in contemporary urban place-making and within the power dynamics that underlie the manufacture of urban space as place, including the construction of place by means of the commission of site-specific artworks. Attention to *Digital Orca* and *Monument for East Vancouver* as case studies of the tensions between place and capital, with their specific narratives of production and reception, also suggests how contemporary space-centric cultures of luxury in Vancouver are developed in a broader sense, according to a controlled narrative premised in cultural tourism and the erasure of marginalized communities.

Public artworks are created for a variety of reasons: to commemorate a person or event; to express community values; to contribute to a shift in the usage of space and a transformation of the landscape; or to encourage engagement with ideas and the questioning of popular assumptions (Anon. 2019). Public artworks are imbued with cultural, social, political and economic meanings at different scales: those assigned at their commission and installation by means of formal documentation and those assigned to artworks by local populations who regularly interact with the works by means of controversy and word of mouth. While public artworks play an active role in 'place-making' and the social negotiation of space, they are also actively enmeshed with systems of capital, whether by means of their commission and/or in how they co-create place. As signs representing complex networks of economic relationships and as objects that become increasingly entangled in value systems, public artworks eventually become forms of capital themselves, contributing to the construction of geocultural mythologies that concern and often generate economic capital.

According to Pierre Bourdieu, capital exists in three interrelated states, each 'convertible' into the others: cultural, social and economic ([1983] 1986: 242). Cultural capital, which can be loosely defined as an individual's social assets as they relate to their social mobility, exists in three forms:

in the *embodied* state, i.e., in the form of long-lasting dispositions of the mind and body; in the *objectified* state, in the form of cultural goods (pictures, books, dictionaries, instruments, machines, etc.), which are the trace or realization of theories

134

or critiques of these theories, problematics, etc.; and in the *institutionalized* state, a form of objectification which must be set apart because [...] it confers entirely original properties on the cultural capital which it is presumed to guarantee.

(Bourdieu [1983] 1986: 242, original emphasis)

For Bourdieu, the various states of cultural capital are at once tangible and transitive, meaning that forms of cultural capital can be sensed and acquired but are also the manifestation of a dynamic, symbolic process. To *spatialize* capital, then, is to codify geographic space according to a dynamic that assigns value based on a related framework for cultural, social and economic signification. Cultural capital, as defined by Bourdieu, is already spatial in that access to embodied, objectified and institutionalized forms of capital are mitigated by geographic access and access to economic capital. Cultural forms like art museums, for instance (which Bourdieu deems 'highbrow' in the tradition of modernist art critic Clement Greenberg), are often more readily available to (affluent) populations living in cities, whereas inhabitants of small rural regions generally have limited access to art museums.[2]

Luxury is a significant component of the consumption of cities-as-cultural-capital, of cities as a set of social and cultural processes and practices. Armitage and Roberts, theorists of the field of critical luxury studies, define luxury as hinging on both a 'dynamic process' and 'socio-cultural practice' concerning, if not centred upon, cultural capital, because of luxury's relationship to the disciplines of art, design and media, which they highlight in their framework of approach (2016b: 1). Luxury 'begins at the point at which humans surpass necessity or whatever constraints determined their natural inheritance' (2016b: 2) and is grounded in the 'practice of "unnecessary" enjoyment' (2016b: 4). Further, luxury has an observable relationship to visual art, which, according to conventional understanding, is generally not considered a necessary aspect of human existence – although theorists such as Thomaï Serdari remind us that this is not the case for many artists and artisans for whom the intellectual, emotional and practical fulfillment of artistic creation is essential to both their livelihood and well-being (2016: 136–37) – but has considerable social and cultural significance, while being intrinsically related to forms of economic value by means of these significations.

Comparing the discursive elements of the commission and reception of Coupland and Lum's works in Vancouver and considering them in the contexts of their commission and reception, I explore how the manufacture of these forms of spatial capital shifts the collective imaginary of place as it relates to urban space and notions of spatial capital and luxury. I observe how the ideas of spatial capital and luxury, as communicated by means of public artworks and their narratives, contribute to tensions that draw out embedded power relations connected to the cycles of capitalism and the production of forms of luxury premised in space and cultural specificity.

With the goal of revealing how sociopolitical, cultural and economic contexts for the creation and display of Coupland and Lum's works intersect with broader fields of cultural and economic production, I analyse how these specific works of public art, as variously 'monuments' and cultural texts, interact with public histories and spaces in Vancouver. I also examine how they correspond with or construct notions of place. Vancouver, as one of Canada's most expensive and global cities, provides an ideal backdrop for examining the dynamics between the concept of luxury and financial and cultural interests and how these become interconnected in conversations about public, social space.

Public art, place-making and Vancouver

Public artworks communicate forms of social, cultural and economic value that relate to geographic space and which might come to physically and symbolically articulate space as *place*. In their critical reconsideration of the social role of public artworks in the mediation of place, geographers Massey and Rose posit that place is typically understood through a relationship between spatial character, boundedness, 'a coherent community', 'a common understanding', 'an essence which is internally generated' and 'inherited traditions' (2003: 3). They suggest that a public artwork exists in relation to these characteristics of place as a form of open-ended spatial intervention. Although the nature of public artworks is inherently relational because *public* can be understood as 'an arena in which many diverse kinds of people can come together and engage', the way the public is imagined tends to be idealized (2003: 6), arguably mirroring the way the artwork might similarly be presumed to affirm a place's socio-spatial character. While the geographers acknowledge that for artists, scholars and broader audiences alike, a primary consideration for a work of public art often concerns its funding contexts and sources (2003: 1), they further insist that public artworks be considered a site of relational negotiation, stating, '[F]or an artwork to be public, negotiation between social differences has to be part of what the artwork does. If negotiation among diverse social identities is not invited, then the artwork is not public' (2003: 19).

While the reaction of the viewer to public art remains indeterminate during the commission process, the artwork's interpretation and ability to convey meaning is a central focus during the selection and commissioning process. Although the 'relational negotiation' (Massey and Rose 2003: 19) inherent to an artwork concerns a number of variables, there is generally an attempt by the artists and commissioning body to harness this outcome during the work's early stages, irrespective of the political intentions underlying the work's commission. Public artworks convey messages about space and can be strategically used to convey meaning within space by means of the relational negotiations between the work, place, context and the work's diverse viewership. However, this means that artworks can be deployed as a tactic to alter the signification of space and can be taken up as a sign to use space to represent and articulate ideologies or ideological messaging. This strategic use and interpretation of space and place by public art can be deployed in such a way as to appropriate place and its social, cultural and economic significance against the grain of its original context and meaning, as a means of harnessing or manufacturing cultural assets.

Public artworks have a complex relationship to cultural capital, in that they can focalize extant social and cultural value or, under the right circumstances, can synthetically produce it. Public works of visual art, as a representation or marker of luxury, play a role in the signification of space and place as participating in luxury as a cultural condition or process. Public artworks – as signs occupying, defining and representing space – can also begin to articulate luxury, as a form of economic excess and enjoyment (Armitage and Roberts 2016b: 4), in contexts where it might otherwise be absent, unwarranted or unwanted. The ways that public artworks come to be integrated into the social and cultural landscape of place, and the ways that these integrations are initiated, play a significant role in how they might participate in the manufacture and generation of cultural and spatial capital and luxury.

As well as being expensive, Vancouver, British Columbia, also offers North America's highest quality of life[3] and has become internationally known for its contributions to contemporary art. This evolving reputation is communicated and celebrated by means of its commissioned public artworks, which are on display in the city's many public and public/private squares, parks and other gathering places. Some works have been in place for generations, such as Coeur de Lion MacCarthy's *The Angel of Victory* (1921), located at Waterfront Station and commissioned to commemorate the Canadian Pacific Railway workers who died during the First World War (Anon. 2017). Many others date from around the time of the city's most transformative moments in its recent history, stemming from the vision of the city's civic and corporate leaders, who sought to highlight the city's potential as a cultural and economic centre in Canada and on the Pacific Rim. The phenomenon of 'Vancouverism' (Beasley 2019: 38) emerged as a result of architectural and organizational interventions particular to Vancouver's contemporary formative period, beginning in the late 1970s. It is a particular and intentional style of architectural design and urban planning that attempts to counterbalance needs for urban density and economic competitiveness with concepts and practices of sustainability and livability. This form of urban planning has had a profound effect on the development of the city as an internationally recognized, geographically distinct destination, with particularized features that can be 'exported internationally' (Bogdaniwicz 2006: 22). Vancouverism also plays a role in the kinds of artworks that have been selected to establish and communicate the city's identity. Typically, artworks celebrate the city's unique characteristics as a destination with a specific colonial cultural past and a proclivity for nature and green space. They also frequently centre the city's international historical fine arts legacy of the Vancouver School of conceptualist photography or other more local or regionalist art histories. While these approaches can be at odds with one another, such critical differences do not preclude them from intersecting in the expression of luxury inherent in public forms of visual art.

As with the majority of major international cities, Vancouver's geo-cultural and geosocial realities exist on a variety of scales. Vancouver is host to extreme wealth as well as extreme poverty. With the rising cost of urban real estate and the rapid gentrification of the metropolitan areas of the city's downtown, spaces that were once known for extreme poverty are slowly making way for new development. This includes the Downtown Eastside neighbourhood, a part of Vancouver known as 'the poorest district in the metropolitan area, while its postal code is reputed to be the poorest in Canada' (Ley and Dobson 2008: 2481). This puts marginalized populations in (often inequitable) dialogue with the super-rich when it comes to debating the politics of urban space, its usage and its meaning.

Local populations interpret the city's spaces by means of lived experience and engage actively in the enactment of both Lefebvre's triadic understanding of space as variously 'perceived-conceived-lived (in spatial terms: spatial practice, representations of space, [and] representational spaces)' ([1974] 1991: 38) and Massey and Rose's characterization of place as formed by means of internal, community-generated understandings (2003: 3), whereas outsiders and tourists might interpret spaces according to reactions couched in the way the city circulates in the cultural imaginary. These differences in both interpretation and lived experience are enacted not only on the basis of the boundaries of the city but also on the smaller regional boundaries of individual neighbourhoods. These boundary definitions play a role in the ways that public artworks construct space and discourses of luxury; a viewership with an intimate, lived relationship with a space comes to have a particular understanding of the public artworks in their neighbourhood, whether aesthetic or economic, familiar or alien. Thus, the inhabitants of a particular place will offer a unique interpretation of the artworks with which they share space and might find external interpretations (those of non-locals) to be contentious, at odds with the history and identity of place particular to the space.

Celebratory and critical: Public monuments and place in Vancouver

In 2009, Douglas Coupland was commissioned to create a public sculpture for the Vancouver Convention Centre Art Project. That same year, Ken Lum was commissioned to produce a public work of art to coincide with the 2010 Winter Olympics in Vancouver. Both artists were funded according to initiatives controlled and organized by governing bodies in Vancouver, conceived in response to the city's successful bid, which would, ostensibly, raise the city's public profile within a global context. Such an increase in profile would, in turn, help to strategically negotiate and construct place-based identities at the sites of the artworks within specific Vancouver neighbourhoods, as conceived by the funding bodies supporting the commissions.

Coupland's sculpture, *Digital Orca* (2009), was created for a high-end waterfront tourist area cast as ground zero for the international broadcasting of the Olympic Games, which has since become a well-loved destination for visitors. According to the City of Vancouver's Public Art Registry, *Digital Orca* is categorized as part of 'Other' public art programs, meaning that it is not part of the city's public art initiatives; the listed owner is 'Pavco' [*sic*], a Crown Corporation founded to manage the B.C. Pavilion during Expo '86. The page provides a map locating the work along the Seawall at Burrard Landing, between the Cactus Club Coal Harbour and the Vancouver Convention Centre. The 3D killer whale is composed of black-and-white cubes made of powder-coated aluminum. The work is stylized to suggest that it is constructed of a material that emulates both pixels and Lego blocks. It is mounted on a stainless steel frame and stands approximately seven and a half metres tall. From dusk until dawn, tiny LED lights embedded in the surface of the orca's body twinkle and shimmer, enhancing the technological theme of the piece and capturing the interest of passers-by.

Coupland has stated that he was seeking to capture elements of the Coal Harbour site's pre-Expo history, as an industrial area featuring a train yard at the harbour, while also speaking to the contemporary site and moment (Tang 2010). The work, which is placed directly on the ground in Burrard Landing at the Vancouver Convention Centre, appears to be leaping from the square but, from many vantage points, can be imagined to bound from the waters of the harbour against a mountain backdrop. Materially, the orca's construction (shimmering LED lights or not) invokes the materials of both the contemporary architecture of the convention centre and the docked cruise ships nearby.

Within Coupland's oeuvre, *Digital Orca* occupies a position that intersects with the well-known author's literary work exploring technology's effects on contemporary thought and his playful, colourful explorations of ubiquitous materials. It fits within the broader, established body of his public sculpture, with a visual

FIGURE 5.1: Douglas Coupland, *Digital Orca*, 2009. Powder-coated aluminum, stainless steel, LED lights. 762 cm. Vancouver, BC. Collection of Pavco (B.C. Pavilion Corporation). Courtesy of Julia Polyck-O'Neill.

relationship to such works as *Monument to the War of 1812* (2008), *Four Seasons* (2014) and perhaps especially *Golden Tree* (2016), a true-to-size golden replica of the Hollow Tree, the enormous stump of a six- to eight-hundred-year-old red cedar in Stanley Park that is a popular tourist attraction. This public sculpture, located near Vancouver's Marine Drive SkyTrain station, can be read as akin to *Orca* in that it also has the potential to invoke the site's past amid the frenzy of perpetual real estate development, this time in the city's southwest Marpole area. Before colonization, Marpole was originally *c̓əsnaʔəm*, a Musqueam (*xʷməθkʷəy̓əm*) village dating back at least four thousand years, and the invocation of the neighbourhood's precolonial past reminds viewers and current residents of Vancouver's colonialist legacy, giving testimony to the city's history before the arrival of European settlers. While *Digital Orca* is more firmly linked to the city's industrial past by means of Coupland's published artist's statements, it also can remind viewers of the area's precolonial roots in that it is located near a former *Skwxwú7mesh* (Squamish) settlement and that the orca has symbolic importance to the majority of Coast Salish peoples.

While Coupland is best known as an author, he was originally academically trained in visual art, a discipline to which he returned full-time after achieving literary success. He has a strong personal relationship to Vancouver, having grown up there (though he was born on a military base in Germany) and as a current resident of West Vancouver. His connection to and knowledge of the city is reflected in the subject matter of his artworks and novels, which frequently explore not only the region's physical spaces but also themes related to the collision between consumer culture, technology and the natural landscape that reflect the city's evolution in the twentieth and twenty-first centuries. But despite Coupland's strong connection to Vancouver as a place, there is also a sense that his works are politically benign and lack critical clarity. This critique is particularly resonant given the contrast between his work and the critical and politically engaged approach to visual arts and arts criticism that has become characteristic of Vancouver's contemporary arts community and remains a dominant expressive mode within the artistic landscape of the city as it is represented both locally and abroad. During the late 1960s and early 1970s, critics lamented a lack of relevant arts criticism in Vancouver while the city emerged as a cultural hub of national and international importance (Wood 2011: 138; Wallace 2011: 30). However, Vancouver visual artists and critics began to develop a globalized artistic and critical consciousness shortly thereafter (Sandals 2016), which contributed to the sense that Coupland's work has an unconscious that is 'entrepreneurial' and that references to external cultures are only at the service of the work, undertaken with an undertone of 'privileged, effortful, [and] performative' detachment (Balzer 2015).

While *Digital Orca* is a work created to appeal to a broad public audience, Lum's large-scale *Monument for East Vancouver* (2010b) is a tribute to one of the city's most marginalized neighbourhoods: Vancouver's Downtown Eastside, an area described in a national newspaper as 'notorious for its poverty, addiction, prostitution, mental illness and homelessness' (Allford 2016). The imposing 'neon' and steel cross – the neon effect being created with LED lighting – is just seventeen and a half metres tall and stands on a concrete post; the full work stands at just over eighteen metres. As opposed to Coupland's *Digital Orca*, the City of Vancouver's Public Art Registry lists the work as being part of its Civic art program, with the

FIGURE 5.2: Ken Lum, *Monument for East Vancouver*, 2010. Concrete, steel, aluminum, impact modified acrylic, LED illumination. 17.5 m. Vancouver, BC. Collection of the City of Vancouver. Courtesy of Ken Lum.

City of Vancouver listed as the owner. The website provides a link to a write-up about Lum and the work and includes a map locating the piece at the corner of Clark Drive at East 6th Avenue near the VCC/Clark SkyTrain Station but does not indicate that the work is positioned at the crest of a hill, in a relatively nondescript area, industrial in aesthetic. The site is located on a slightly elevated point above the treetops, at the busy intersection of a six- and five-lane street, and as such, the cross is highly visible from a number of vantage points in the city. Because of its topographically elevated standpoint and the lack of tall buildings around the site,

FIGURE 5.3: Ken Lum, *Monument for East Vancouver*, 2010 (illuminated). Concrete, steel, aluminum, impact modified acrylic, LED illumination. 17.5 m. Vancouver, BC. Collection of the City of Vancouver. Courtesy of Robert Keziere.

the 'monument' seems to overlook the urban landscape like a beacon, particularly when illuminated at night.

The Latin cross features the words 'EAST', running vertically, and 'VAN', running horizontally, which intersect at a shared letter 'A'. The form is borrowed from a colloquial text-based symbol that is said to have originated in graffiti in the neighbourhood and is also attributed to the large population of Roman Catholic residents who once inhabited the area (Campbell 2010). Lum created the work as an homage to the historically economically downtrodden area, where he was born in 1956. The concept of a monument commemorating the history of an infamously marginalized part of the city as well as the work's religious symbology and placement is quite striking. In a variety of ways, the work formally mimics the neon crosses of contemporary roadside churches, which adds an element of camp to its premise, which is simultaneously celebratory and critical. The large cross also recalls recognizable religious monuments such as the Mount Royal Cross (1924) in Montréal, Québec and the statue Cristo Redentor (Christ the Redeemer) (1931) in Rio de Janiero, Brazil, and this contributes to the work's gravitas, which might be further inferred by means of the local public's enthusiastic embrace of the work as a symbol for not only the neighbourhood but also the 'fabric of the city' (Public Art Program cited in Brend 2018).

With his unambiguously critical sensibility, Lum is a member of the group of artists commonly referred to as the 'Vancouver School' of photography, a name that 'began to be applied to a number of artists in Vancouver around 1990' and 'refers to a common critical sensibility towards subject matter, rather than one unified through common formal attributes' (Modigliani 2018: 2). He has worked in photography and is well known for both his photography and text-based works, most often interested in exploring themes and issues relating to diasporic identity. His public artworks are similarly implicated in such explorations; *Monument for East Vancouver* maps Vancouver's east end onto the cultural landscape. The ironic interplay of the work's title suggests a kind of commentary on the social hierarchies of the city, by offering a 'monument', a structure traditionally reserved to commemorate or honour an important person or event, to a historically oppressed population in a historically poor neighbourhood, most often redacted from the social landscape of the city by its notoriously affluent residents.

Lum has produced a number of public artworks in Vancouver that resonate with residents, such as *A Tale of Two Children: A Work for Strathcona* (2005) and *from shangri-la to shangri-la* (2010). Both reflect Lum's interest in site specificity. Although the work has been removed, *A Tale of Two Children* was installed at the corner of Thornton Street and Malkin Avenue in the National Works Yard, an industrial area described as an 'urban hinterland' (Laurence 2005). The work, a large-scale photographic diptych portraying a crying Caucasian child next to the text 'What an idiot / What an idiot you are! / What an utterly useless idiot you are!' beside an image of an Asian mother and child paired with the text 'You so smart. / You make me proud / you so smart. / I so proud you so smart.', explores issues of cultural identity and childhood connected to the Strathcona neighbourhood. In 2010, *from shangri-la to shangri-la* was temporarily installed at the Vancouver Art Gallery's offsite location in a plaza adjacent to Living Shangri-La, a luxury hotel and condo development located on West Georgia Street in the city's downtown core. The installation replicates three squatters' cabins on stilts that used to occupy Maplewood Mudflats, an intertidal area on Vancouver's North Shore, known for its nonconformist inhabitants, including many culturally significant

Vancouver writers and artists. In fact, the reproduced cabins belonged to novelist Malcolm Lowry, Greenpeace activist and cetologist Dr Paul Spong and visual artist Tom Burrows (Laurence 2010). The work is a critical intervention, disrupting the illusion of permanent abundance and opulence that the architecture attempts to distill on the site and imbuing the austere, modernist plaza with a sense of historic memory. The contrast between the steel, glass and characterless landscaping of the Living Shangri-La complex and the hand-hewn wooden boards of the shacks, and their disparity in scale against the backdrop of the towering buildings, inspire a kind of sympathy for the city's modest past, which has predominantly been erased from the landscape. Like these works, *Monument for East Vancouver* seeks to claim a presence in the distracting, ever sleeker topology of the contemporary city.

Public artworks interconnect with other artworks and sites, and their histories and identities, creating a broadened network of site- and place-specific meaning. Like Coupland, Lum also has deep roots in Vancouver, having been born and raised in Strathcona, and these connections inform his work, particularly in how he connects identity and place with a sense of acute specificity. The oftentimes critical messages underlying the creation of Lum's public artworks inform the space of display and their mutual interconnection and, in turn, begin to construct meaning in the city more generally. Although Coupland's messages are frequently more ambiguous, his works function similarly, and his oeuvre of public works also tells a site-specific story. In turn, these stories are altered by the reception of their publics, creating collaborative narratives of place.

Cultural capital, 'spatial luxury' and public art

To better understand the mechanisms underlying the role of public artworks such as *Digital Orca* and *Monument for East Vancouver* as forms of cultural capital – or as objects promoting the generation and circulation of cultural capital – it is useful to consider the relationship between cultural capital, space or place and public art, and to examine how public artworks might realize multiple forms of interpellation, as a means of address, according to multiple kinds of viewership. But the interplay of cultural capital and space has other, less-obvious significance. Sociologist Laurie Hanquinet (2016) identifies that, in contemporary life, the 'mechanisms of social positioning and position-taking in a social field according to the level and types of resources at disposal' that Bourdieu originally described remain operational, though his 'modernist emphasis on strongly classified high and lowbrow cultures' (see Greenberg 1961) no longer reflects mainstream socio-cultural values, which have adapted to 'new aesthetic criteria' (1961: 67). Indeed, following Lash and Urry, Hanquinet argues that '[w]ith postmodernism, a more participatory and inclusive vision of cultural artefacts has sprung up and this has modified people's relationship to their material environment. This environment has an aesthetic component containing sign-values or images' (2016: 68). She further asserts the spatial dynamics of these shifts, noting that

> [i]n their cultural consumption, people are increasingly preoccupied by the styliza-tion of their everyday life. In the establishment of these lifestyles, places, and espe-cially cities, have become central arenas for display and consumption, and have become part of the aesthetic experience itself. Art has become 'contextual' (Ardenne 2004) and directly depends on place.
>
> (Hanquinet 2016: 68)

Aesthetic experience tied to context underlies what Hanquinet and Mike Savage have termed 'urban cultural capital' (Hanquinet 2016: 68), to account for the ways in which 'cities are now lived and consumed as resources of cultural capital because our aesthetic relationship to things has profoundly changed' (Hanquinet 2016: 68).

Building on Hanquinet's adaptation of Bourdieu's theories to consider the atomization of cultural capital within urban space, the relationship between urban populations and public art can be understood both as lived signification – related to Lefebvre's triadic interpretation of space ([1974] 1991: 38–39) – and as consumer experience. It is precisely in the ways that works of public art are *consumed* that the social and cultural dynamics of cultural capital and luxury might be identified; the relationships between the specific ways that geographic *space* is perceived (spatial practice), conceived (representations of space) and lived (representational spaces) contribute to the manufacture of *place* and also signal how the idea of luxury is folded into *place* in the collective imaginary of both local and wider communities.

Public art can become intertwined with the daily lives of many of its viewers in a number of ways. It becomes part of what Massey and Rose call the 'internal diversity and complexity (rather than coherence) [...] at the core of the sense of place' (2003: 4) and of the 'making of a sense of identity' (2003: 5). It is also worth observing that the process of choosing, commissioning and placing public artworks is seldom democratic, although practices of community-driven selection and cre-ation processes are gaining popularity. The question of the public artwork's own-ership is also somewhat unclear, given that certain populations have more agency than others in the work's underlying production processes. The dynamics inherent to place-making as expressed by commissioned public artworks also hinge on the concentration of power at the core of the commission; as Paris and Fang note, the fusion of local contexts and the 'specific rituals and seasonalities' of luxury are often an expression of both prestige and economic power (2017: 12). As such, public artworks have an unclear and potentially uneasy relationship to the notion of luxury, despite some obvious connections to systems of cultural and spatial capital, in that they are intended to imbue space with meaning and express value.

Vancouver and the 2010 Olympic Games

Local populations rarely respond evenly to the economic effects inherent to the international and spectacular event of hosting Olympic Games.[4] Most often, celebrations in response to the announcement of a winning bid for the games are countered by widespread public backlash. This counter-response is motivated in part by the financial and societal impact, which is predominantly incurred at the local level and hinges on social and ethical issues related to globalization, such as poverty, terrorism, commercial exploitation by multinational corporations and nationalism (Milton-Smith 2002: 131). This is especially the case when the city in question is renowned for its activist culture and uneven social, political, cultural and economic topology. Vancouver was no exception, and the effects are ever more intriguing when taking into account the mandate of the International Olympic Committee (IOC), introduced concurrently with the 2010 Games, for host cities to address local impacts and ensure social inclusivity. Furthermore, it has been revealed that the Olympic Games Impact (OGI) Study in Vancouver, slated to measure the impact of the Games, used quantitative strategies that overlooked 'contextual details necessary to evaluate impacts and legacies in context' (Pentifallo and VanWynsberghe 2015: 278).

In 2003, when it was announced that the Vancouver bid was successful, the local response was largely negative. In the months leading up to the events, there were widespread protests decrying the impact of the construction and amplification of public space, venues and infrastructure (Hill 2009). While cultural institutions largely benefitted thanks to the increase in tourism and the proliferation of subsidies and cultural initiatives, economically and socio-politically precarious populations suffered. Attempts were made to drive homeless and underprivileged people away from the city centre to make way for luxury accommodations. Local governance, using the IOC's new policies, created ad hoc committees to strategize oblique ways to obfuscate the city's underprivileged from global media while ostentatiously creating outreach initiatives. However, local special interest groups, such as the Anti-Poverty Committee, undermined these strategies. Vancouver's new Convention Centre, a site discursively tied to the Olympic bid, opened in 2009; according to many accounts, its emergence had similarly dismal – if not disastrous – effects on marginalized local populations. The centre opened at the peak of the economic downturn and was massively overbudget. Having more than doubled its estimated construction costs, the project became infamous for having the 'largest [financial] overrun of any public project in B.C. history' (Dembicki 2009).

As two of the works commissioned by publicly funded governing bodies in Vancouver, *Digital Orca* and *Monument for East Vancouver* reveal how economic capital made such commissions possible as well as the inherent inequities in the city's preparations to host the Olympic and Paralympic Games. *Digital Orca* was commissioned and is owned by B.C. Pavilion Corporation or PavCo, which emerged out of the 2008 amalgamation of B.C. Pavilion Corporation and Vancouver Convention Centre Expansion Project Ltd. PavCo is governed by a Board of Directors appointed by the provincial government. The financial reports of this Crown Corporation are decidedly obscure and do not outline the acquisition of Coupland's work directly. Instead, they merely list generic categories such as 'Buildings and Improvements' and 'Art/Theming Collection' (2009: 42). The City of Vancouver's Public Art Registry cites Coupland's artist statement: 'The raison d'etre [sic] of the piece was to commemorate the workers in and around Burrard Inlet and Coal Harbour. The site's owners, Pavco specifically wanted artists to consider the past, present, and future of the site.' The naming of PavCo in his statement and the clinical nature of the public documentation of the artwork's commission point to a certain sterility reflecting the social hygiene of the site, near the Jack Poole Plaza adjacent to the West Building of the Convention Centre. There is little evidence of the controversy that had come to underlie the identity of the site for many Vancouver communities, such as the history of how Poole was responsible for securing the 2010 Games bid. Neither is it evident that the original B.C. Pavilion was constructed on the site as part of the efforts to prepare for Expo '86, the World Exposition on Transportation and Communication, which had displaced more than a thousand low-income residents of the Downtown Eastside and disrupted many local communities (Baker 2016), and which, like the Olympic Games, became a catalyst for social and cultural change and a critical intervention into the local politics of public space.

In contrast to the opacity of PavCo's public records, the City of Vancouver's documentation of its own public commissions process and records is significantly more transparent. According to the final review draft of the 2008 Vancouver Public Art Program (Bressi et al 2008), works including Ken Lum's *Monument for East Vancouver* were conceived and funded according to the municipal mandate called 'Legacy Art Projects' within the $800,000 Olympic and Paralympic Public Art Program, although funding was also 'generated by development', which is to say that profits from the city's contracts with the private sector also helped fund the program. These permanent commissions were, and continue to be, mandated to 'leave a lasting mark on the city' (2008: 52) and remain signs for Vancouver's prosperity and its availability of economic capital, while also materializing cultural and symbolic capital.

Orca and *Monument* each represent aesthetics particular to Vancouver. Both were intended to become landmarks at a time when the city would be center stage, but each was conceived and produced according to differing authorial intentions. As previously mentioned, Coupland's work is intended to commemorate the historic diversity of workers operating in Coal Harbor and the Burrard Inlet but also attests to PavCo's specific request that artists consider and respond to 'the past, present, and future of the site' (Public Art Registry 2010a). Lum, on the other hand, seems to have created his work according to a predetermined intention to memorialize and render permanent a local symbol and site with which he closely identifies on a personal level, as he was raised nearby (Public Art Registry 2010b). These works not only reflect contrasting formal and discursive narratives – a difference intrinsic to the Vancouver art market – but also have very little in common aside from the proximity of their commission to Vancouver's preparation for the Olympic Games. Their proximity to socio-economic issues specific to Vancouver's complex and storied spatial politics provides a common pathway to understanding how public art can translate complex spatial debates, histories and systems. This contingency is tied to a shared relationship with a symbolic framework that is, intriguingly, materialized within a system of commodities discursively and materially related to Vancouver's developing reputation as an international luxury destination.

Public art often represents a balance between private and public interests in public space; public art's place-making role interacts with space on a wide variety of scales, and, as such, a public artwork comes to represent the polyvalence inherent to the site. American urban arts specialist Tom Finkelpearl's argument for what he observes as 'a very basic dialectic between top-down, "pro-growth" development initiated by or for business elites' and ' "community-oriented" development initiated by or for people outside the traditional mainstream of power' (2000: 5) makes sense in the context of how *Orca* and *Monument* have gained social significance beyond their association with the Olympics as their context of production. However, Finkelpearl's idea that such a dialectic produces a sociocultural dynamic that contributes toward 'sharing power rather than imposing solutions, toward healing wounds inflicted by the fragmentation and social segregation of contemporary public spaces' (2000: 5) is in many ways a utopian approach to the understanding of how public art contributes to social contexts. *Orca* and *Monument* each convey a complex web of meaning and relations both at the level of the site and at the broader scale of the city. Their contexts for production and reception play an important role, although the differences between the commissions, sites and reception are significant to their interpretation, as are Coupland's and

Lum's individual relationship to the city and its visual art. Now *Orca* and *Monument* have come to stand not simply for a wave of rapid urban development but also for the broader networks represented by the politics of Coupland's and Lum's careers, of their other works, actions and civic interventions.

These artists' public artworks continue to be both popular and controversial, although their meanings have shifted as the intensity of the Olympic period has been relegated to the annals of history. This is to say that although the potential controversy of their context of production remains relevant, the framework for their acquisition began to fall into the background as the works became integrated with the landscape of the city. For example, as early as the summer of 2014, *Digital Orca*'s reception began to shift when the Vancouver Art Gallery hosted Coupland's first comprehensive retrospective exhibition, *Everywhere Is Anywhere Is Anything Is Everything*, by Daina Augaitis, chief curator and associate director of the Vancouver Art Gallery from 1996 to 2017. *Orca* remained in its permanent location, but thanks to the gallery's ambitious and prolific promotional campaign for Coupland's show, as well as the public installation of his large three-dimensional self-portrait *Gumhead* (2013) on the gallery concourse, *Orca* gained greater attention as Coupland's profile and stable of public artworks gained attention. Indeed, thanks to the proliferation of materials promoting both the exhibition and Coupland's affiliation with the city in such places as the airport, on public transportation, on telephone poles and in newspapers, his already established position within Vancouver's vernacular was further cemented. Coupland came to stand for a certain set of relations inherent to Vancouver's identity.

Lum also encountered a number of controversies surrounding *Monument*'s spatial narratives and its relationship to gentrification. While Lum has always publicly contended that the sign is not something he created, the topic of the potential appropriation of the East Van cross came to a head in 2011 when a Vancouver resident, Rocco Dipopolo, who claimed to have copyrighted the East Van cross, challenged Lum's use of the symbol in court. Dipopolo was unsuccessful, but the news story allowed Lum to clarify that the cross design is ubiquitous in the Eastside area, noting that its folkloric narrative dates back to the 1940s. He remembers having seen the symbol first-hand in the 1960s and 1970s. Most significantly, in response to the lawsuit, he explained that the trademark for the symbol (in its manifestation in neon) is now owned by the City of Vancouver and that it is impossible for anyone to claim ownership of the immaterial *sign*, which is intrinsic to the history of the city (Cole 2011, emphasis added).

The controversy around Lum's artwork as a place-based sign recently entered the public spotlight again in a different way, after Vancouver developers Nature's Path claimed that they had received Lum's permission to build a tower at the western side of the work that would obstruct views of *Monument*; it turned out that no such permission had been granted (Brend 2018). The city's public art planners are also considering moving the work, despite Lum's concerns that the work is site-specific and should remain in place and that the work should be protected because of its cultural and spatial significance, locally (Brend 2018) as well as nationally and internationally (Sandals 2019). *Monument* points to the circulation of Lum's ideas and works as a form of mythology, but the work also reveals the city's own mythology as well as its economic and political systems. As such, the work has thus taken on several scales of meaning; not only materializing the struggle of the Downtown Eastside's residents against the forces of gentrification, *Monument* is also the direct subject of these debates, rendering them visible to a wide audience.

The East Van cross's origins as an immaterial sign related to place imbue Lum's *Monument* with a sense of collective mythology, and the work's location and relationship to the well-known artist's biography suggest a sense of authenticity that adds to the perception of the work's value in the urban imaginary of the city. Historian Catherine Kovesi argues that sign, space and mythology contribute to an object's *aura* (after Benjamin 1968) and become entangled in the manufacture of the aura of luxury, observing that '[w]here that object is now made, and its true value and worth, becomes less important than the mythic story woven around its origin, the [name] stamped upon it, and the quasi-sacral space given to its display' (2016: 120). In similar ways, Lum's work draws auratic power from a sense of being intrinsic and thus invaluable to the unique texture of its site, imparting a form of spatial capital within the landscape of the neighbourhood. The East Van cross design, much like the designs and aesthetic of Coupland's works, can be understood as a node within the aporetic network comprised of both marginalized residents of the Downtown Eastside and varying forms of capital.

Merchandise and the commodification of place

While the cultural value of consumer goods varies according to a number of factors, there is something to be said for how commodities related to real, physical spaces communicate and represent political and social imaginaries and how these might link to broader aspects and forms of cultural capital. Commodities are a kind of mass cultural text, and objects that connect directly to works of fine art bear a message tied to taste and luxury. Further, such items evoke spatial narratives and systems of spatial luxury.

In considering Bourdieu's definition of cultural capital as an amassing of embodied, objectified and institutional forms of capital in relation to the holders' dispositions, that is, their schemes of perception, thought and action ([1983]

1986: 242), and the fact that cities are also associated with cultural capital (Hanquinet 2016: 68), it is conceivable that identifying oneself with particularized narratives of a city and expressing familiarity with the intimate social and cultural workings of its spaces communicates a desirable form of symbolic and cultural capital. As such, there is a market for city-signs-for-purchase, driven by the desire for consumer items that represent a sense of knowing or awareness of the culture of certain cities, albeit in a flattened and highly aestheticized form.

Both Coupland and Lum's works and sensibilities have been translated, directly and indirectly, into the form of wearable signs, though for markedly different motivations and generating different results and meanings. Coupland's 2014 exhibition *Everywhere Is Anywhere Is Anything Is Everything* expanded upon his already well-known geographic relationship to the city. Moreover, the merchandise available in the gift shop increased the circulation of his brand, literally and figuratively. The products available, a series of graphic t-shirts and a statement scarf, relate directly to his fashion collection for Roots Canada, which debuted in 2010. *Roots × Douglas Coupland* was a collaboration between the author and the Canadian brand; the press for the collection listed 'women's, men's and children's clothing, leather goods, design items, furniture, limited editions, original art and a series of pop-up stores', noting that '[t]his is Coupland's first time designing fashion wearables and includes t-shirts, polos, hoodies, leather jackets, accessories and more. He has also created a special coat-of-arms that many of the items are adorned with' (Michael 2010).

Lum's work, on the other hand, is replicated more faithfully in the form of a jewellery collection; specifically, the East Van cross is available in the form of a variety of pendants (Fiedler 2012). Importantly, jewellery designer Susan Fiedler's collection is endorsed by Lum and is part of a fundraising initiative for the Pivot Legal Society, a not-for-profit organization working to create social and systemic change in the Downtown Eastside. The cross is available in various forms and ranges in price from CAD 125 to CAD 325. The cross campaign is displayed in her portfolio alongside collections raising money for cancer research charities and collections endorsed by or endorsing Sarah McLachlan, the Rolling Stones, *The X Files* and the mass fashion brand *Roxy*. While the ongoing East Van cross campaign has resulted in the increased dissemination of the work as a notable art object to broader markets, replicating the symbol and connecting it to Lum and his work has also intensified the fetishization of a controversial site and associated it with forms of popular commerce. Effectively, those who purchase and wear Fiedler's pendant are disseminating a sign for the vulnerable area, while also wearing a symbol that concentrates different points of relation, including to Lum himself, his messaging and the pendant's origins and ontology as a consumer object.

Read in light of Bourdieu's notion of capital and fashion scholar Susan B. Kaiser's (2012) argument for the relationship between dress (as self-presentation) and geography, these altered iterations of the artists' works, as signs meant to be worn on the body as an expression of identity, point to how fashion systems play an active role in establishing forms of capital, while also shifting the meaning of the works and their uneven spatial contexts. While Coupland's *Orca* is not physically represented in his *Roots × Coupland* collection, nor was it depicted on any of the merchandise available for purchase at the Vancouver Art Gallery gift shop,[5] there is something of the work in the multitude of consumer items available. Coupland's specific and various sensibilities are represented, and along with these sensibilities come a set of aesthetic, material and conceptual representations fundamental to his praxis. Because he and his work have become synonymous with Vancouver, the city's identity is also entangled in this set of relations.

Are these consumer objects inherently luxurious, or do they attempt to harness the innate luxurious imaginary of Vancouver as a place? In fact, the objects themselves might more closely relate to kitsch than luxury, in that they participate in accessible, mass commercial cultural systems (Greenberg 1961: 9–10). However, it is important to note that mass-produced t-shirts and affordable pendants are not accessible to everyone and certainly not to the marginalized populations at stake in the spatial debates central to Coupland's and Lum's artworks. The consumer objects are priced at a point amenable to the budget of the average global consumer of luxury goods, who might wish to express a form of symbolic ownership of the city's spatial narratives. If cultural capital can be 'spatialized', distributing the process of 'becoming-luxury' (Armitage and Roberts 2016b: 2, 4) across geographic (physical) space and lending it a geo-cultural and geosocial dimension, then consumer objects can be imbued with a sense of spatial luxury. Cultural capital can be converted into social and economic value (Bourdieu [1983] 1986), meaning that forms of culture have direct social and economic significance for populations, so items that signify these relations come to represent social and cultural status – and luxury.

Capital's multifarious nature explains the urge to physically bear signs of Vancouver's determining cultural and spatial discourses, which communicate familiarity with the city and its topographies. This gives these commodified urban signs symbolic and social value as well as political, economic and cultural significance. As such, they express taste and cultural and social consciousness intrinsically related to the capitalist class structure. Such a paradigm also helps differentiate between motivating factors for the purchase of these signs as 'fashion objects', which vary in form, content, and price and value. But how are these signs disseminated, and how do they communicate a knowing position?

Coupland's and Lum's art commodities are most frequently marketed to women, as the predominant promotion of feminized items such as scarves and pendants suggests. Kaiser explains how representations of geographic identity more frequently than not occur 'on the backs of women's bodies and that such dress is often indicative of hegemonic values'. She posits that this is because 'power relations are operating, and these relations tend to be based, at least in part, on the ability to persuade' (2012: 72–73). While Kaiser is referring to more traditional forms of place-centric dress, her ideation translates to discussions of how signs of urban capital communicate a specific message centred in a framework of both hegemonic values and forms of persuasion. Following Benjamin, the reproducibility of the image creates potential for it to be deployed for ostensibly political purposes (Sturken and Cartwright 2009: 201) and subsequently tied to commercial interests. Further still, power dynamics – such as agency expressed in the control of the means of production – have significant impact on the broader population, particularly marginalized communities. The dissemination of signs emanating from and reinforcing such frameworks becomes increasingly intertwined with neoliberalist, capitalist production systems.

As Vancouver becomes increasingly gentrified, cultural signifiers and signs are beginning to represent and stand in for histories that are being systemically erased and homogenized. *Digital Orca* and *Monument for East Vancouver* are objects imbued with the histories of their sites and continue to accrue meaning as they evolve as place-making landmarks. While each intervenes in space according to the different intentional frameworks of the artists and the sources of their commissions, the artworks have been given new collective meaning over the course of their presence in the fabric of the city. They are each part of a much broader network of meaning-making that informs the co-creation of place in Vancouver. As physical space in Vancouver becomes increasingly desirable, signs representing space and place in the city, especially according to intimate, local scales, gain new significance. In Vancouver, space is luxury and, even more so, so is place.

Understood within the complex frameworks of the reproduction of images, as well as the appropriation and circulation of nonlinear historic and contemporary narratives of Vancouver and its spaces, the manufacture and distribution of signs, such as those designed by Lum and Coupland, are a mode of communication that reinforces hegemonic systems specific to Vancouver. Both Coupland and Lum created artistic objects that become shorthand for geographic discourse. While there are notable differences between the artists' creative and authorial positions, the complexity of the economic, political, social and cultural frameworks from which *Digital Orca* and *Monument for East Vancouver* emerged and remain situated plays an active role in the mutual construction of collective, place-based identity. The bearers of their commodified and codified signs, whether cognizant or not, partake in the fetishization of Vancouver's spatial paradoxes – its place-making and social justice imbroglios – and participate in the city's dense and manifold systems of capital. If place is luxury, public artworks, in their active and intentional role in place-making, are an expression both of this luxury and of the dynamics of power at its foundation.

NOTES

1. Place is here defined according to geographer Yi-Fu Tuan's idea: 'What begins as undifferentiated space becomes place as we get to know it better and endow it with value' (1977: 6). In short, place is space that has been attributed with a specific identity.

2. For further reading on the topic of art museums and their relationship to systems of capital, consult Bourdieu and Darbel (1991).

3. Cf. Mercer (2019), whose study evaluated 'local living conditions in more than 450 cities surveyed worldwide' according to 39 factors grouped in 10 categories, such as 'Political and social environment', 'Economic environment', 'Socio-cultural environment', 'Medical and health considerations', 'Housing' and 'Natural environment'.

4. See, for instance, the public reaction to human rights controversies that drove the 1993 'Stop Beijing' campaign (Keys 2018).

5. Interestingly, the merchandise was identical when the exhibition later travelled to Toronto's ROM and to the Museum of Contemporary Canadian Art in Winter 2015.

PART 3

FUTURE OF CANADIAN LUXURY

This final section of *Canadian Critical Luxury Studies: Decentring Luxury* challenges the reader to rethink luxury from the perspective of technology to imagine the future potential of an idiosyncratic luxurious experience emerging from interactive fashion and fashion-adjacent innovation. The field of fashion is perhaps the most amenable to discussions of luxury since fashion as a practice is both a highly personal and creative endeavour for the individual yet remains equally a social and economic activity for both producer and consumer. This dense network of meanings constitutes fashion's added value. However, this section's contributors approach the experience of fashion's luxuriousness not as a measure of status or a means of self-styling, but as the enriching potential that technology adds to the field and its players.

In Chapter 6, Marie O'Mahony's intervention calls attention to gaps in the Canadian luxury fashion market that can be addressed by looking to smaller European craft centres as models that, paradoxically, counter the move towards globalization and consolidation that typify the practices of luxury conglomerates. Using the example of a 2019 award-winning ski jacket by the Norwegian luxury sportswear brand Kjus, whose development brought together a number of tech creatives and specialists from government, industry and academia, O'Mahony concludes that '[i]n a global economy, the geographical closeness of the different partners is remarkable. Although discipline brings its own technical culture, the regional proximity allows for a cultural closeness to ease the collaboration process'. This chapter argues that to remain exceptional, luxury cannot operate only in the globalized commercial realm. Adding value to fashion's creative process can be ensured through technological innovations that engage a number of social and cultural domains in the process of creative collaboration that remains true to regional identities. The small-scale, high-luxe players that O'Mahony highlights provide inspiration for the smaller-scale cultural producers that make up various Canadian markets. The application of this chapter's thesis could be usefully considered by Canadian cultural players, for example, the organizers of Toronto Fashion Week, discussed in Chapter 4. Instead of adopting a model that demands more formalized and ideological institutionalization, in the model of Paris's *Fédération de la Haute Couture et de la Mode,* or backing by a more developed commercial culture, in the model of a New York Fashion Week, buttressed as it is by political and economic hegemony, Canadian markets could look to localized networks for collaboration with input from the public and parapublic sectors. A fruitful example of ways that the privileging of local ties and regional interests can create added value in the field of fashion occurred in November 2020 during the online Indigenous Fashion Week Toronto. Forging partnerships with the three levels of Canadian government, Ryerson University, the Ontario College of Art and Design, la Maison Simons (a Québec-based department store) and a number of Indigenous designers and media, Indigenous Fashion Week Toronto 2020 transformed the conventional fashion week model to create space for discussions and panels with artists, makers, curators and scholars that foregrounded the traditions and cultural specificities with which Indigenous making engages. These discussions, made possible by the collaborative efforts of regional, cultural and industry players, much like O'Mahony's Norwegian example, foregrounded the luxuriousness of Indigenous fashion design, featured in the event's fashion films (see Lezama 2021).

Bookending this volume, the final chapter by Valérie Lamontagne (1968–2019) is an edited version of four case studies that comprised Lamontagne's doctoral thesis. This innovative scholar and maker shares her research from working in four fashion-tech laboratories in Europe and Québec. Lamontagne's analysis leads the way for Canadian luxury makers to embrace the boundary-expanding possibilities that technology brings to the individual and individual expression. Contrary to what is commonly inferred when technology meets fashion, human experience is both deepened and widened in the case studies in this chapter. What Lamontagne brings to light is not that technology is the added value that elevates fashion to the status of luxury, in the way that, for example, Apple and Hermès harness each brand's capital in their much discussed wristwatch collaboration. Rather, the luxuriousness of technology becomes ultimately humanist. One of the case studies focusing on the work in the lab of Montréal professor Joanna Berzowska highlights the subversively playful and idiosyncratic experience of donning fashion-tech. Lamontagne shows that when technology meets fashion, there is more to be had than mere quantification. Rather, Berzowska's wearables focus 'on creating meaning as opposed to efficiency, productivity' through an *il*logical relationship to the wearer. It is the human experience that is made richer without the technocratic imposition of quantification. What's more, this chapter proposes that technology allows for personal investment in the fashions that adorn the wearer. The work in Lamontagne's own atelier 3lectromode, in Montréal, Québec, is an example of wearables breaking down the barriers between consumer and maker through a collaborative process that involves those working in the atelier with a larger community of pattern makers, textile specialists, graphic designers and engineers. The finished product is not a garment for sale, but 'a library of executable open-source fashion designs that may be assembled as kits by anyone with an interest in wearables, electronics, or fashion'. Interestingly, Lamontagne proposes that the fashion-tech field, while perched at the cutting edge, 'has much in common with the cottage industries that existed before the Industrial Revolution, with small artist/artisan spaces playing critical roles in fabrication processes and choices, all the while retaining control over the end-product or design'. In this way, this chapter closes with a Benjaminian leap from the most futurist practices into the past. Contemporary luxury marketing has often used craft as the metaphor for putative surplus value and a mystification of its industrial reality. Lamontagne's chapter guides us to a true craft revival that does not mislead the consumer, but transforms them into their own luxury maker.

6

Beyond the Catwalk: What Happens When Luxury Meets Digital?

Marie O'Mahony

It is paradoxical that this digital age should cause demand for luxury to both speed up and slow down. This chapter looks at the role of digital technologies in responding to this contradictory impulse for the luxury fashion market, specifically through technology's ability to introduce innovation and creativity in ways that are not possible in traditional supply chain production, brand communication and public-facing commerce.

In his study of the history of the factory, *Behemoth*, Joshua Freeman (2018) examines the many technological innovations that have created efficiencies in production, from Richard Arkwright's spinning machine of 1768 to the introduction of robots that have replaced or work alongside human labour. Furthermore, Lewis Mumford (1895–1990) credits the clock as 'the foremost machine in modern technics' (1934: 15). The ability to determine quantities of energy and its expenditure through a standardized measurement of accurate timing affords a level of perfection that 'machine thinking' aspires to. The introduction of the computer and the internet has exponentially increased the speed of communication and production. As a consequence, manufacturing has been scattered across the world to supply chains with a labyrinth of sub-contractors and workers. Low-cost labour and factories alone would not have been enough to prompt this shift, but combined with the 'need for speed' and continuing financial gain, off-shore production – at a previously unimagined scale – became necessary, out of which fast fashion was born. To exist, the luxury industry has to be clearly distinguishable from this mode of industrial mass production both in its physical form and in its visual culture. This refinement in image is possible through digital platforms. This chapter examines some of the ways that digital technologies can differentiate luxury, often working in tandem with more traditional atelier techniques. Further, this chapter asks how to achieve this digital distinction while retaining core values and reputation that are key to the consumer perception of luxuriousness.

> Production is organized in such a way that we have unbelievably high productivity. The atelier is a place of amazing discipline and rigor. Every single motion, every step of the process, is carefully planned with the most modern and complete engineering technology. It's not unlike how cars are made in the most modern factories. We analyse how to make each part of the product, where to buy each component, where to find the best leather at the best price, what treatment it should receive. A single purse can have up to 1,000 manufacturing tasks, and we plan each and every one.
>
> (Bernard Arnault quoted in Thomas 2007: 21)

If this description of luxury production invokes an image of lowly factory production, it is because Arnault himself makes the comparison between 'atelier' and 'factory'. Thomas (2007) and others have documented many of the cost-saving practices adopted by luxury brands. These range from sourcing in China and assembling in Italy (to retain the highly prized 'Made in Italy' label) to using foreign workers to reduce the labour cost. While seemingly economically sound, these practices challenge both luxury's ethics and its ontology. For example, the diner in a fast-food restaurant or in a Michelin star restaurant will check their bill for mistakes. Whatever the cost, no one likes to be short-changed. In the same vein, if in the eyes of the luxury fashion consumer – in light of the tensions elicited from profit-driven corporate concerns – the time or cost involved or the provenance of the luxury good is called into question, what *new* signifiers of refinement can a brand offer without abandoning the carefully honed heritage story? Ironically, digital technology, so instrumental in the rise of fast fashion, is seen by many as an opportunity for luxury to redefine itself as 'Digital Luxe'.

These questions have geopolitical dimensions in the ways that national industries have mobilized digital luxe to enhance their standing in a global luxury scene. This chapter proposes that the following examples, drawn from smaller-scale European luxury producers, foreground potential models for future developments in the localized Canadian economy. As Valérie Lamontagne shows in this volume, Canada's wearable technology scene, and particularly that of Montréal, is a vibrant site of new development in the relationship between luxury and tech. However, there remain further avenues through which Canadian developers and producers could engage the global digital luxury market. The global examples spotlighted in this chapter suggest the dynamic possibilities of digital luxury available to future generations of Canadian designers and makers, particularly in light of the strong growth history and potential of the Canadian tech industry.[1,2]

This chapter examines how digital technology fits within existing aspects of luxury such as tradition, craft and exclusivity. Going beyond traditional categories, I explore new and emerging forms of digital luxury. This includes the enhanced client experience through the digital and the hybrid physical-digital. Inference is drawn on the consumer's likely engagement with digital luxe and how this extends conventional notions of what is considered to be luxury. The ultimate goal of this chapter is to provide examples that can inspire Canadian luxury producers, whose smaller scale and more recent presence in the industry allow for the necessary agility to build the refinement that recent technological developments permit.

When digital meets with tradition

Luxury is closely associated with tradition and handcraft (cf. Kapferer and Bastien 2009: 311–22), the latter idea in itself denoting the time taken to develop that skill. When Hermès's 'craft roadshow', titled *Festival des Métiers*, came to the Design Exchange in Toronto in 2013, the digital was notable only for its absence. Parisian artisans silk-screen printed the brand's much-coveted *carrés*, meticulously mixing inks and setting the screens by hand. Glove makers stretched, cut and stitched butter-soft leathers, while handbag makers explained the métier's long heritage back to the fashion house's origins in saddle-making in 1837. The purpose of the exhibit, as explained by Jennifer Carter, president and CEO of Hermès Canada, was to provide 'an opportunity for visitors to have an intimate dialogue with artisans and discover the exceptional know-how that the *maison* has embraced for over 175 years' (Schelling 2013: n.pag.). Visiting the exhibition, I spoke with many of the artisans who each emphasized the apprenticeship system that appeared unchanged since the nineteenth century. Craftsmanship is readily associated with skills built up over time, repeating and refining actions between the eye and the hand. The consumer of Hermès also embraces the digital as a route to closer association with their favourite artist's brand, as Thomaï Serdari reminds us in 'Experiments in suchness: Hiroshi Sugimoto's silk *Shiki* for Hermès' (2016). Sugimoto's images are based on a series of twenty Polaroids, arguably the most immediate of the photographic processes and almost the antithesis of the photographer's usual painstaking process involving elaborately long exposure. The inkjet printing process is also more immediate than the multiple screens normally used. The project website (Hermès n.d.) shows technicians overseeing the machine process with no physical contact being made. Serdari argues that 'an object-based study of luxury explains the encounter between the object and the individual as well as the individual's neurological and emotional responses to it' (2016: 147). The craft is present in the Hermès–Sugimoto series, but less visibly so and as such cannot be taken as an immediate signifier of luxury. In the bringing together of art, technology and craft, the viewer is called upon to engage with the luxury object in a way that is personal and unique to them.

However, between the eye and the hand, technology can play an essential role in adding value to the maker's process. 'Mutual understanding [between craft and industry] will do much for both. It will help build up a feeling of craft in industry, to industry's and the craftsman's [sic] and society's benefit', expounded industrial designer Charles Eames, in a presentation titled 'The making of a craftsman' given at *Asilomar: First Annual Conference of American Craftsmen* in June 1957 (Demetrios 2013: 279). In the industrial textile sector, craft can be seen in advanced applications. Yet even here the nature and form of craftsmanship is evolving. For example, in my 1998 book, co-authored with Sarah E. Braddock, titled *TechnoTextiles: Revolutionary Fabrics for Fashion and Design*, an account of the manufacturing process for a British Aerospace (Systems and Engineering) Ltd. nose radome for the Tornado F3 (Braddock and O'Mahony 1998: 46–47) shows the early potential in the digital to enhance handcrafting. Woven D-glass and E-glass fibres are used in the composite structure to achieve the desired transparency needed for the antenna's radar waves to scan ahead. Both are woven as preforms with one slightly larger than the other and pulled down over the radome mould before injecting epoxy resin between the layers and then leaving it to cure (harden) and remove for use. Although highly technical with vitally high precision, in the image that accompanied the text, it is, remarkably, the two industrial craftspeople who stand out, rather than any manufacturing or diagnostic equipment.

Twenty years later, digital technology, as much as human labour, is as likely to deliver the craft component. The 2016 Elytra Filament Pavilion at London's Victoria and Albert Museum exemplifies this process, where, like the aircraft radome, both human and machine are responsible in the refinement process of the e-textile. The architect Achim Menges, with structural engineer Jan Knippers, brought together a process of robot fabrication to build the construction. The KUKA industrial robot was programmed to undertake a filament winding procedure to build a canopy structure that spanned over 200 square metres. Sensors embedded in the fibres collected data on how visitors inhabited the pavilion that allowed for further 'growth' of the structure over time. The repetitive process of winding, based on a pre-programmed skill set with the ability to learn and refine, can be considered as a collaborative craft process between maker, engineer and programmer. While the advances in artificial intelligence (AI) may one day see this type of technology used to create luxury bespoke fashion, for the moment at least, the relationship between industry and craft in haute couture is taking a different route.

The Swiss town of St. Gallen exemplifies the possibility of bringing together tradition and technology in a way that brings benefit to both in the field of luxury fashion. Founded in 614 CE by the Irish monk St. Gall, it was known as a centre of learning in the Middle Ages, and its textile heritage can be traced back to the period around 800 CE. Originally focused on creating linen products using locally grown flax, sixteenth-century examples show the use of silk and metal thread. At the time of the Industrial Revolution, emphasis shifted to cotton and intricate hand embroidery. The invention of the first hand embroidery machine by Alsace-born Joshua Heilmann in the early nineteenth century increased many aspects of production. Refined and commercialized by F. E. Rittmeyer and F. A. Vogler in St. Gallen, over twenty thousand machines were used in the region. The new machines had the capability to use over three hundred needles at once. This allowed for the rapid transfer of pattern to fabric and the beginnings of mass production.

The growth of St. Gallen lace is in marked contrast to Borris lace, introduced to the region that it is named after in Ireland. The Irish lace is based on Greek lace and was brought over by Lady Harriet Kavanagh, a local landowner, as a means of establishing gainful employment for local women. The Borris lacemaking process was never refined through technological advances. In the absence of technology, Irish lacemaking went into decline in the early twentieth century. Conversely, St. Gallen lace achieved world renown and is often referred to as Guipure or etched embroidery. The Textile Museum St. Gallen holds a large collection, including a House of Worth ballgown (c.1860), that was said to have belonged to Empress Eugénie, wife of Napoleon III. Contemporary textiles in the region continue to weave together luxury and tradition via companies such as Jakob Schlaepfer, Forster Rohner, and Schoeller.

The most defining feature of Swiss Jakob Schlaepfer fabrics is their ability to combine luxury with heritage and technology in a way that creates a sense of mystery. Until his retirement in 2018, Creative Director Martin Leuthold stressed the importance that it is the company's choice to remain in St. Gallen, which grounds its heritage. 'You need culture, the past and roots which is why we stay in St. Gallen. I believe very much that industry has to have roots, in the landscape, people – this is life! This is why Jakob Schlaepfer is so different' (O'Mahony 2014).[3] Leuthold describes the benefit of drawing on the region's long history, culture and high level of expertise in lacemaking, but he is quick to tie tradition to technology, asserting that, 'when both come together you have a lot of potential'. In fact, Leuthold introduced laser-cutting over a decade ago and, more recently, introduced Emboscan technology, which integrates laser-cutting with embroidery. This allows for a very precise manipulation of fabric and embroidery previously only possible using different machines and manual processes. Now, two or three layers of fabric can be brought together, embroidered and the top layers cut, leaving the base fabric intact. The designer introduces large sequins and stitching, then laser-cuts them to create a dramatic new luminescent look. Couture fashion houses use the fabrics. The designer agreed that the use of digital technologies such as laser-cutting by fast-fashion brands is something about which to be vigilant. His mindset remains ever positive, viewing it as a challenge to push creativity even further. In an interview with *Women's Wear Daily* in 2004, Leuthold likens the labour-intensive process of their approach to digital ink-jet printing (Murphy). A team of fourteen designers in the atelier first take photographs of flowers and flower arrangements, then proceed to alter them digitally and print high-resolution images on large computer-controlled rigging. In addition to the time taken to arrange, photograph and digitally manipulate the images, textile printing takes around three hours for every ten metres. 'We've been working on this for about three years', Leuthold explains, '[i]t takes a long time. But as soon as it is rolled out too broadly, it will no longer be for Schlaepfer' (Murphy 2004). One of the key innovations of Jakob Schlaepfer is bringing craftsmanship to technological equipment and processes so that the machines used become a hybrid of technology and the handmade. This is not an area that fast fashion has ventured into, so far.

In 2016 Jakob Schlaepfer became part of the Forster Rohner Group, retaining its brand Jakob Schlaepfer Ltd. The homepage for Forster Rohner's website shares their philosophy of 'Fascination through Creation, Innovation and Tradition' (Forster Rohner n.d., translation added). Founded in 1904, Forster Rohner AG specializes in embroidery for haute couture, ready-to-wear, lingerie and, within the Forster Rohner Textile Innovations business unit, electronic or e-embroidery. This business unit was established in 2011 with an aim to combine material science with visionary embroidery technology and electronics. Crucially, the business and technological development moves beyond apparel to markets including construction and automotive. At the biannual TechTextil trade show in Frankfurt 2019, the company exhibited in their own booth as well as with ATN GmbH Kreative Produktionen, synthetic textile producer, with whom they showcased illuminated e-textiles on vinyl artificial leather and microfibre fabrics with embedded LEDs for interior applications. In a personal interview, Adis Causevic, head of technical development at Forster Rohner Textile Innovations, also stressed the importance of lighting for markets such as interiors for building capability and consumer acceptance of the technology (O'Mahony 2019). Extending the technical capability of luxury textiles has meant that the company has to address the challenge of developing additional competencies from outside the embroidery or even the textile industry itself. Causevic is a graduate in electrical engineering and sees the need for more multidisciplinarity within teams both in-house and as collaborators.

In 2012 a Swiss-based start-up called Osmotex introduced smart membrane technology. The thin membrane has the capability to transport water from one side to the other when subjected to an electrical stimulus. Electricity, when reapplied, reverses the process. In discussion with one of the developers, Trond Heldal, it was clear that Osmotex has a vision for its potential in clothing to transport moisture away from the body, regulate temperature and keep the wearer dry. To date, however, the company has not developed a blueprint for how this could be achieved. In 2019, the 7Sphere Hydro_Bot smart sweat technology ski jacket was awarded a gold medal at the ISPO Munich trade fair, an annual event for the sports business. The partnership list that brought about the luxury sportswear garment illustrates the degree of complexity involved. Osmotex is the technology innovator. Schoeller AG, specializing in high-end performance and technical textiles for a number of end uses including luxury sportswear, provides the textile component. Kjus is the sportswear brand and, working on the electronics, APPLYCON is a young company, founded in 2005, that focuses on bringing together interdisciplinary knowledge for wearable technology and intelligent textiles in processes for integration with the Swiss Center of Electronics and Microtechnology (CSEM) for engineering research and development (R+D). Also participating in the development of this e-textile are the Swiss Federal Laboratories for Materials Science and Technology (Empa) bringing their electro-chemistry expertise, R+D and testing, as well as another dozen universities and research labs in the Swiss region. 'Collaboration is key', as Milan Baxa, managing director at APPLYCON, explains. 'We aspire to be a significant force in the field of wearable electronics and its integration into mass production and our collaboration with Osmotex represents an exciting innovation for us to be involved in' (O'Mahony 2019). In a global economy, the geographical closeness of the different partners is remarkable. Although discipline brings its own technical culture, the regional proximity allows for a cultural closeness to ease the collaboration process.

Emerging forms of digital luxe

In 1989 Scott Crump of Stratasys patented fused deposition modelling, a technique that fuses material layer by layer until a 3D object is created. This style of additive manufacturing is what is most commonly associated with what we refer to as 3D printing. iam Media, which uses IPlytics to aggregate 3D printing patents, positions Stratasys at the bottom of the top ten list, with the list headed by General Electric Company, then HP Inc. and United Technologies Corporation (Pohlmann 2019). Clayton M. Christensen makes the point that when new technologies emerge in a field, it is very rare for the dominant company to retain its position over subsequent generations (2016: xxiv). Although no longer holding top market share, Stratasys maintains a strong position as innovators, demonstrated in their work with artists and fashion designers for products such as the 'Anthozoa' 3D printed Cape and Skirt (2013) with the Dutch fashion designer

FIGURE 6.1: Iris van Herpen's 'Aeriform' dress produced in collaboration with the Canadian architect Philip Beesley. Acquired by the Royal Ontario Museum (ROM) and exhibited at the museum's 'Iris van Herpen: Transforming Fashion' show in 2018. Courtesy of Marie O'Mahony.

Iris van Herpen and American-Israeli designer Neri Oxman. The inspiration for the work comes from the *Book of Imaginary Beings* (1969) by Jorge Luis Borges. The garment looks at human augmentation that is inspired by nature and was first shown at Paris Fashion Week for Spring–Summer 2013. It was produced using Stratasys's Objet Connex 3D printing technology that allows for a range of materials to be printed in a single building process, from hard to soft. This combination is essential to the form, texture and movement of the piece when worn. Garments such as these are haute couture, and although 3D printing is considered simply as creation by the push of a button, these garments demonstrate the complexity of design that is possible with the meeting of 'hand and machine'. Neither is it a fast process, particularly when compared to techniques such as laser-cutting.

In the summer of 2018 the Royal Ontario Museum (ROM) in Toronto exhibited the work of Iris van Herpen and Canadian architect Philip Beesley in two separate shows, but also included a specially commissioned collaborative work. Van Herpen and Beesley have been collaborating since 2013. The commissioned 'Dome Dress' forms part of the fashion designer's *Aeriform* collection (Fall 2017). The collection examined the nature and anatomy of air,

FIGURE 6.2: Philip Beesley, shown here with his *Transforming Space*. The installation uses 3D printed forms to create an artificial nature, reanimated by an artificial intelligence (AI), sensors, sound, lighting and movement to interact with visitors to the exhibition. Courtesy of Marie O'Mahony.

looking to communicate a feeling of airborne materiality. Metal, a deliberately heavy material, was used for the garment. However, laser-cutting the imposing material transformed it to reveal a gossamer-thin biometric form. To the viewer it is lace, rather than metal. In van Herpen's words, 'This *Aeriform* dress is like fine lace so it is very connected to the traditional idea of textile' (O'Mahony 2018). Importantly, the technology used is not a shortcut to mass production, as APPLYCON's Baxa envisions as the key potential of technofabrics. The Dome Dress demonstrates that it is because of its technologically advanced nature that the human hand is so vital to its creation. In fact, the dress took 240 hours of handmaking to construct, while 62 hours of machine making was needed for the laser-cutting, according to the accompanying documentary. The laser-cutting could not have been done without human support and participation – recalling Eames's industrial craftsperson. Human craft is more easily attributed to 240 hours of studio craft plus 62 hours of industry craft, making a craft total of 302 hours. By contrast, in fast fashion, whole collections are delivered in much less time:

While the fashion industry largely operates on a seasonal calendar, fast fashion retailers deliver new garments and accessories to their stores every four to six weeks, sometimes even more frequently. Inditex brand stores (including Zara), for instance, receive deliveries of new clothes twice a week.

(Anon 2016)

The digital luxe experience

Outside of innovations in design and manufacturing, digital technologies have become omnipresent, from consumer analytics to social media platforms to online shopping and virtual and augmented technologies that offer new experiences of luxury. ' "A Luxury 4.0" operating model is emerging', according to McKinsey & Company, 'in which brands and retailers use data to build customer intimacy, capture merging customer preferences, and streamline the process of turning ideas into new products' (2018: 2). While much of these data-based innovations are interlinked, I will use a few examples to illustrate some of the opportunities for industry and how they are responding.

AI is having a profound effect on consumer analytics that in turn influences the prediction of seasonal trends. As with the design process, the digital tool is not used in isolation because of its limitations. AI is exceptionally good at 'crunching' large data sets and offering predictions based on the findings. 'It's important to remember that AI is always restricted by what it knows', advises Joshua Gans, chief economist with Creative Destruction Lab, Rotman School of Management, in Toronto. 'As it advances, we'll be able to input even *more* data, and AI's breadth of understanding and ability to learn from data will increase' (2019: 8, original emphasis). This is leading to a growth in data-analytics platforms for industries, including luxury, that operate globally, such as MakerSights in San Francisco, the Future Laboratory based in London and EDITED operating in both New York and London.

There is an argument to be made that the digital technology platform brings so much potential to the luxury industry. Miu Miu has used the iCoolHunt AI software to look at the social media behaviour of 300,000 influencers and their followers (McDowell 2019). Because the NextAtlas software targets fast-moving large data sources such as Instagram, Twitter and Pinterest, it can seem more reflective of nuanced shifts. However, it can also expose gaps where usage may vary because of geographies, culture or demographics. Ultimately, used in conjunction with human insights, it becomes a much more powerful tool.

In *The Age of Digital Darwinism* (McKinsey & Co. 2018), the report's authors use Euromonitor and Forrester sources to predict that one-fifth of personal luxury sales will take place online by 2025. Already, they indicate that 80 per cent of sales in the sector are 'digitally influenced'. The discrepancy between these two figures points to a convergence – yet not quite a merger – between online and off-line consumption. Both in-store and online luxury sales respond to the desire for luxury's 'added value', with much of this revolving around the combined virtual and bricks-and-mortar experience that can be offered.

Holition, a London-based marketing firm specializing in digital content, prom-ises to 'engineer the experiences of tomorrow' for their clients' predominantly luxury brands (2019). The London practice works in the space between digital and physical, as well as the purely digital. *Alexander McQueen: Savage Beauty Virtual Makeup* is one of their earliest projects, from 2015. Commissioned for the McQueen exhibition at the Victoria and Albert Museum, visitors were immersed in virtual make-up looks from the designer's catwalk collections *What a Merry Go Round* (Autumn–Winter 2001) and *La Dame Bleue* (Spring–Summer 2008). Facial-tracking technology and projection mapping were used. Exhibition iPads were available to visitors allowing them to see the designer make-up virtually mapped onto their own features. The following year saw the technology evolve to appear in stores as Charlotte Tilbury's augmented reality 'Magic Mirror'. This innovation brought a number of benefits for the brand and the consumer as it allowed users to 'try-on' make-up and looks without the need to physically apply products and then remove them. This innovation eliminated hygiene concerns – particularly pertinent in the wake of the pandemic – and improved dwell time and the number of store interactions. It also combined both digital and physical experiences while providing strong novelty and a 'selfie opportunity' linked to the brand and the store. The pace of technological evolution at Holition reflects the expectations of the luxury consumer they are looking to reach. *The Age of Digital Darwinism* report asserts that consumers are engaging with brands that wield as many as fifteen touch points in what the authors describe as a journey that is both fragmented and highly personalized (McKinsey & Co. 2018). Interestingly, the authors find that Chinese luxury consumers lead the way for this digital-based consumption.

At an event held at London's Design Museum in 2017, the online luxury shop-ping platform Farfetch unveiled its vision for the future of luxury fashion in the founder and CEO José Neves's presentation 'The store of the future'. The online platform envisioned bringing together fashion and technology with data collection to strengthen the connection with the consumer. Two years prior they had made a key purchase of the iconic London luxury fashion boutique Browns, located – since the 1970s – in five Georgian townhouses on South Molton Street. Browns East was launched in 2017 combining an immersive technology experience with art installations, events and luxury fashion all promising to change constantly, echoing the capability of online platforms in a bricks-and-mortar space. The East London store has become a test-bed for technologies and customer experience. A shopping app allows customers to create a wish list of items, make special appointments and access the store through a special entrance (Shannon 2019). Similar innovations were brought to the main Browns store in its new Mayfair site in 2020. The move is indicative of the changes that luxury brands and retail need to face and the ways that the digital needs to be about technology that is itself creative and not merely a means of harvesting large quantities of data.

In an earlier era of luxury, founder Louis Vuitton would write personalized letters to customers suggesting travel products for their next trip. Today, the brand's clients may not expect to receive a handwritten note, but they do expect to be made to feel noticed, special or unique by a luxury label. In an era when so much is possible, the competition for the dollar, the pound and the yuan has never been fiercer. The experience of luxury has become key, and to realize this, established brands are merging the digital and the physical in a convergence that embraces technology, creativity and, perhaps most vitally, the consumer.

NOTES

1   I would like to acknowledge the work of the late Valérie Lamontagne as the inspiration for this chapter and humbly dedicate this writing to her.

2   Cf. *Canadian ICT Sector Profile 2018*, https://www.ic.gc.ca/eic/site/ict-tic.nsf/eng/h_it07229.html. Accessed 31st July 2019.

3   The quotes used here are taken from a personal interview that formed the basis for 'Jakob Schlaepfer, luxe embellishment meets tech', published online by *Stylus Fashion*, 7 January 2015. The quotes used here do not appear in the published article.

7

Contemporary Case Studies of Performative Wearables

Valérie Lamontagne

The Wearable Performs

This chapter presents case studies of four fashion and technology ateliers, which are shaping and inventing the wearables[1] landscape. These are: the internationally known, Dutch-born, San Francisco-based fashion-tech designer Anouk Wipprecht; the Danish design studio Diffus, based in Copenhagen and run by Hanne-Louise Johannesen and Michel Guglielmi; my own DIY atelier, 3lectomode, located in Montréal; and Concordia University's XS Labs, directed by Joanna Berzowska, also in Montréal.[2]

The four sites were chosen both for their excellence in the field (all have won prestigious awards, commissions and grants, and are headed by internationally reputed thinkers and makers) and for their uniqueness and diversity of approach. Such a comparative analysis is necessary to articulate the argument that artistic wearables stem from a hybrid, multifarious and expanding set of practices, overlapping with fields that include computer science, interactive design, architecture, fashion, media arts and DIY. Each case study's particular epistemic culture shapes its material outcomes via its studio/atelier/laboratory's intermingling of tools and experts. This diversity of approaches aids further in cementing the argument that the performative layer enveloping artistic wearables is not limited to only one method, practice, technology or material, but that it is transversally modular and exportable to expansive arrays of methods and approaches – each containing its own formula for 'performativity'.[3]

My relationships with some of these laboratories and their members span years and comprise many meetings, interviews, encounters at conferences and expert workshops, as well as repeated visits to familiarize myself with the sites, designers and methods found at each studio/atelier. In each case, the individuals involved have become allies, even friends; we have collaborated through the process of this research in elevating and sustaining the field of wearables within the design, tech, education, fashion and art milieux. The process of conducting this extensive and often intimate research has meant that the study participants have also contributed significantly to the direction and depth of my research, for which I am grateful and indebted.

Using some of the tools that inform my previous work – from the various material forms that encompass wearables to the historical context of computational and pre-computational wearables and finally the performative-theory perspectives from sociology, media arts, fashion and science, technology, society (STS) – we will presently investigate contemporary wearables and their links to performance (see Lamontagne 2017: 1–158). Specifically, we will consider how the laboratory in itself is a research-social-materials space where humans and nonhumans and their 'dance of agency' (Pickering 1995) converge and create the wearable designs of today. Next, we will analyse the wearable in relationship to its technologies as a path to a better understanding of its effects on the body as well as its role in shaping aesthetics and performativity. Further, we will examine how concepts of fashion and style influence wearables' various expressions. Finally, we will consider wearables in their body/interaction dimension to gauge how the totality of their parts (technology, design, interactivity with the body and other bodies) performs. Hence, we will work our way from the outside in – that is to say, from the laboratory, via technology and fashion, to the performatively social – as a way of situating the places, moments and contexts wherein performance is visibly tuning the wearable.

Anouk Wipprecht: 'Spider Dress' (2014)

Context

The first case study begins in 2011 at V2_ Lab for the Unstable Media in Rotterdam, where I met Anouk Wipprecht, fashion-tech designer-in-residence at the time. While at V2_ for a three-month Ph.D. residency stay, I participated in the E-Textile Workspace research cluster, which conducted monthly meetings on the themes of craft and DIY wearables. I also organized a Test_Lab (single-evening events dedicated to showcasing new works) entitled 'Clothing without Cloth', which featured members of the European wearables community (Italy, England, France, the Netherlands) involved in active material experimentation that pushes the limits of 'clothing' and textiles.[4] Since this research stay, Wipprecht and I worked on organizing the TechnoSensual exhibition, which took place at

FIGURE 7.1: Anouk Wipprecht, 'Spider Dress', 2014. Courtesy of Jason Perry.

the MuseumsQuartier in Vienna (2012) for which I curated the symposium. We have also sat on panels together, including a recent one on 'Embracing Fashion + Technology' at the Atelier Néerlandais in Paris (2016), and we have collaborated on a fashion-tech festival in Montréal in 2017.

Background

Wipprecht, trained as a fashion designer and later in engineering for design, is one of the few mavericks in the field of wearables to straddle skill sets in aesthetics and engineering with equal virtuosity. With the mindset of an inventor and the ambition of a fashion star, she has built an impressive collection of works, collaborators and followers, influencing the field of fashion-tech. Capitalizing on the growing maker movement, multimedia entertainment events and opportunities for fashion-tech to tell its story and be at centre stage, she has developed a style that combines robotics and techno-aesthetics. As a researcher, she is keenly invested in wearables' interactive and interrelational dimensions and in the potential for wearables to offer the body new capacities for expression that traditional fashion cannot. In short, Wipprecht has crafted a fine creative balance, in which her designs – combining fashion, technology and the body – permit us to visualize, experience and dream how we may wish to perform with the fashion-tech of the future.

Laboratory culture

To begin with the laboratory or studio context in which Wipprecht works, one should first mention her nomadic and collaborative praxis approach to fashion-tech design. Unlike other designers, who may have set places and spaces of production, Wipprecht prefers to embed herself within R&D work settings such as Intel, Autodesk or Microsoft. Once on site, she builds partnerships with internal teams to develop new designs that respond to technical needs, embark on explorations or undertake media showcasing of new fashion-tech technologies. The majority of Wipprecht's work since 2013 has been the result of client-based commissions and sponsorships from some of the biggest tech industries in America, allowing her unheralded access to new technologies, materials and processes, not to mention high-profile platforms for the presentation of her completed designs. As an epistemic culture, it is one that is oftentimes predicated on a client's need to create better aesthetics and/or stories around emergent technologies in the form of desirable fashion-tech displays. In this way, one of the biggest challenges is balancing the need to showcase a client's technology while maintaining a consistent signature design. Keeping this goal in mind, Wipprecht's fashion-tech has been structured around a techno-futurist aesthetic that (to date) consistently features 3D printing, robotics, sensors, exoskeletons and leather.

Wipprecht's works often result from opportunities to forge into new materials and technical or expressive explorations with both clients and collaborators, in what she calls a 'collision of practices'. As she notes: 'The best context for collaborating is when someone wants to get into fashion' (Wipprecht 2017). For example, the *Smoke Dress* collection, developed for a 2013 Volkswagen car show, resulted in a collaboration with Italian architect Niccolo Casas. Harnessing the opportunity to fund a new series of works, Wipprecht invited Casas to participate in developing the new pieces for Volkswagen. Their collaboration provided an opportunity for Casas to experiment in the field of fashion (he has since become one of Iris van Herpen's main collaborators in the fabrication of her 3D-printed fashions), while Wipprecht benefitted from the hands-on tutelage of Casas to master the 3D software Maya for fashion-design use. In this way, both designers could benefit by expanding their skill sets while creating new work, a common strategy for Wipprecht.

Technology

In fact, the *Smoke Dress* had an earlier iteration, presented at the TechnoSensual exhibition (prototyped with Dutch fashion technologist Aduen Darriba), prior to its Volkswagen redesign. In explaining the initial prototyping process for the 'Smoke Dress' collection, Wipprecht describes how she (and Darriba) first experimented with the use of smoke machines to visualize the effects on the body. Wipprecht often begins with ideas, images or concepts that later spur and feed technical experimentation. Examples of this process include: the visual effect of ink floating in water, as a starting point for the *Pseudomorphs* dresses (developed at V2_ in 2009); the idea of a 'disappearing' garment, which informed the *Intimacy 2.0* dress (also developed at V2_ in 2009); and finally the notion of social invisibility, propelling the idea of the 'Smoke Dress'. Once the concept is established, Wipprecht engages in a process of visualization – both through tangible mock-ups and collage/moodboards – in order to map the placement of technologies, as well as the interactive system's architecture on the body, thus defining the garment's shape. As Wipprecht cautions, 'You can visualize through photos or drawing, but with interaction you need to physically see it in action' (2017).

Early in the design process, accommodation for technical needs and limitations is at the forefront of the design parameters. For example, questions around battery and wire placement can dictate the shape and style of the garment, as in the case of Fergie (of the Black Eyed Peas, who performed at the Super Bowl 2011 halftime show), where the batteries were located on the shoulders as epaulettes, instead of around the waist, in order to preserve the pop star's silhouette. In the case of the 'Smoke Dress', the overall shape of the garment was structured in an hourglass form as a consequence of accommodating the smoke machine in the lower-torso section, while the 'Spider Dress' features black spheres (that look like eyes) integrated into the design in order to conceal the proximity sensors. Wipprecht notes, '[M]y style is created out of the spaces that I create around the body in order to place the electronics' (2017). Hence, as a design process, it is one that is predicated on action and tacit experiments that oscillate between the concepts and technical possibilities. This performative model of discovery – which engages in a process of virtual-to-tangible modelling – dictates the final garment's shape, style and materiality.

The idea for 'Spider Dress' stemmed from a short, experimental stop-motion video featuring an analog puppet mechanism placed on the body, which was produced in collaboration with Viennese programmer/technologist Daniel Schatzmayr. After posting the video online and receiving an enthusiastic number of 'likes' literally overnight, the duo proceeded to create the piece in earnest. In this way, the internet could even be considered as a collaborator/performer, as it instigated the development of the piece.

'Spider Dress' is based on the idea of creating personal space for its wearer. Conceived as an 'aggressive' and perhaps even antisocial wearable, it features animatronic arachnid limbs that are activated by the presence and approach of others. Protecting its human 'prey', this exoskeleton can enact twelve different behavioural states, depending on the type of approach (fast/slow, back/front, etc.), featuring different speeds and combinations of activations for the spider legs. 'Spider Dress' was developed in two iterative processes (Wipprecht often reworks previous designs): the first version was created with Schatzmayr; the second, in collaboration with Intel. The principal difference, other than the showcasing and embedding – and the Intel Edison chip in the second design – is the colour. In our interview, Wipprecht emphasizes the importance of aesthetic choices in choreographing wearables' interactions and notes how the first version, fabricated in black, was too menacing and thus antithetical to interaction (2017).

Fashion-tech

'Spider Dress' was manufactured using PA-12 material via 3D printing using selective laser sintering (SLS) techniques at Materialise in Belgium. Meanwhile, the upper dress bodice was developed in collaboration with Studio Palermo in Austria. Wipprecht describes the inner workings of the 'Spider Dress' as follows:

> The Edison module runs embedded Linux, the design is programmed in Python. The dress interactions are defined in 'twelve states of behavior' through two Mini Maestro twelve channel USB servo controllers from Pololu, and uses inverse kinematics. I am working with twenty small 939MG metal gear servos (0.14sec.60o/0.13sec.60o – stall torque 2.5kg.cm/2.7kg.cm). All servos run back to the system. I am also working with Dynamixels (XL-320 series) of Robotics, which are supernice to work with, as they are smart, strong, and very accurate.
>
> (Svadja 2014: n.pag.)

'Spider Dress' works via a series of embedded sensors that react intelligently to the ambient interactions it encounters. The 3D-printed robotic shell is enabled with proximity and breath sensors that trigger the carapace's movements. Wipprecht explains: 'Using wireless biometric signals, the system makes inferences based on the stress level in your body. It can differentiate between twelve states of behavior' (Kaplan 2015: n.pag.). The behaviour of the legs modulates depending on the speed at which one approaches the devices as well the wearer's physiological reaction as measured by her breath. The technology powering these effects are a combination of an Intel Edison Bluetooth controller and a Maxbotix prox-imity sensor encased in the dark globe at the front of the wearable. Wipprecht's arachnid wearable thus operates as a collaborative visualization of events both within the wearer (breath and proximity) and through the actions and reactions of those surrounding the wearer (speed of approach, distance to fashion-tech garment, length of stay and sequence of movements). Hence, the movements of the legs are an amalgam of the performance of fashion, body and technology as encountered both on the wearer's body and through the public's interactions. In this way, the 'Spider Dress' is a co-created performance involving wearer, device and public.

Collaboration

While Wipprecht is hired by companies and sponsors to create fashion-tech designs that promote and showcase their technologies (software, hardware, automobiles), the element of social interaction, relatability or 'readability' is paramount in her design choices, from both an aesthetic and an interaction standpoint. For the designer, a wearable piece has several layers of interaction, of which approachability is the first. The white, Intel version (or albino, as she calls it) of the 'Spider Dress' was altered in order to enhance this first layer of interaction. Wipprecht had felt that the first (black) design was too ominous and hence did not invite the public/user to approach it. Second, the shape of the design itself, explains Wipprecht, should reveal, or announce, its nature/character from afar (2017). Thus, the 3D-printed, spider-like legs and overall dress structure announce early on that the garment will feature animalistic qual-ities. Furthermore, for the designer, fashion-tech should speak to all audiences, including (perhaps most of all) those uninitiated to wearables, fashion-tech or this type of technology. With the 'Spider Dress', because of the strong visual spider theme, the behavioural dimension of the design is easily relatable to almost anyone, as a spider is both recognizable and behaviourally predictable. This known, or 'readable', motif makes the garment that much more successful, according to Wipprecht, because it can be immediately accepted and understood and does not require initiation or special knowledge. Like fashion, which at all ends of the design spectrum must be socially recognizable (e.g. what is the value of a luxury item that cannot be recognized as such?), the wearable, too, must fit into an ecology of fashion.

Considering Wipprecht's design process, we may surmise that her epistemic cul-ture is one of demand, availability and co-design: the *demand* of the client/market to create something for a specific context (a spectacular Super Bowl halftime-show garment, an Audi/Volkswagen brigade of tech-dressed car presenters or an Intel/

Edison intelligent dress); availability because through tech-industry partnerships like Intel, Autodesk and Materialise, Wipprecht secures access to special resources, which she engineers towards fashion-tech outcomes; and, finally, *co-design*, as the internal workings of this nomadic studio practice is primarily choreographed around friendships, the sharing of skills and the collective pursuit of developing new technologies for the body. Thus, Wipprecht's pieces are rarely a solo process – or a solo vision, for that matter – and the public is often invited to witness, provide aid (crowdsourcing via social media for help and tips) and weigh in on the evolution of the designs as she posts process images online and via social media platforms (Instagram, Facebook).

Bodies/interaction

When planning the body's actions and the 'attitude' of the wearable, Wipprecht works through a number of different scenarios. The piece's attitude comes together in the final stages, often in the context of the photo shoot, which is also often the first time all the parts are seen together and on a body. The styling and choice of model further influences the feeling of the piece, together with choices over how to perform for the camera, all the while emphasizing certain parts of the wearable above others. Wipprecht describes the process:

> For example, in the 'Spider Dress' photo the model is looking down, the system gets more attention this way. It depends what you want to highlight. Do you want to take away a little bit of the face and the information through that? And, what kind of attitude do you want to create with it? That is what you mostly do with the photo shoot. This is the place where you figure out the piece's identity and the DNA.
>
> (2017)

The performance and presentation contexts of the 'Spider Dress' were guided by Intel's need to promote a new product – the Intel Edison chip. Hence, presentations of this iteration of the 'Spider Dress' took place principally at tech events, such as the Consumer Electronics Show (CES), held in Las Vegas every January. As trade fairs are focused on 'demo-ing' new technologies to industry and media audiences, the 'Spider Dress' was presented in a format Wipprecht calls a 'walking act', wherein the model walks among the attendees and demonstrates the work. In the case of CES, the 'Spider Dress' was additionally accompanied by a small flock of 3D-printed robotic spiders, mirroring the wearable via an ambulatory cluster of similarly designed creatures.

Beyond the need to promote industrial clients is Wipprecht's overarching aim to craft new forms of intimacy via wearables. Inspired by the social challenges faced by many in their efforts to connect, assimilate and build appropriate social 'fronts' (as theorized by Goffman 1959), Wipprecht's designs speak for the socially awkward, resistive and ambivalent. For Wipprecht, social malaise is a universal concern, which is perhaps most directly tackled in her recent project Agent Unicorn. Developed in collaboration with the Ars Electronica Center in Linz, Austria, Agent Unicorn is a wearable adapted for children with ADHD. Playfully designed to look like a unicorn horn, and fabricated via 3D printing, it monitors moments of concentration (when the wearer is still and focused) and communicates this information back to the child/wearer. In this way, affected children can better identify and understand their own patterns of attention/inattention and thus act on them in a more deliberate fashion.

However, Wipprecht is adamant that the interactions and experiences offered by wearables go well beyond the panacea of health, fitness and happiness too often marketed via consumer wearables (2017). Rather, she pushes her wearables into uncomfortable emotional terrains of anger, shyness, indecency or misfire.[5] As Wipprecht notes, she is interested in how 'these systems around our bodies intuitively might both behave and misbehave [...] wearables should not behave, because we are misbehaving most of the time, or at least I do. Wearables should provoke the idea of making us better, by calling us out'. Hence, in the choreography of her fashion-tech wearables, Wipprecht aims at the co-structuring of experience with the garment. She is chiefly interested in how we perform with the wearable as well as the potential for it to perform for us and even solicit better or more authentic performances from us. As notes the designer, 'If you wear a design that you partly control and it partly extends your agency through its autonomous actions, you start to question where you end and my system begins' (see Svadja 2014: n.pag.).

This symbiotic performance proposes new ways of thinking about how wearables can extend performatively around and with our bodies, as well as through our mental and emotional states. In a way, one could argue that Wipprecht is interested in breaking the artificiality of the 'front' and other social constructions proposed by sociologists like J. L. Austin (1962) and Erving Goffman (1959) more than half a century ago. Her work expresses a dimension of social breakage and reinvention that both resembles König's concept of sartorial deviance (Goffman 1974) and elucidates the states of non-closure and transition as described in Turner's theory of 'liminoid' states (1967, 1974). Given this line of thought, is it possible to imagine a future in which it will be acceptable for our garments to push people away or obliterate us in a cloud of smoke when we grow tired of someone or are uncomfortable speaking to them? To be sure, these scenarios, in being more complex and contradictory, are also richer than many of the socially interactive platforms that we engage with today.[6]

FIGURE 7.2: Diffus, 'Climate Dress', 2009. Model: Anne Sophie Fioritto Thomsen. Courtesy of Anni Norddah.

Diffus Studio: 'Climate Dress' (2009)

Context

The second case study considers the work of Danish design studio Diffus. In the fall of 2011, invited by Diffus, I participated in the Copenhagen Artist in Residency programme (CPH AIR) and, later that fall, in the Danish International Visiting Artist (DIVA) programme via an invitation from Aarhus University. The CPH AIR provided me with an atelier space at the Fabrikken: Factory of Art and Design, where artists have access to traditional fine-arts workshops for wood, metal and painting. During this residency, I worked with Diffus's co-directors, Hanne-Louise Johannesen and Michel Guglielmi, at their research office/atelier. While at Diffus, I familiarized myself with their various wearables and interactive textile designs as well as their material libraries and collaborated on brainstorming sessions with local and international partners: Alexandra Instituttet (Denmark), Forster Rohner (Switzerland) and Cetemmsa (Spain).

Background

Diffus design is a multidisciplinary, materials-focused studio working at the intersection of theory and application in art, industrial design, architecture, smart fabrics and wearables. In existence since 2004, they have developed a number of client-based works and projects that highlight material innovation with design excellence. Wearables have comprised a part of their research focus, though not exclusively. Johannesen has a master's degree in art history, has worked as an assistant professor in visual culture at the University of Copenhagen and now teaches at the IT University of Copenhagen, while Guglielmi is an architect working with tangible media and interaction design, who teaches at the Royal Danish Academy of Fine Art in the schools of architecture and design.

Laboratory culture

Diffus describes its approach as both practical and theoretical, wherein art, culture, aesthetics and technology all play equal parts in informing design decisions. Particularly, they are interested in experimenting at the intersection of traditional know-how (and craft) combined with new materials in order to create both 'soft' and complex technologies. Recognized for their attention to detail in design, Diffus is increasingly sought out by international companies and universities to contribute to the conceptualization of new 'smart' designs. Their added value, they assert, is in creating aesthetic objects from technological and innovative materials from various textile and research industries (Diffus 2017). In their quest to create designs (and meaning) out of brute materiality, Guglielmi and Johannesen often approach their task from a philosophical point of view, wherein feelings and concepts about materials, bodies and interaction guide the decision process and feed into the final design. In this way, the firm seeks to innovate designs that 'appeal to our emotional self and open up to the sensibility of a large public'.[7]

The Diffus studio is a small, intimate space located in Copenhagen's central Vesterbrø neighbourhood and situated in a former residential building with other creative studios. The Diffus workspace, however, also extends to remoter spaces, including their personal and teaching settings and the laboratories of collaborators and service industries – all depending on material needs or convenience of workflow. Many collaborators intersect in their design development process, including seamstresses, engineers, 3D printers and other textile/material professionals. Because of Diffus's location in the European Union, many of their clients, partners and collaborators come from government-funded research grants (such as Horizon 20/20), putting them in direct contact with small and medium enterprises, notably in the field of industrial design – Pilotfish (Germany), VanBerlo (Netherlands), Fuelfor (Spain) and Zaha Hadid Architects and Base Structures (United Kingdom) – as well as research universities – Delft University (Netherlands), University of Southampton (United Kingdom), Politecnico di Milano (Italy) – and graduate students. In this way, Diffus is able to benefit from a large network of materials and research resources that both inspire and feed the direction of their projects. As Johannesen mentions in the course of our interview, these collaborations open up the studio to new and not-yet-distributed (or published) processes and materials, which guides the design concept phases and tangible possibilities. Furthermore, says Guglielmi, the EU grants also offer precious time for reflection and discussion – key to developing aesthetic and material concepts and ideas.

Technology

Materials are the essence, or core, of Diffus. As Guglielmi explains, 'We always try to remember where we come from, which is, exploring the possibilities of creating reactive materials from a design standpoint. Sometimes we try to go back to those roots, as a way of remembering' (2016). A key way in which this materiality is concretized, from a research point of view, is through an ever-expanding 'sample book'. Functioning much like a materials library, this sample book permits Diffus to archive and collect materials (which they may have encountered or tested during research) as well as to communicate their skill set to potential clients or collaborators. Johannesen explains, '[T]he sample library acts as a very active communicator' (Diffus 2017). In these sample books are contained various kinds of conductive materials (yarns, textiles, metal components) and processes (inks, embroidery), through which they highlight their past projects, breakthroughs and expertise. While these tests are often the result of contracts and requests on the part of collaborators, Guglielmi notes that the process is not always systematic, but consists more of 'making associations from materials that you use in one field and looking at the possibilities of translating them through small adaptations that you find interesting as a designer' (Diffus 2017). In either case, experimentation and research are 'more or less equal' for the design process at Diffus (2017).

Through their EU and client networks, and via their extensive experience and expertise, much of the work at Diffus is client-oriented. In this way, the epistemic culture of the lab is driven by external needs and opportunities (both financial and materials-based). It is in part through such a process that the 'Climate Dress' was developed in 2009.[8] The dress was conceived as a proof-of-concept collaboration with the Swiss textile company Forster Rohner, funded in part by the Alexandra Instituttet, a Danish technology think tank. Seeing a need to diversify their core business of haute couture embroidery and lace manufacturing, Forster Rohner has embarked upon engineering embroidery for smart fabrics. Led by Dr Jan Zimmermann, head of textile innovations at Forster Rohner, the company has been developing smart fabrics for various textile and design uses (from fashion to architecture to auto industries) adapted to the integration of hardware, such as LEDs, sensors and batteries. The partnership with Diffus emerged from mutual needs: that of Forster Rohner, to showcase their new expertise in smart embroidery fabrication; and of Diffus, to secure access to emergent processes and industry techniques for smart textiles. The 'Climate Dress' features a combination of conductive embroidery parts, embroidered LEDs, a CO_2 sensor and an Arduino to compute and manage the data inputs and outputs. The dress is designed to be wearable as a visible air-quality sensor, which can navigate various geolocated spaces and assess environmental air quality. The dress alerts the wearer and those near the dress to distressing levels of CO_2, both to warn the public over air quality and to sensitize them to the dangers of pollution.

Fashion

The partnership between Diffus and Forster Rohner was initiated through an invitation to showcase a design within the context of the COP15 Climate Summit in Copenhagen in 2009. Some of the parameters that the design duo took into consideration when developing this piece included creating a garment using traditional craft, revealing information through aesthetics and creating a new relationship with embroidery that featured technology. Hence, the 'Climate Dress' was born from a desire to fuse craft and tech in such a manner that would aesthetically reveal its functionality. Inspired by the methods of turn-of-the-century French architect Gustave Eiffel and his decorative use of metal structures, Diffus set out to create a garment that could build on the concept via embroidery rather than steel. Created in under two months, the process saw meetings between students from the Danish Design School, technicians from the Alexandra Instituttet and the technical team at Forster Rohner. Diffus describes their primary work as mediating between the various participants and collaborators in order to arrive at the results they aimed for. Along the way, considerations had to be made for the capacity of the conductive thread and LEDs to adequately illustrate CO_2 levels in a visually cohesive and pleasing manner. Guglielmi describes the process of negotiating needs with aesthetics:

> The interaction played a major role in the design of the embroidery and indirectly in the design of the garment on which the embroidery would be applied. More LEDs with more processing abilities could have been added but we needed to constrain ourselves to clear interaction rules between CO_2 levels and the LED patterns as pulse. Those clear rules influenced the design of the circuit layout as well as the design of the required algorithm.
>
> (Genova and Moriwaki 2016: 142)

Because the departure point for research at Diffus is materials exploration, it makes sense that the fashion (and aesthetic) frameworks are built around technical and interaction needs. Instead of seeing this as a limitation, the Diffus team is inspired to make 'form follow function', as coined by American architect Louis Sullivan.[9] Interestingly, Johannesen refers to Adolf Loos, also a proponent of functional architecture, as an inspiration for their design ethos. She explains,

> I think that because of someone like Loos, I was scared to go into something to do with embroidery, because embroidery is just ornament. I think it is really interesting, then, to give this ornament a functionality. Trying to respect Loos, and at the same time subvert him, or being subversive towards him.
>
> (Diffus 2017)

Another concrete example of this philosophy in action is the Solar Handbag, created in collaboration with Forster Rohner, the Alexandra Instituttet and the Hochschule für Technik Rapperswil, in Switzerland – and also the outcome of an EU-funded research grant.[10] The bag uses solar cells to power portable devices; instead of concealing the solar cells, Diffus approached the problem similarly to the 'Climate Dress', making the square cells an integral part of the exterior fabric and design.

In this way, the Diffus studio is closely guided by the quest to discover appropriate form and function through materiality. In describing his action- and time-based performative laboratory, Andrew Pickering (1995) outlines how human agency's intentionality must be mediated through the nonhuman agencies of matter, machines and things. Because Pickering's 'dance of agency' proceeds across this human–nonhuman negotiation, which unfolds via *temporal emergence*, outcomes can be neither forced nor predicted. Diffus's philosophical approach to integrating new technologies into design in a holistic and self-evident way is, in my opinion, indicative of a performative laboratory approach. Rather than force ideas about interaction, use or aesthetics onto a material or a technology, the studio embraces the process of discovering these things, of seeing them revealed *through* the process. In this way, their studio often arrives at results that fittingly display and propose a logic (and aesthetic) of use that may have not been readily apparent at the start, but which springs from the nature of the initial material. For these reasons, it is not unreasonable to see their process – focused primarily as it is on creating interaction and design out of technology – as inherently performative.

Body/interaction

The designs of Diffus – wearables or otherwise – are always informed with the body in mind, in consideration of both how the body will react to the design and how the design will interact with the body. Concern over touch, texture, manipulation and interaction feeds many of their form and material design decisions. In this way, the emphasis on materiality subscribes to the project of the re-embodiment and re-materialization of the technical object, as opposed to screen and data streams. Johannesen explains their position on materiality: 'When you work with technology and you work with human beings using the technology, it has to somehow occur within an experience. I think that we are working with technology that wants to be noticed and thereby, it enters the fashion area' (Diffus 2017). For Diffus, interaction, aesthetics and technology are inextricably intertwined.

One could also argue that Diffus's performative design matrix builds on new-media concepts of embodiment and experience. Foregrounding the body (touch, sight, movement, etc.), they bring a phenomenological dimension to the experience of their wearables. Diffus's work thus focuses on how design objects can, through good design and style, enter into the world of body-centric, sensuous and interactively rewarding experiences, which reposition the body at the centre of the technological question. Not surprisingly, as Diffus works for clients seeking new forms of expression for materials that have yet to find a use, meaning or shape, their work often consists in unlocking (and scripting) the interactive and poetical dimensions of matter. More than orchestrating new functionalities for technologies and smart materials, the Diffus team believes their design objects should also offer a respite and meditation for the future user, opening a door to deeper experiences. However, as they are well aware, designing for technology, as Guglielmi notes, is 'a polarity, really. On the one side, the need to do things simpler, and on the other side, exploring the complexity of structures, materials, and so on. It is about finding the balance between those things' (Diffus 2017). As a performative platform, their designs invite the sensing, sensitive, living, touching body back

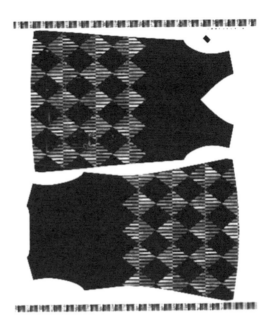

FIGURE 7.3: 3lectromode, *Strokes&Dots*, 2013. Models: Mathilde & Yollie (Dulcedo). Courtesy of Julia Marois.

into the technology, both through attention to detail and a sensibility towards form that follows function.

3lectromode: Strokes&Dots *(2013)*

Context

The third case study concerns 3lectromode, my own DIY atelier for craft and e-textiles wearables. For several years, I have been active in creating accessible DIY wearable platforms that borrow equally from the culture of at-home garment sewing (i.e. *Vogue* and McCall's patterns) and hobbyist electronics. These platforms and communication devices have been produced at my label's atelier as well as at various collaborative institutions – Hexagram Institute (Montréal), V2_ Lab for the Unstable Media (Rotterdam), Fabrikken for Kunst & Design (Copenhagen), Oboro (Montréal) and InterAccess (Toronto) – and been funded primarily through grants from the Canada Council for the Arts, the Conseil des arts et des lettres du Québec and the Concordia University Part-Time Faculty Association. During this time, I have also participated in a number of residencies, conferences and other events to trace the limits and potentials of this emerging field. Residencies have included the Danish International Visiting Artist Programme (DIVA), hosted by the Department of Information and Media (IMV) Studies at Aarhus University, where I delivered a conference presentation titled 'Kitchen Table Wearables', together with a series of workshops with design students titled 'How to Knit Your Own Computer'. Other conferences on the subjects of DIY and performance include an 'Open Wearables' panel and workshop, which I led at ISEA 2011 in Istanbul, Turkey; an 'Open Hardware Summit', held at Eyebeam Art + Technology Center in New York City in 2012; MEDEA's 'Prototyping Futures' conference in Malmö, Sweden, also in 2012, which examined emergent DIY technologies; and the MODE@MOTI symposium in Breda, Netherlands, in 2013, as part of a master class in fashion and technology, where I tested my ideas on the link between fashion-tech and modern-era innovation.

Background

In short, I have been active in researching and testing the limits of e-textiles and DIY culture (and various other themes such as performance, materiality and the history of wearables) to inform wearable aesthetics and production methods. The field of e-textiles, while lacking the finesse and resources of more industrial or academic research projects, offers a rich platform of collaborative and self-directed explorations for embedding electronics in garments.[11] In this sense, my atelier is more like an artist studio than a design company or service-oriented studio. Due to the nature of the funding – arts exploration grants – the projects are, for the most part, self-directed and independently developed. That said, the techno-arts atelier of today relies on a number of external industries and resources that directly impact onto the design. As I argued in my talk 'Open Design Practices + Wearables + 3lectromode' (Lamontagne 2011), there is a growing body of research describing the shift in production paradigms taking place as a result of the proliferation of new technologies, machines and shared expertise, as seen in the 'Maker' movement. Examples of this increased access range from the multiplication of shared physical spaces offering access to rapid-prototyping technologies (fab labs and hacker spaces) to the expanding networked possibilities of 'print-on-demand' services for remote 3D printing, as well as textile and circuit printing. Increasingly, the arts and design 'laboratory' has much in common with the cottage industries that existed before the Industrial Revolution, with small artist/artisan spaces playing critical roles in fabrication processes and choices, all the while retaining control over the end-product or design – an element that modern production chains had all but erased (Anderson 2012; Gershenfeld 2005; Openshaw 2015). Hence, for a field such as wearables, design, access to machines, technicians and materials can make all the difference. This dimension of DIY wearables has been explored in a number of how-to and instructional publications (Buechley et al. 2013; Genova and Moriwaki 2016; Hartman 2014; Pakhchyan 2008). Much like fashion designers who began their careers with a collection of accessible equipment, like home sewing machines and sergers housed in basement studios, the wearables designer and techno-crafter of today has access to a fast-growing palette of technologies and tools – from LilyPad Arduinos, conductive threads and inks to remote technical resources like laser-cutters, textiles and 3D printers – to create her/his creations.

Laboratory culture

3lectromode is a small design atelier run by myself as designer/owner, together with a variety of other experts from textiles, fashion and engineering and media arts who work on an ad hoc basis on various aspects of designing, developing, making and disseminating or marketing fashion-tech designs. Our designs range from material explorations, fashion-tech design and workshops that straddle the communities of high-tech, craft, arts, product design and speculative design. Key to 3lectromode's design ethos is the desire to create a library of executable open-source fashion designs that may be assembled as kits by anyone with an interest in wearables, electronics or fashion.

Performativity in the 3lectromode laboratory occurs among the individuals on-site in the atelier, together with the extended community of users and collaborators, from pattern makers to textile specialists, graphic designers and engineers. The team works towards a functional wearable aimed at satisfying a number of parameters, from the aesthetic to the technical, while one central concern is to create a wearable template that could be built by anyone. For this reason, all steps for producing (and reproducing) 3lectromode wearables are integrated and communicated via the design itself. This is done by means of graphically illustrating the placement of all necessary parts – from electronics, batteries, sensors, circuit layout to buttons and garment sewing – needed to assemble a functional wearable. Hence, many of the design parameters depend on the construction of a product that can be translated into a functioning wearable design. In this way, DIY culture expands the possibilities for anyone and everyone wishing to participate in it. By making the design and electronics open-source and accessible, 3lectromode, like many electronics companies that publish instructional videos, blogs and schematics, including Arduino and Adafruit, allows the general public access to various toolkits for the construction of wearables, thus contributing to the collective effervescence and activity in the field.

Technology

As a case in point, *Strokes&Dots* was designed with the intention of communicating the fabrication process of wearables to a general audience. Part of a micro-collection of sixteen garments, *Strokes&Dots* was inspired by early Modernist representations of speed, graphic design, abstract art and technology – as well as the print work of Russian/French textile visionary Sonia Delaunay. We began the design process by looking at early Modernist textile pattern and fabrication processes, which flourished during the early twentieth century. To begin with, a series of watercolour graphics inspired by Delaunay were created as design explorations. Next, we created four different garment patterns around which to build the collection: a top, a shirt, a skirt and a dress. Then we digitized the watercolour graphics and made them into textile patterns that could later be integrated into the (also) digitized garment patterns, created on a 1:1 scale in large Adobe Illustrator files. Finally, we integrated the layout guidelines for the placement of the electronics, which could later be machine- or hand-sewn with conductive threads onto the wearable. The digital document, now containing schematics of the transformed watercolour graphics, the garment pattern layout for sewing and the electronics placement guides, was printed on Japanese Habotai silk with a Mimaki digital textile printer at the Hexagram Institute at Concordia University. While the electronics guides were printed on a 'bottom' layer along with the textile graphics, the 'top' layer, a slightly thinner fabric, acted as light diffuser for the integrated LEDs. From a material standpoint, the *Strokes&Dots* kit contains a textile printout featuring the outline of the garment pattern and the layout placement for the electronics, which include a LilyPad Arduino, an accelerometer or light sensor and five to twelve (depending on the design) embroidered, responsive LEDs. The garments are reactive depending on the types of movements made by the individual wearing them. Three states of LED light displays were embedded into the design to communicate with the wearer and those nearby. The first state is when the wearer is at rest, and the lights cycle through lighting each LED to display its presence. When the wearer moves more dynamically, the LEDs respond by lighting up more actively and randomly, as though they had been 'woken up' or charged. Inversely, when the wearer stops moving for a long period of time, the LEDs display a warning sequence, in which all the lights light up at once and flash, indicating that the person should perhaps move. This playful communication between the wearer and the garment expresses the interactions taking place and having taken place, for all to see. In this way, they become a second layer of communication for all to 'read'.

As kits, which can be sold, constructed at home or in DIY wearables ateliers, or sewed in workshops or educational contexts, they are design objects that reveal their fabrication process and thus transform the user into a maker (or at the very least, a 'learner'). This method takes some of the initial guesswork out of electronics assembly, while allowing the user to create a customized and fashionable design. As each piece is uniquely designed and comes with customizable options for different print patterns, colours and sizes, the designs aim to give the user/designer agency in fabricating his/her own iteration. Computational variations are also included to modify the LilyPad Arduino programme, with the aim of simplifying the programming one step further. So far, 3lectromode designs have focused on integration of LEDs with various sensors, using the LilyPad Arduino platform for electronic components and programming. However, this is but a starting point for later iterations, which may integrate other emerging DIY technologies, as well as customizable options, thus adding to the landscape of maker-directed wearables. The 3lectromode label's next goal is to develop a maker/meeting space to foster community exchange and building around DIY wearables, as seen internationally in events such as Fashion Hack Day (Berlin) and the E-Textiles Summer Camp (Loire Valley, France).

Fashion

Beyond the mission to create a kit that can visually communicate how they can be built, a second important driver in the *Strokes&Dots* project is the creation of a collection of interactive objects that can stand on their own in the world of fashion. As many fashion-tech projects are one-off designs, this element of reproducibility in the studio was ever important to create a large collection, as opposed to a singular prototype. In this way, the sixteen stylistically connected garments could be deployed as a micro-collection on the runway or in other live events. Furthermore, the wearability – the ability for the garments to be worn in the everyday, on a variety of bodies, of varied ages and for a prolonged period of time, like at a cocktail party, an art opening or a fashion show – further reaffirmed their viability as fashion objects. Aesthetically, the *Strokes&Dots* garments had to 'pass' as fashion first and electronics second in order to make headway into the universe of fashion. With this goal in mind, the wearables were fabricated with silk and followed the shape of *prêt-à-porter* fashion; in other words, the garments are meant for 'everyone' and for 'anytime' contexts. These stylistic and functional factors meant that the studio was able to mount traditional fashion shows (*D-Moment* 2014; *Academos* 2015) with the interactive garments as well as participate in a number of public events (Augmented World Expo 2014; Boston Consulting Group 2014; CES Las Vegas and New York 2012, 2013, 2014, 2015). Having the garments stylistically echo fashion trends was important, enhancing visibility and, in this way, providing ample testing grounds to engage in live presentations as well as encounters with a diverse public.

Body/interaction

Finally, as a performative object, what does the wearable communicate? In the case of *Strokes&Dots*, a few elements can be identified. First, as they are disseminated as kits, the garments are often worn by their makers and hence are tangible testimony of their makers' process and skill, as expressed in the wearing. A close collaboration with the technology is enacted, as the wearable's 'performance' runs parallel to that of the lived – and creative – body that wears it. As the technology (the accelerometer or light sensors that give information on the body's movements or environment) is set into motion, the effects (LEDs, in the case of the DIY Social Skin) have an expressive dimension not fully controllable by the actual and situated body. At times, one might have the impression that the technology speaks with, for or even on top of the body. This duplicitous relationship between a self-unfolding technology, a garment as fashion expression (what says 'technophile' more than embedded technologies in your clothing?) and a body in action, reflects the complex, negotiated performativity that is the wearable.

Two strong messages arise out of the culture of DIY wearables, as exemplified in 3lectromode's design strategy. The first concerns the individual's participation in the construction of technology, or otherwise getting dirty, beyond the smooth surfaces of the Web 2.0 culture of input apps and content interface screens.[12] The second touches on the political act of wearing your technology as a craft movement. As a performative object, the DIY wearable is not a consumer item, but rather an object of technological affirmation for the masses. More than putting on a wearable gadget, DIY electronics and interfaces are about the storytelling and the individual's David-versus-Goliath struggle to have a voice in an increasingly technologized environment. One could even argue that it is a creative form of performative resistance to popular consumer tech culture, which forces the wearer and others to position themselves vis-à-vis the greater landscape and politics of an increasingly technocratic society.

XS Labs: Captain Electric and Battery Boy *(2010)*

Context

The last case study explores XS Labs, situated within the Milieux Institute (formerly Hexagram Institute) at Concordia University and directed by Joanna

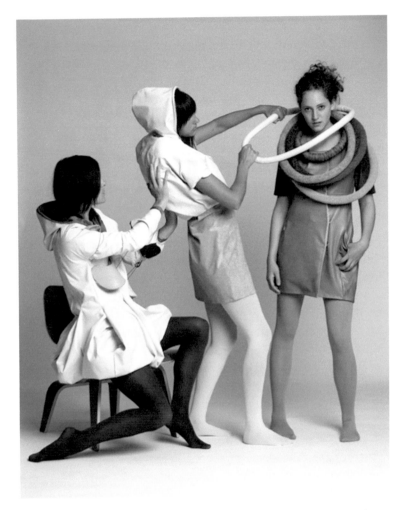

FIGURE 7.4: XS Labs, *Captain Electric and Battery Boy*, 2010. Models: Émilie Grenier ('Sticky'), Marjorie Labrèque ('Stiff') and Lisa Small ('Itchy'). Courtesy of Guillaume Pelletier.

Berzowska, associate professor of design and computation arts. Joanna and I have been colleagues in the same department for over a decade, and by virtue of intersecting interests, I have had the privilege of witnessing the evolution of her studio and even curating some of its works in international exhibitions, such as Sartorial Flux (A+D Gallery, Columbia College, Chicago, 2006) and Electromode (2010 Vancouver Olympics). With XS Labs nearby in the same institution where I teach, I have benefitted from its proximity by intersecting with and learning from the research conducted in its laboratory and in sharing resources and information. Furthermore, in being embedded at Concordia, XS Labs has provided a research focus on wearables engineering and crafting, thus attracting researchers and collaborators both locally and internationally, to the benefit of the local academic milieu, as well as the wider professional wearables community.

Background

Berzowska's background combines degrees in design and mathematics in an era before computation arts, interaction design or digital-arts education. As an academic researcher, her lab is focused on innovation, knowledge building, education, publishing and lecturing in the field of e-textiles, new materials for wearables and interaction design. Important research grants from the Fonds de Recherche du Québec – Société et culture (FRQSC) and the Social Sciences and Humanities Research Council of Canada (SSHRC) have guided the lab's focus towards a combination of fundamental research, design concerns and the training of what Berzowska calls 'highly qualified people' (HQP). XS Labs seeks to innovate in design via new technologies, while responding to such design's impact and poetic resonance on the body's actions. In this way, how interactive garments script the body is a central question for the lab. Having studied at MIT's Tangible Media Lab, the founding institution for wearables technologies, Berzowska is well versed in the challenges and aims of creating meaningful designs that can inspire both industry and art.

Laboratory culture

XS Labs, a design research studio founded in 2002, focuses on innovating in electronic textiles and responsive garments. Berzowska says, 'A core component involves the development of enabling methods, materials, and technologies – in the form of soft electronic circuits and composite fibres – as well as the exploration of the expressive potential of soft reactive structures' (Berzowska 2012: n.pag.). XS Labs works at the intersection of two communities: researchers and students. In this way, the laboratory's epistemic culture combines material and design innovation via the continuing education of her student researchers. Berzowska describes her lab as a playful and experimental space where students are encouraged to try new ideas and materials, thus creating a collaborative, collegial approach to research creation.

Technology

Core research at XS Labs is focused around the creation of design platforms for emergent technologies. The studio approaches new technologies with a concern and sensibility to make design 'softer' and hence more wearable. Motivated by the lack of e-textiles and poor wearability in traditional human–computer inter-action (HCI) applications, XS Labs has cultivated a palette of techniques and materials better suited to embodied and worn-interaction platforms. Berzowska explains that XS Labs is

> particularly concerned with the exploration of interactive forms that emphasize the natural expressive qualities of transitive materials. We focus on the aesthetics of interaction, which compels us to interrogate and to re-contextualize the materials themselves. The interaction narratives function as entry points to question some of the fundamental assumptions we make about the technologies and the materials that drive our designs.
>
> (Berzowska 2010: n.pag.)

From a technical standpoint, the studio works with materials including con-ductive fibres, reactive inks, photoelectrics, shape-memory alloys, conductive inks, LEDs, thermochromic inks, motors and more. While cutting-edge material inventions propel the studio's designs forward, the cultural history of tex-tile fabrication processes (weaving, stitching, embroidery, knitting, beading, quilting) also informs how this innovation will take shape. These experi-ments allow the construction of 'complex textile-based surfaces, substrates, and structures with transitive properties' (Berzowska 2010: n.pag.). Examples of this high-tech craft approach include the Karma Chameleon research pro-ject, carried out in collaboration with Dr Maksim Skorobogatiy, Canada Research Chair in Photonics at the École Polytechnique de Montréal, which involved a mixture of nanotechnology and traditional weaving (Berzowska and Skorobogatiy 2009, 2010).

Body/interaction

XS Labs' designs reconsider how interaction through soft and textile networks can foster novel and at times ludic or even dark-humoured forms of physical and body-based interaction. As Berzowska notes, new materialities 'promise to shape new design forms and new experiences that will redefine our relationship with colour, texture, silhouette, materiality, and with digital technology in general' (Genova and Moriwaki 2016: 24). This body-material-focused design approach has influ-enced many of the studio's early designs, like the *Memory Rich Clothing* series (Berzowska 2005; Berzowska and Coelho 2006a, 2006b), featuring dresses that invited strangers to touch the wearer in order to activate the material transform-ation of thermochromic inks (*Spotty Dress*, 2004) or garments that beckoned you to whisper into them so as to activate a series of lights and thus tangibly display the act of intimacy (*Intimate Memory Shirt & Skirt*, 2003). In this way, the technology arrives at its logical (or illogical, in the case of self-described absurdist or transgressive projects) placement and interaction, focused on creating meaning as opposed to efficiency, productivity or other wearable tech strategies discussed previously.[13]

This visceral and whimsical approach to designing new modes of interaction with emergent materialities is succinctly illustrated in the *Captain Electric and Battery Boy* (CEBB) research project (2007–10) (Berzowska et al. 2010a, 2010b). Initiated on the occasion of a class titled 'Second Skin and Softwear', which Berzowska taught at Concordia in the winter of 2008, the project took off with a student brief to create 'Human Powered Illumination'. The results propelled further investigations (and a 2008 summer workshop) into haptic platforms for power generation and storage via wearables. Exploring the potential for garments to harness the body for electricity, the project produced three designs, which playfully highlight our co-dependent relationship with electricity. Inspired by conceptual frameworks of co-dependence, parasitic systems or even extreme power relations between users and their need for or use of electricity, the designs stage a series of physical interactions that both amplify and visualize this exchange or power dynamic.

The results of CEBB showcase erratic, intransigent garments that provoke the user to pull, scratch and wrestle comically with its materiality, in the aim of generating future available wattage. Fittingly named 'Itchy', 'Sticky' and 'Stiff', the garments stage body-generated energy systems, capitalizing on various strategic, gestural platforms of activation. Building on intuitive actions, such as pulling, pushing and rubbing, the garments activate both the collection of energy and its visualization through a variable output (sound or light). For example, 'Itchy' invites the wearer (or others) to rub the concentric circles of its wool collar, thus creating static energy that powers a series of LEDs. 'Stiff', meanwhile, projects a parasitically passive platform for energy creation that necessitates the participation of an external player, who must push its attractive little back hump in order to activate a recording device available only to the wearable's wearer. Alternately, like a cat trying to scratch its own back, the wearer can also seek to collide with objects so as to activate the awkwardly placed bump. Finally, 'Sticky' features a waist-activated lever system that both restricts and benefits from the wearer's natural arm/hand actions to feed its need for energy. Admittedly, these are at once awkward and provocatively thoughtful systems that force us to consider the human–energy relationship in a new light as well as the concept of 'natural' forms of wearable interaction scenarios.

These three CEBB wearables force the wearer to 'work' in order to have access to energy. Each fashion-tech garment forces the wearer not only to negotiate awkward or uncomfortable textiles and sartorial shapes but also to engage in unnatural movements in order to create electricity friction. In the case of 'Itchy', the wearer must rub the collars together or invite others to do so in a way that is 'normal', or socially condoned. We all know that static is the enemy of good fashion, yet here, fashion invites the creation of static friction through robust movement. In the case of 'Stiff', the garment is literally stiff – the antithesis of textile garment comfort. The hump-like protrusion embedded into the garment is not only anti-fashion in shape but also rather inaccessible, as an interactive platform for the wearer. In this way, the garment becomes a parasitic system, in search of participants to activate it, or proposing unconventional ways of interacting with the environment, such as repeatedly bumping into walls or other objects in order to charge it. The final design, 'Sticky', is a bully system that requires the wearer to pull the device in order to be charged. However, the device also influences normative movements such as picking things up, because any movement using the hands must interact with the pulley. In this way, any movement of the hand has no choice but to participate in the kinetic ecosystem of energy gathering, whether the wearer wishes to do so or not. An inverse way of looking at the interaction is to think of the wearables as hosts who make use of the body to power themselves, thus inverting the power dynamic of wearable and wearer.

Furthermore, such projects exacerbate the limits of 'smart' design by highlighting both the very real and absurdist nature of our present-day technological demands. This work highlights current concerns over energy, environment and climate issues, which are at once distant and day-to-day concerns. Perhaps it could even be argued that, as transitional objects of an absurdist nature, CEBB designs demonstrate a 'liminoid' quality, as they neither fully adhere to the expectations of an HCI system nor are purely art. Not quite functional, and not quite purely playful, the CEBB designs reside at the limit of what we might expect or be willing to engage in when using a wearable. Berzowska reminds us that we 'need wearable computing that is irrational, poetic, musical and theatrical. We need wearable computing that stimulates magical and literary experiences in our everyday life rather than just trying to improve productivity or our efficiency' (Genova and Moriwaki 2016: 24). In this way, XS Labs' designs question the form and meaning of the wearable through their choreography of distinctly 'off' interactions.

Conclusion: Wearables as performative

The above four contemporary case studies invite us to reflect on how performance informs wearables and fashion-tech's epistemic cultures of production and internal systems of performance occurring in the studio/atelier/laboratory. By following key works produced within each studio, we see how performative potentials are seeded though the course of their conceptualization and developmental processes. Furthermore, we can see how contemporary wearables are pushing the boundaries of performance through design, style, interaction and use of technology by infusing their works with questions of social interaction, emotions, poetry, agency, bodies and politics. In each case study, we encounter the processes, agendas, tools, materials, dreams and struggles at play within the theatre of wearables creation. Furthermore, each case study proposes a new angle on the kind of performance unfolding in the studio, from those of collaborative industry research in fashion-tech (Wipprecht) to smart-fabrics innovation via fashion and design (Diffus) and from DIY e-textile production (3lectromode) to the rethinking of HCI scenarios via wearable design (XS Labs). Most importantly, however, we become aware of performance's role as central to the raison d'être of the wearable, as it is present in its logic of use. In other words, wearables need bodies, fashion and technology, and each of these facets contributes to how a wearable is experienced. The performance of robotics mixed with emotion, as seen in the world of Wipprecht, and the acrobatic interaction scenarios proposed by Berzowska through CEBB both point to the body performing with technology. Furthermore, these examples confirm how the wearable would be devoid of meaning without a body to push up against it (sometimes literally) and without the shapes and materials that inform/comprise them. The same can be said of how matter performs over the course of its process towards becoming an 'intelligent' design, as seen in the Diffus studio, or the proposition that DIY wearables can offer appreciation and knowledge through their hands-on production and deployment. In the contemporary wearables atelier, we encounter a positioning vis-à-vis wearables' capacity to offer new experiences for the body as well as new relationships to fashion and technology.

NOTES

1. I frame wearable technologies as body-worn devices that use electronics to modulate and transform materiality in real time.

2. Much of the content of this chapter derives from a series of audio interviews conducted in early 2016 with each of the contemporary case-study subjects. The interview transcripts can be found in Lamontagne (2017: pp. 243–309).

3. The past 50 years have seen an increase in the use of the terms *performance* and *performativity* in non-theater/stage-associated research fields, such as linguistics, anthropology, ethnography and sociology. The 'performative turn', a paradigmatic shift in humanities and social sciences from the 1960 to the 1980s, adopted performance-inspired methods and situations as subject, object and research methodology. These utilized grounded,

intimate and embodied practices to source experiences and material from which to understand society at large. The modes of research employed stemmed principally from first-person and everyday interactions, observations and analyses, while embedded within an intimate social context, thus stepping away from representational and symbolic models of inscribing the 'real' world. This type of research methodology can be seen in the work of numerous linguists, sociologists and anthropologists, like J. L. Austin, Erving Goffman, Victor Turner and Dwight Gonquergood (cf. Lamontagne 2017: 62–63).

4. Participants in 'Clothing without Cloth' included: Emily Crane, a recent MA graduate from Kingston University, London, working with edible textiles (United Kingdom); Christien Meindertsma, a materials designer from Rotterdam (Netherlands); Carole Collet, then director of the Textile Futures MA program at Central Saint Martins, London (France/United Kingdom); Giada Dammacco, lead designer at Grado Zero Espace, a technology and design company in Florence (Italy); Pauline van Dongen, an independent fashion-tech designer (Netherlands); and Brian Garret, a 3D designer at Freedom of Creation (Netherlands).

5. For more on emotional wearables, see Stead et al. (2004).

6. In the interview conducted for this case study, Wipprecht repeatedly brings up the malaise of social media. She makes it clear that she is interested in creating more 'authentic' interactions than the veneer of happiness and sociability afforded by likes and brags, as seen in many social media exchanges. See interview with Wipprecht in Lamontagne (2017: pp. 243–59).

7. See http://www.diffus.dk. Accessed 6 July 2012. The website has since been updated and the statement removed.

8. The 'Climate Dress' is also at times referred to as the CO_2 Dress; for purposes of this study, I will refer to it in the former manner.

9. Similar to Eiffel, Sullivan was interested in how steel, in this case in the construction of American skyscrapers, could create new architectural aesthetics.

10. The Solar Handbag has since been re-branded as Eclipse, but for purposes of this case study I will refer to it in the former manner.

11. For a more detailed exploration of the field, see Lamontagne (2017: ch. 1, pp. 1-26).

12. I take this opportunity to thank Hanne-Louise Johannesen for mentioning Katherine N. Hayles's book, How We Think, during our interview. As Johannesen notes, referencing Hayles, it is important that, 'all of us do hands-on stuff, because digital media and technology is such an integrated part of our society, it is so important that we all contribute to it'. See 'Diffus Interview' in Lamontagne (2017: pp. 260–81) and Hayles (2012).

13. For more on speculative and confrontational design, see DiSalvo (2012), Dunne (1999), and Dunne and Raby (2001, 2013).

Epilogue

Jessica P. Clark and Nigel Lezama

Warning: This chapter contains details about residential schools that may be distressing.

The field of critical luxury studies (CLS) encourages thinkers, industry players and observers to examine relationships of power that undergird contemporary and historical luxury systems. Recent scholarship has urged us to further unpack the field's focus on particular ideas about luxury and specifically western sites and developments that have, for historical reasons, dominated both the industry and our understanding of what is and is not luxurious. This volume contributes to this pursuit, by situating Canadian luxury in the context of colonial and neocolonial systems; highlighting the power dynamics at play in luxury markets, including the ways that commercial luxury can impoverish the lives of certain constituencies; and foregrounding the very real consequences for those finding themselves on the losing end of contemporary luxury systems. Its contributors join other scholars of luxury who are refocusing the epistemological lens and critically interrogating inequitable processes underpinning understandings of luxury rather than replicating them (see Iqani and Dosekun 2019a).

In doing so, the essays in *Canadian Critical Luxury Studies: Decentring Luxury* offer alternate entry points into analyses of luxury that do not turn on traditional European production or dominant markets in global fashion capitals. While Canada is situated in the Global North, the current focus of most scholarship on luxury (Iqani and Dosekun 2019b: 3), this collection nonetheless demonstrates the ways that some 'secondary' or 'peripheral' luxury markets operate in relation to the enduring cultural and economic hegemony of European and American producers and consumers. The interventions in this volume lay bare the European domination that positioned Canada and Indigenous and settler-colonial producers, products and markets in a subordinate position to the metropole and its so-called refined production. While Canadians sought out their own means to engage in luxury production

200

and consumption, and specifically through nationalist understandings of surplus value, Canada nonetheless operated outside a cultural imaginary that determined what was and was not luxurious in relation to dominant luxury markets.

Contributors to this volume further reveal the ways that space and place function as key nodes of luxury market development, albeit in ways that do not always serve existing populations with their respective histories and subjectivities. Recent attempts to forge Canadian luxury events and public art in urban centres like Toronto and Vancouver have arguably come at the expense of those subject to the damaging effects of displacement and gentrification. In some cases, Canadian luxury experiences such as Toronto Fashion Week have failed to make headway because the wholesale adoption of hegemonic structures that function in dominant fashion capitals fails to resonate in secondary markets. But other instances, such as those in Vancouver, confirm the levelling effects of some luxury developments, as people and places are priced out of the tenuous twenty-first-century real estate landscape, and the historical and cultural specificity of these spaces is homogenized through the deployment of capital and power in the form of public art monuments.

Essays in this collection nonetheless suggest some promising moves towards the future. This includes the resurgence of Indigenous values and cultural production, which is, by its very nature and creation, luxurious (Kucheran 2019a). There remains work to be done to establish this reality among global communities of luxury consumers and players, in efforts to renounce hundreds of years of colonial rule with its violent processes of dispossession, dependency and oppression against Indigenous peoples (Manuel and Derrickson 2017: Part 1). In the Canadian context, rather than hinder Indigenous and other makers, chapters suggest that the intimate scale and independent nature of the nation's luxury scenes could foster connections to land, sustainability, local production and innovation. This onus on localized communities is also evident in Canada's movement towards digital and wearable tech in the nation's creative fashion and fashion-adjacent industries. Contributors' studies of Canada's fashion luxury scene, and particularly their attention to ethical practices in sourcing, production and distribution, point to a future of Canada's standing in global luxury markets that engages with the diversity of cultural actors that constitute the country's luxury cycle of production, consumption and circulation. As authors have shown, the Canadian case can stand as a model for developing more inclusive definitions of luxury, dislodging traditional western axes of power and prestige, and prioritizing community in the development of alternate luxury markets on a national scale.

This volume thus offers insights into future possibilities for redefining Canada's relationship to luxury as well as that of the field of CLS more broadly. And yet, at the time of writing, the future of luxury is especially unclear given recent developments that could – and should – dramatically transform definitions of luxury, worldwide commodity flows and luxury providers' relationship to social justice and equity. In March 2020, in the midst of a global pandemic, many Canadian provinces shifted into isolation, shuttering most brick-and-mortar businesses for an unknown duration. In May and June 2020, protests broke out across North America and beyond to challenge the enduring power of systemic racism and particularly that of anti-Black racism and state-sanctioned violence. One year later, in May 2021, preliminary investigations by the Tk'emlúps te Secwépemc First Nation located the remains of 215 Indigenous children's bodies on the former site of the Kamloops Indian Residential School. The ties binding these developments are myriad; from the disproportionate impact of COVID on people of colour to the ways that our broader structures of power systematically discriminate against and endanger the lives of our most economically and culturally vulnerable populations, these ruptures reflect broad, longstanding inequities defining western – including Canadian – systems of governance and the economy. In the wake of these developments, it is all the more essential to notions of democracy to interrogate our current definitions of luxury. How does luxury function in a moment when so many find themselves in a position of vulnerability, and how could it function in new, more responsive ways?

In light of the global pandemic and the wide-ranging movement for social justice, luxury markets worldwide and their most assured assets find themselves in a period of unprecedented destabilization (Beauloye 2020: n.pag; Amed et al 2020: 7; Chaboud 2020: n.pag.). While analyst Luca Solca's determination, during the first wave of the pandemic, that '2020 is [...] shaping up to be "the worst year in the history of modern luxury"' (quoted in Amed et al. 2020: 11) has proven almost oracular, the current social context has provided luxury companies around the world with the opportunity to develop their own responses to this crisis, as conceived and articulated by luxury brand marketers and strategists. To counter these major declines, and help quell widespread anxieties, industry-facing publications have called for companies' 'flexibility', 'business agility' and 'brand humanity'. This will allegedly allow major luxury providers to adapt to post-COVID 'survival of the fittest' conditions (Amed et al. 2020: 29–31), as if the neoliberal, hypercapitalist reality of western hegemony were not already a zero-sum game. Responses have included practical and symbolic transformations, such as LVMH and Hermès's shift to produce hand sanitizers and other disinfecting agents (Chaboud 2020: n.pag.) in the early months of the pandemic. More broadly, developments also include a renewed emphasis on online points of contact via the ongoing 'digital transformation of luxury' (Amed et al. 2020: 20–22). An onus on 'community building' via networking events and other online spectacles allegedly maintains connections with luxury customers who will, according to some estimations and recent consumer patterns in mainland China, take up 'revenge shopping' when finally released from COVID-related restrictions (Williams and Hong 2020: n.pag.). In other words, luxury industries not only hope for a return to the status quo but are also working towards (and literally banking on) an intensification of pre-pandemic hyperconsumption.

It is not only in relation to consumer connections that we may see changes in luxury markets. Advisors also foresee shifts in luxury conglomerates' dependency on global supply chains, many of which were destabilized in the major outbreak of COVID in Wuhan (Amed et al. 2020: 7). 'A less efficient phase of globalization might be dawning', posits Stéphane J. G. Girod. 'Luxury goods players would need to continue to balance sales internationally, but they would also need to tighten their link with their place of origin (reshoring manufacturing) and start keeping buffer inventories in each region or even country' (2020: n.pag.). Rather than see this localization of production as a detriment to luxury profits, however, commentators point to the potential appeal to luxury consumers and particularly those in specific geographies. Girod observes, '[T]he crisis might tilt Western consumer behaviours' preference towards locally-made products, particular for highly-priced goods' (2020: n.pag.).[1] One can only sigh, *plus ça change* …

An onus on the local reflects a trend across luxury market projections emphasizing the centrality of 'meaningful luxury' to post-COVID industry reconfigurations. Focusing on values prized by millennial consumers including 'environmental, sustainability and social issues' (Beauloye 2020: n.pag.; Amed et al. 2020: 19), commentators position this crisis as a moment to rethink their approaches to luxury production – or at least 'their brand perceptions' as those who care about such values (Beauloye 2020: n.pag.). 'It's a chance for luxury businesses to pause and ponder about the very essence of their brands', argues Florine Eppe Beauloye, 'to deliver a timeless and timely form of meaningful value' (2020: n.pag.). Bain & Company echo this sentiment, arguing that this could 'be a transformation for the good' (quoted in Beauloye 2020: n.pag.). This means accepting that post-COVID consumers may not, in fact, be interested in luxury in the same ways. 'Experience […] suggests that, after a large-scale crisis with a heavy emotional toll, consumer preferences could shift, at least for a time, toward "silent luxury"', note Antonio Achille and Daniel Zipser of McKinsey & Co. This entails 'paying more attention to classic elements, such as craftsmanship and heritage, and less to conspicuousness and "bling"' (2020: n.pag.). Predictions of less conspicuousness and 'bling' are nevertheless a racially loaded mystification of luxury and an idealized 'in-the-know' consumer who lives beyond the reach and understanding of the hoi polloi. Worse yet, invoking such language suggests that pundits are hoping for a deeper whitening of privilege.

When initially invoking 'large-scale crises with a heavy emotional toll', business commentators were describing the COVID pandemic and its effects. But this 'heavy emotional toll' was also evident in the social justice movement that rose up in many nations in response to the May 2020 police murder of George Floyd in Minneapolis, Minnesota. The fundamental ideas of human rights, equity and diversity expressed by Black Lives Matter protesters are also themes that many luxury brands purportedly embrace, and vociferously so, in the wake of the recent cultural movement. And yet, unlike in previous moments of social unrest and demands for justice, consumers have more openly questioned – if not outright dismissed – branded attempts to meet calls for racial equity. Writing in *GQ*, for example, Rachel Tashjian called out brands' mixed success at navigating 'tepid support for social justice issues and true activism' (2020: n.pag.; Jung 2020).

More recently still, Canada has been witnessing its own history of white supremacy and genocide and the ongoing effects thereof. Myths of Canadian exceptionalism have long been challenged by Indigenous communities, including Survivors of Canada's Residential School System as outlined by the Truth and Reconciliation Commission of Canada (TRC), which operated between 2008 and 2015. The TRC noted that its findings 'are sometimes difficult to accept as something that could have happened in a country such as Canada, which has long prided itself on being a bastion of democracy, peace, and kindness throughout the world'. But the reality is that '[c]hildren were abused, physically and sexually, and they died in the schools in numbers that would not have been tolerated in any school system anywhere in the country, or in the world' (Truth and Reconciliation Commission of Canada 2015: v–vi). The discovery of the mass grave in Kamloops in late May 2021 brought to the fore this collective history and the enduring, lived effects of Canada's Residential School System, as well as many settler Canadians' willful ignorance of this reality. ' "The outrage and the surprise from the general public is welcome, no question," Assembly of First Nations National Chief Perry Bellegarde said. "But the report is not surprising. Survivors have been saying this for years and years – but nobody believed them" ' (quoted in Editorial 2021). What this confirms, and what the TRC argued six years ago, is that '[r]econciliation is not an Aboriginal problem; it is a Canadian one. Virtually all aspects of Canadian society may need to be reconsidered' (TRC 2015: vi). This includes the valuation of not only the human dignity, history and lived experiences of First Nations, Métis and Inuit peoples but also their centrality to Canadian culture and identity, in all its forms. 'At stake', argued the TRC, 'is Canada's place as a prosperous, just, and inclusive democracy within [a] global world' (TRC 2015: 7).

It can be troubling to speak of, if not advocate for, luxury in such an urgent moment when so many live in precisely opposite conditions. However, luxury is culture or at the very least a form of cultural production. As the various chapters in this volume demonstrate, a distinctly Canadian luxury must take into account the regional and cultural specificities that make up the country and its history.

In concert with the TRC, CCLS affirms that Canada's status as a 'prosperous, just, and inclusive democracy' demands both reconciliation and realignment with First Nations, Métis and Inuit peoples and their cultures. By decolonizing luxury, it becomes possible to conceive of a truly meaningful luxury that centres sustainability, equity and community as grounding principles and expected outcomes. Canadian luxury can be a redefinition of the term and an example for how luxury can operate outside of neoliberal and hypercapitalist systems by embracing regional realities and historical specificities. Luxury in the Canadian context can be a force for change.

Accordingly, the essays in this volume respond to calls for more rigorous redefinitions of meaningful luxury, offering alternate means to conceptualize and reconfigure luxury as an idea and in its practice that do not necessarily depend on those systems that have come to dominate luxury production through the post-war period (McNeil and Riello 2016: 225–51). By emphasizing the local, including localized values shared by communities of invested parties, a national approach to luxury need not be bound by multi-billion-dollar interests or global supply chains (see Hitchcock 2016: 68). Rather, it turns on localized parties to invest in – and subsequently redefine – what it means to create luxury in a time of change.

In the Canadian context and elsewhere, what this means, in large part, is participating in broader processes of decentring. As chapters in this volume demonstrate, the decentring of traditional European hegemony can, and should, be applied to luxury industries – and scholarly efforts to document them (see also Dosekun and Iqani 2019a). The inaccessibility of luxury, in its current form, for the vast majority of global consumers confirms that it remains a purview of the 1 per cent. And yet, this does not capture the ways that luxury shapes global experiences of consumers, labourers and those communities operating adjacent to luxury and subsequently affected – for better and for worse – by its reach (see, e.g., Noris, Kalbaska and Cantoni 2018: 285). This volume has shown how luxury, and conceptions of it, influence the economic possibilities for local communities; the legacies of leading national corporations; the valuation of Indigenous- and immigrant-made luxury as racialized productions; the coopting of public space in the name of luxury spectacles, art and development; and the potential of digital luxury to expand human experience and deepen community ties.

It is not only in the Canadian context that these conditions apply. This volume's case studies can thus function as productive models for any localized economies that have historically functioned as 'secondary' markets: where raw materials were harvested, Indigenous peoples subjugated and immigrants made to feel inferior to a colonial metropole. By decentring definitions of luxury, we can begin to ask what is truly meant by *meaningful* luxury. In the Canadian case, this involves prising open current definitions of luxury to include processes previously overlooked, experiences available to all and items that hold meaning beyond their price or brand valuation. Chapters in this volume, in concert with recent postcolonial critiques in fashion studies (Gaugele and Titton 2019; Kucheran 2019a; Elan 2020), demonstrate that these processes can extend to the study of CLS in a few key ways. This includes the naming of Eurocentric language and systems and the ways they underpin contemporary luxury markets and, at times, CLS; a critical interrogation – and destabilizing – of the *expected* geographies of luxury production and consumption; and attention to the role of community capital as a fundamental component of everyday luxury for diverse constituencies around the world.

A key theme to emerge from this volume is the development of a more inclusive, dynamic study of luxury via the recognition – and naming – of global systems of power that shape it. There have been critical discussions around definitions of luxury, but what of hegemonic western values that underpin these explanations of markets, consumers and goods? An interrogation of the language of luxury, as demonstrated in these chapters, suggests there is further work to be done to determine its value in critical enquiries. For example, how do 'exclusivity' and 'rarity' function as social or political tools to not only signal luxury status but also oppress or marginalize global actors? How are luxury-adjacent players – sweatshop labourers, global migrant workers, those displaced by luxury development – included or excluded by current conceptualizations of luxury?[2] To develop a more expansive understanding of who and what is affected by current luxury systems, authors in this volume show that we must actively name and grapple with the colonial foundations of many central tenets of luxury as a concept, industry and field of study. Luxury is a value system that, from before and after the early modern period, bolstered the power of imperial nation states and their metropolises. We live with the enduring afterlives of these historical realities, which continue to shape the ways we conceptualize developments like the movement of luxury production to offshore locations or the emergence of East Asia as a primary site of luxury consumption. As proponents of *critical* luxury studies, then, our job is to not only interrogate luxury as a discrete phenomenon but also interrogate the broader logics that sustain distinctions of luxury, many of which postcolonial critics – and growing numbers of people around the world – are currently trying to dismantle. In other words, the study of luxury is not separate from pressing questions of decolonization (Kucheran), gentrification (Franklin and Halliday and Polyck-O'Neill) or rethinking our digital futures (O'Mahony and Lamontagne). The approaches in this volume, alongside strategies from postcolonial criticism, offer productive guidance for future avenues of study (see also Dosekun and Iqani 2019a; Kucheran 2019a; Gaugele and Titton 2019). This includes the nurturing of interdisciplinary practices, true engagement with

Indigenous and postcolonial methodologies (Kucheran 2019a) and prioritizing the lived experiences of those directly involved in but also adjacent to luxury as labourers, contractors, migrant workers, aspirational consumers, makers and disruptors. These disruptive approaches would deliberately engage with the vestiges of historical Eurocentric luxury systems, all while foregrounding new dynamics that situate the human and humanity (care, community, identity) at the centre of the luxurious experience.

A second theme highlighted in these chapters, and another means through which to destabilize existing modalities of power, is space and place. Specifically, chapters offer a critical dislodgement of traditional locations of power and prestige in studies of luxury (Kucheran, Clark and Lezama). Indeed, their work challenges any notions of 'naturalized' geographies of luxury, owing to history, culture or economic standing (Franklin and Halliday and Polyck-O'Neill). Current luxury economies historically privilege the European context, which precludes opportunities for more expansive explorations of non-traditional forms of luxury. While metropolises like Paris and London or nation states like Italy historically dominated modern luxury production – and while these histories are crucial in contemporary luxury brand management (McNeil and Riello 2016: 285–87) – these antecedents should not preclude the identification and study of other forms of luxury in historically 'secondary' sites. To solely focus on traditional sites of luxury would risk replicating historical binaries – west/the rest, art/artefact, whiteness/otherness – that still hold very real power in global capitalist systems (Hall 1991 cited in Gaugele and Titton 2019: 16; see also Said 1978). This means acknowledging enduring colonial logics that shape perceptions of a given location, good or brand and asking how and why something is deemed a luxury in one locale and not another. This also means active pursuits of new actors, archives and stories beyond traditional centers of study in CLS. Historically secondary markets may not be main venues in contemporary capitalist systems or may have adjacent relationships to luxury capitalism via exploitive systems of sweated labor undertaken by its citizens. But regardless of a location's connection – or lack thereof – to our modern luxury economies, all sites can lay claim to some form of luxury experience or object. There is arguably even greater power in those markets deemed 'liminal', as therein lay expansive possibilities for negotiation, hybridity and new imaginings of what luxury could mean (Bhabha 1994, cited in Haehnel 2019: 176–80; Gaugele and Titton 2019: 29).

These pursuits should not be undertaken in isolation, and a third and final contribution of these chapters to CLS is the foregrounding of community as the foundation of a new approach to luxury (Kucheran, Lamontagne, Lezama and O'Mahony). The rise of globalization, characterized by offshore production, the expansion of transnational commodity flows and new possibilities in building global communities of consumers and producers, has transformed late twentieth- and twenty-first-century luxury markets (McNeil and Riello 2016: 225–88). These global networks can produce disjunctures and destabilize localized relationships – economic, cultural, political – upon which a new type of social luxury may be predicated. Chapters from this volume suggest the enduring importance of what we have termed 'community capital', a valuation that has become even more urgent as neoliberal politics and its discourse widen the divide separating those with from those without. Even before the crises of 2020 and 2021, the dynamic possibilities of deep, collective relationships to luxury were evident. For those taking a critical approach to luxury studies, the benefits of foregrounding community approaches are certainly clear. For one, a tight focus on community units helps push back against universalism or essentialism (Haehnel 2019: 171) that continues to characterize some commentary on luxury consumers, including that of China, which Jean-Noël Kapferer and Pierre Valette-Florence have dubbed an 'emerging country' despite its long historical relationship to luxury (2016: 120; see also Hall 2020: 36–40; Anon. 2020; Simpson 2017). Not only a focus on community but also a *valuation* of shared principles among groups allows appreciation for multifarious, heterogeneous examples of luxury production, experience and service. On a material level, chapters in this volume show that it is in the community that meaningful relationships to luxury can be forged, not to mention meaningful dynamics of power – including resistance – that help advance issues of social justice and equity. Critical studies of luxury need not be separate from these pursuits, but only through a dramatic reimagining of what luxury can mean on a deeply local, community level.

An emphasis on community in conceptions of luxury could, in time, have an effect on its ethics, not to mention the ways we study it. In describing current luxury brands' efforts at social responsibility, Peter McNeil and Giorgio Riello point to regulation, charitable fundraising and arts sponsorship as key contributions (2016: 265–70; see also Noris et al. 2018: 283). However, more urgent demands, as discussed above, now face luxury brands, consumers and those adjacent to luxury. Issues of social justice, economic and racial equity and sustainability are at the forefront of global concerns and are, in many ways, essential if luxury is to regain its lustre (Kucheran 2018). As these chapters demonstrate, it is here that the role of community can come to the fore as a means to forge new definitions of luxury that prioritize the needs of individuals based on their humanity rather than their socio-economic standing. This will no doubt destabilize the importance of 'rarity' and 'exclusivity' in current definitions of luxury. But it will also reflect the current realities of global constituencies who are demanding a radical revision of dominant systems. This includes 'luxury' and all its trappings.

As volume contributors show, a dedicated focus on naming hegemonic western structures as they continue to shape luxury systems, the locating of luxury beyond conventional European geographies and a valuing of community capital bring the promise of meaningful relationships to luxury and also change how we study it. To find meaning requires a parsing of luxury from exploitive capitalist systems and imbuing the systems with value in new ways that are predicated on community, culture and investment in the future rather than luxury's exclusive – and frequently oppressive – past. As Canadian scholars of luxury, we are implicated in these processes, as we classify, study, define and redefine what luxury is and is not. We are active participants in establishing value around and attention to luxury objects, systems and economies. We can also contribute to the future of these pursuits by instilling value in new forms of luxury that turn on global inclusivity, community and, ultimately, meaning.

NOTES

1. Notably, luxury analysts have not, at the point of writing, addressed the collapse of many subcontracting systems in global luxury production in the wake of COVID-19. This has, however, been a major point of conversation in the fashion world. See, for example, Bramley (2020).

2. Some exceptions in CLS that go beyond European contexts or study luxury-adjacent actors include Dosekun and Iqani (2019a), Sekhon (2015), Hitchcock (2016) and Noris et al. (2018).

References

Absolon, Kathleen E. (2011), *Kaandossiwin: How We Come to Know*, Halifax: Fernwood.

Absolon, Kathleen E. and Willett, Cam (2005), 'Putting ourselves forward: Location in Aboriginal research', in L. Brown and S. Strega (eds), *Research as Resistance: Critical, Indigenous, and Anti-Oppressive Approaches*, Toronto: Canadian Scholars' Press, pp. 97–126.

Achille, Antonio and Zipser, Daniel (2020), 'A perspective for the luxury-goods industry during – and after – coronavirus', McKinsey & Co., 1 April, https://www.mckinsey.com/industries/retail/our-insights/a-perspective-for-the-luxury-goods-industry-during-and-after-coronavirus. Accessed 2 June 2020.

Adamson, Glenn (2013), *The Invention of Craft*, London: Bloomsbury.

Allford, Jennifer (2016), 'Walking tour of Vancouver's Downtown Eastside reveals good in the community', *The Star*, 6 August, https://www.thestar.com/life/travel/2016/08/06/walking-tour-of-vancouvers-downtown-eastside-reveals-good-in-the-community.html. Accessed 1 September 2019.

Amed, Imran, Berg, Achim, Balchandani, Anita, Hedrich, Saskia, Rölkens, Felix, Young, Robb and Ekeløf Jensen, Jakob (2020), *The State of Fashion 2020: Coronavirus Update*, New York: Business of Fashion and McKinsey & Co.

Anderson, Chris (2012), *Makers: The New Industrial Revolution*, Toronto: Signal.

Anon. (1916), 'Big departmental to be all-Canadian', *The Globe*, 16 November, p. 6.

Anon. (1927), 'Only 20 per cent. of all merchandise imported by Eaton's', *The Globe*, 8 February, p. 11.

Anon. (1928), 'Eaton's huge store to tower 670 feet above street level', *The Globe*, 14 November, p. 13.

Anon. (2016), 'Fast fashion', *Fashion Law*, 3 October, http://www.thefashionlaw.com/learn/fast-fashions-green-initiatives-dont-believe-the-hype. Accessed 30 September 2019.

Anon. (2017), 'Explore Vancouver public art from Convention Centre', City of Vancouver, https://vancouver.ca/files/cov/public-art-brochure-waterfront-downtown.pdf. Accessed 1 September 2019.

Anon. (2019), 'What is public art?', Association for Public Art, https://www.associationforpublicart.org/what-is-public-art/. Accessed 1 September 2019.

Anon. (2020), 'Fashion victims: How slow times in the luxury world will separate the bling from the chaff', *Economist*, 20 June, https://www.economist.com/business/2020/06/20/how-slow-times-in-the-luxury-world-will-separate-the-bling-from-the-chaff. Accessed 3 July 2020.

Appadurai, Arjun (1986), 'Introduction', in A. Appadurai (ed.), *The Social Life of Things: Commodities in Cultural Perspective*, Cambridge: Cambridge University Press, pp. 3–63.

Appiah, Kwame Anthony (2016), 'There is no such thing as western civilisation', *The Guardian*, 9 November, https://www.theguardian.com/world/2016/nov/09/western-civilisation-appiah-reith-lecture. Accessed 12 December 2019.

Armitage, John (2020), *Luxury and Visual Culture*, London: Bloomsbury Visual Arts.

Armitage, John and Roberts, Joanne (eds) (2016a), *Critical Luxury Studies: Art, Design, Media*, Edinburgh: University of Edinburgh Press.

Armitage, John and Roberts, Joanne (2016b), 'Critical luxury studies: Defining a field', in J. Armitage and J. Roberts (eds), *Critical Luxury Studies: Art, Design, Media*, Edinburgh: Edinburgh University Press, pp. 1–22.

Armitage, John and Roberts, Joanne (2016c), 'The spirit of luxury', *Cultural Politics*, 12:1, pp. 1–22.

Armitage, John and Roberts, Joanne (2017), 'Luxury: from the idea to the reality of prestigious places', in M. Paris (ed.), *Making Prestigious Places: How Luxury Influences the Transformation of Cities*, New York: Routledge, pp. 23–33.

Austin, John L. (1962), *How to Do Things with Words*, Oxford: Clarendon.

Bain, Alison L. (2006), 'Resisting the creation of forgotten places: Artistic production in Toronto neighbourhoods', *Canadian Geographer*, 50:4, pp. 417–31.

Baker, Rafferty (2016), 'Expo 86 evictions: Remembering the fair's dark side', *CBC News*, 4 May, https://www.cbc.ca/news/canada/british-columbia/expo-86-evictions-remembered-1.3566844. Accessed 1 September 2019.

Balzer, David (2015), 'Douglas Coupland doesn't care about you', *Canadian Art*, 12 March, https://canadianart.ca/reviews/douglas-coupland-doesnt-care-about-you/. Accessed 1 September 2019.

Barman, Jean (2015), *French Canadians, Furs, and Indigenous Women in the Making of the Pacific Northwest*, Vancouver: UBC Press.

Bartlett, Cheryl, Marshall, Murdena and Marshall, Albert (2012), 'Two-eyed seeing and other lessons learned within a co-learning journey of bringing together Indigenous and mainstream knowledges and ways of knowing', *Journal of Environmental Studies and Sciences*, 2:4, pp. 331–40.

Baudrillard, Jean (1988), 'Consumer society', in M. Poster (ed.), *Selected Writings*, Cambridge: Polity, pp. 32–59.

Baute, Nicole (2008), 'Our lost Greenwich Village', *Toronto Star*, 26 December, https://www.thestar.com/news/gta/2008/12/26/our_lost_greenwich_village.html. Accessed 31 July 2019.

Bayly, Christopher A. (1999), 'The British and Indigenous peoples, 1760-1860: Power, perception and identity', in M. Daunton and R. Halpern (eds), *Empire and Others: British Encounters with Indigenous Peoples, 1600-1850*, London: UCL Press, pp. 19–41.

Beasley, Larry (2019), *Vancouverism*, Vancouver: On Point Press.

Beauloye, Florine Eppe (2020), 'Luxury in times of crisis: How should brands react to COVID-19', *Luxe Digital*, 4 June, https://luxe.digital/business/digital-luxury-trends/covid-19-crisis/. Accessed 3 July 2020.

Beker, Jeanne (2014), 'Why we need more than Fashion Week for Canadian talent to thrive', *Globe and Mail*, 16 October, http://www.theglobeandmail.com/life/fashion-and-beauty/jeanne-beker-why-we-need-more-than-fashion-week-for-fresh-canadian-talent-to-thrive/article21094348/. Accessed 31 July 2019.

Belisle, Donica (2003), 'Toward a Canadian consumer history', *Labour/Le Travail*, 52:2, pp. 181–206.

Belisle, Donica (2011), *Retail Nation: Department Stores and the Making of Modern Canada*, Vancouver: UBC Press.

Belisle, Donica (2020), *Purchasing Power: Women and the Rise of Canadian Consumer Culture*, Toronto: University of Toronto Press.

Benjamin, Walter (1968), 'The work of art in the age of mechanical reproduction', in H. Arendt, trans. H. Zohn (eds), *Illuminations*, New York: Harcourt, Brace and World, pp. 219–54.

Berg, Maxine (2005), *Luxury and Pleasure in Eighteenth-Century Britain*, Oxford: Oxford University Press.

Berg, Maxine and Clifford, Helen (1999), *Consumers and Luxury: Consumer Culture in Europe 1650-1850*, Manchester: Manchester University Press.

Berg, Maxine and Eger, Elizabeth (2003), 'The rise and fall of the luxury debates', in M. Berg and E. Eger (eds), *Luxury in the Eighteenth Century: Debates, Desires and Delectable Goods*, Basingstoke: Palgrave Macmillan, pp. 7–27.

Berger, John (1972), *Ways of Seeing*, London: Penguin.

Berry, Christopher J. (1994), *The Idea of Luxury: A Conceptual and Historical Investigation*, Cambridge: Cambridge University Press.

Berry, Christopher J. (2016), 'Luxury: A dialectic of desire?', in J. Armitage and J. Roberts (eds), *Critical Luxury Studies: Art, Design, Media*, Edinburgh: Edinburgh University Press, pp. 47–66.

Berson, Seemah C. (2010), *I Have a Story to Tell You*, Waterloo: Wilfred Laurier University Press.

Berzowska, Joanna (2005), 'Memory rich clothing: Second skins that communicate physical memory', *5th Creativity and Cognition Conference*, Goldsmiths College, University of London, 12–15 April.

Berzowska, Joanna (2010), *XS Labs: Seven Years of Design Research and Experimentation in Electronic Textiles and Reactive Garments*, Montréal: XS Labs.

Berzowska, Joanna (2012), 'Programming materiality', in *Proceedings of the Sixth International Conference on Tangible, Embedded, and Embodied Interaction, TEI '12*, Kingston, ON, 19–22 February, New York: ACM, pp. 23–24.

Berzowska, Joanna and Coelho, Marcelo (2006a), 'Memory-rich clothing', *Conference on Human Factors in Computing Systems (CHI '06), ACM SIGGHI*, Montréal, 22–27 April.

Berzowska, Joanna and Coelho, Marcelo (2006b), 'SMOKS: The memory suits', *Conference on Human Factors in Computing Systems (CHI '06), ACM SIGGHI*, Montréal, 22–27 April.

Berzowska, Joanna and Skorobogatiy, Maksim (2009), 'Karma Chameleon: Jacquard-woven photonic fiber display', *SIGGRAPH 2009: Talks, SIGGRAPH '09*, New Orleans, 3–7 August, New York: ACM, p. 1.

Berzowska, Joanna and Skorobogatiy, Maksim (2010), 'Karma Chameleon: Bragg fiber jacquard-woven photonic textiles', in *Proceedings of the Fourth International Conference on Tangible, Embedded, and Embodied Interaction, TEI '10*, Cambridge, MA, 25–27 January, New York: ACM, pp. 297–98.

Berzowska, Joanna, Beaulieu, Marc, Leclerc, Vincent, Orain, Gaia, Marchand, Catherine, Cournoyer, Catou, Paris, Emily, Frankel, Lois and Sesartic, Miliana (2010a), 'Captain Electric and Battery Boy: Prototypes for wearable power-generating artifacts', in *Proceedings of the Fourth International Conference on Tangible, Embedded, and Embodied Interaction, TEI '10*, Cambridge, MA, 24–27 January, New York: ACM, pp. 129–36.

Berzowska, Joanna, Beaulieu, Marc, Orain, Gaia and Laflamme, Anne Marie (2010b), 'Captain Electric: Human powered electronic garments', *The 7th International Conference on Design and Emotion*, Chicago, 4–7 October.

Bhabha, Homi K. (1994), *The Location of Culture*, London: Routledge.

Bickham, Troy (2005), *Savages within the Empire: Representations of American Indians in Eighteenth-Century Britain*, Oxford: Oxford University Press.

Bird, Louis (2002), 'Story 0027 – *Our Voices* – original Cree culture', *Our Voices*: *Omushkego Oral History Project*, https://www.ourvoices.ca/filestore/pdf/0/0/2/7/0027.pdf. Accessed 15 April 2020.

Bockstoce, John R. (2009), *Furs and Frontiers in the Far North: The Contest among Native and Foreign Nations for the Bering Strait Fur Trade*, New Haven: Yale University Press.

Bogdanowicz, Julie (2006), 'Vancouverism', *Canadian Architect*, 51:8, pp. 22–24.

Borges, Jorge Luis, Guerrero, Margarita and Di Giovanni, Norman Thomas (1969), *The Book of Imaginary Beings* (trans. N. T. Di Giovanni), New York: Dutton.

Bourdieu, Pierre ([1979] 1984), *Distinction: A Social Critique of the Judgement of Taste* (trans. R. Nice), London: Routledge.

Bourdieu, Pierre ([1983] 1986), 'The forms of capital', in J. Richardson (ed.), *Handbook of Theory and Research for the Sociology of Education*, Westport: Greenwood, pp. 241–58.

Bourdieu, Pierre and Darbel, Alain (1991), *The Love of Art: European Art Museums and Their Public*, Stanford: Stanford University Press.

Bourdieu, Pierre and Delsaut, Yvette (1975), 'Le Couturier et sa griffe: Contribution à une théorie de la magie', *Actes de la recherche en sciences sociales*, 1:1, pp. 7–36.

Braddock, Sarah E. and O'Mahony, Marie (1998), *TechnoTextiles: Revolutionary Fabrics for Fashion and Design*, London: Thames & Hudson.

Bramley, Ellie Violet (2020), ' "Lockdown has been a wakeup call for the industry": What next for fashion?' *The Guardian*, 22 April, https://www.theguardian.com/fashion/2020/apr/22/lockdown-fashion-wakeup-call-coronavirus-lockdown. Accessed 2 June 2020.

Brend, Yvette (2018), 'Artist fears development will cast long shadow over East Van Cross', *CBC*, 4 October, https://www.cbc.ca/news/canada/british-columbia/east-van-cross-art-public-ken-lum-vancouver-city-development-clark-east-6th-1.4848946. Accessed 1 September 2019.

Bressi, Todd W., McKinley, Meridith and Otani, Valerie (2008), 'Vancouver public art program: Program review and design framework for public art', City of Vancouver, 17 April, https://vancouver.ca/files/cov/CulturePlan-Phase1-PublicArt-Review-Plan.pdf. Accessed 1 September 2019.

Brown, Jennifer S. H. (1980), *Strangers in Blood: Fur Trade Company Families in Indian Country*, Vancouver: University of British Columbia Press.

Brown, Jennifer S. H. (2003), 'Doing Aboriginal history: A view from Winnipeg', *Canadian Historical Review*, 84:4, pp. 613–36.

Brown, Jennifer S. H. and Vibert, Elizabeth (eds) (1996), *Reading beyond Words: Contexts for Native History*, Peterborough: Broadview.

Brown, Judith (2009), *Glamour in Six Dimensions: Modernism and the Radiance of Form*, Ithaca: Cornell University Press.

Brydges, Taylor and Hracs, Brian J. (2018), 'Consuming Canada: How fashion firms leverage the landscape to create and communicate brand identities, distinction and values', *Geoforum*, 90, pp. 108–18.

Brydges, Taylor and Hracs, Brian J. (2019), 'The locational choices and interregional mobilities of creative entrepreneurs within Canada's fashion system', *Regional Studies*, 53:4, pp. 517–27.

Buckley, Réka C. V. and Gundle, Stephen (2000), 'Flash trash: Gianni Versace and the theory and practice of glamour', in S. Bruzzi and P. Church-Gibson (eds), *Fashion Cultures: Theories, Explorations and Analysis*, London: Routledge, pp. 331–48.

Buechley, Leah, Peppler, Kylie, Eisenberg, Michael and Kafai, Yasmin (eds) (2013), *Textile Messages: Dispatches from the World of E-Textiles and Education*, New York: Peter Lang.

Bunch, Adam (2013), 'William Gibson and the Summer of Love – the author's drug-fuelled days in Yorkville', *Spacing*, 8 January, http://spacing.ca/toronto/2013/01/08/william-gibson-and-the-summer-of-love-the-authors-drug-fuelled-days-in-yorkville/. Accessed 31 July 2019.

Butler, Judith and Athanasiou, Athena (2013), *Dispossession: The Performative in the Political*, Cambridge: Polity.

Campbell, Paloma (2010), 'Ken Lum: Monument for East Vancouver', City of Vancouver, https://vancouver.ca/files/cov/public-art-brochure-monument-for-east-vancouver.PDF. Accessed 1 September 2019.

Canadian Urban Institute (2016), 'TOcore neighbourhood population profiles', City of Toronto, 4 July, https://www.toronto.ca/wp-content/uploads/2017/12/9386-city-planning-tocore-neighbourhood-population-profiles-aoda-07-04-2016.pdf. Accessed 31 July 2019.

Cariou, Gail (2004), 'Enduring roots: Gibb and Co. and the nineteenth-century tailoring trade in Montréal', in A. Palmer (ed.), *Fashion: A Canadian Perspective*, Toronto: University of Toronto Press, pp. 182–202.

Carlos, Ann M. and Lewis, Frank D. (1999), 'Property rights, competition and depletion in the eighteenth-century Canadian fur trade: The role of the European market', *Canadian Journal of Economics*, 32:3, pp. 705–28.

Carlos, Ann M. and Lewis, Frank D. (2010), *Commerce by a Frozen Sea: Native Americans and the European Fur Trade*, Philadelphia: University of Pennsylvania Press.

Castello, Lineu (2017), 'Prestige and luxury: Places of urbanity in paramount locations', in M. Paris (ed.), *Making Prestigious Places: How Luxury Influences the Transformation of Cities*, New York: Routledge, pp. 95–112.

Chaboud, Isabelle (2020), 'How the Covid-19 crisis could remodel the luxury industry', *The Conversation*, 13 May, https://theconversation.com/how-the-covid-19-crisis-could-remodel-the-luxury-industry-138137. Accessed 2 June 2020.

Chevalier, Michel and Mazzalovo, Gérald (2008), *Luxury Brand Management: A World of Privilege*, Singapore: John Wiley.

Christensen, Clayton M. (2016), *The Innovator's Dilemma: When New Technologies Cause Great Firms to Fail*, 3rd ed. Boston: Harvard Business Review Press.

Clapperton, Jonathan (2013), 'Naturalizing race relations: Conservation, colonialism, and spectacle at the Banff Indian Days', *Canadian Historical Review*, 94:3, pp. 349–79.

Cole, Yolande (2011), 'EastVan cross symbol has been around for decades, says Vancouver artist Ken Lum', *Georgia Straight*, 12 July, https://www.straight.com/news/east-van-cross-symbol-has-been-around-decades-says-vancouver-artist-ken-lum. Accessed 1 September 2019.

Colpitts, George (2013), 'The domesticated body and the industrialized imitation fur coat in Canada, 1919-1939', in P. Gentile and J. Nicholas (eds), *Contesting Bodies and Nation in Canadian History*, Toronto: University of Toronto Press, pp. 134–54.

Conn, Hugh R. (1956), 'Careful fur preparation brings bigger cash returns', *Indian News*, 2:1, p. 4.

Corntassel, Jeff (2018), *Everyday Acts of Resurgence: People, Places, Practices*, Olympia: Daykeeper Press.

Coulthard, Glen (2014), *Red Skin, White Masks: Rejecting the Colonial Politics of Recognition*, Minneapolis: University of Minnesota Press.

Craik, Jennifer (2013), 'Fashion, tourism, and global culture', in S. Black, A. de la Haye, J. Entwistle, A. Rocamora, R. A. Root and H. Thomas (eds), *The Handbook of Fashion Studies*, London: Bloomsbury, pp. 353–70.

Cree Nation Government (n.d.), 'The Eeyou of Eeyou Istchee', https://www.cngov.ca/community-culture/communities/. Accessed 15 April 2020.

Currid-Halkett, Elizabeth and Scott, Allen J. (2013), 'The geography of celebrity and glamour: Reflections on economy, culture, and desire in the city', *City, Culture and Society*, 4:1, pp. 2–11.

Cushman & Wakefield (2017), 'Main streets across the world 2017', http://www.cushmanwakefield.ca/en/research-and-insight/2017/main-streets-across-the-world-2017. Accessed 31 July 2019.

Dari-Mattiacci, Giuseppe and Plisecka, Anna (2010), 'Luxury in ancient Rome: Scope, timing and enforcement of sumptuary laws', *Legal Roots*, 1, pp. 1–27, https://papers.ssrn.com/sol3/papers.cfm?abstract_id=1616712. Accessed 31 July 2019.

Davis, Fred (1992), *Fashion, Culture, and Identity*, Chicago: University of Chicago Press.

de Bussierre, Zoé (2018), *Luxe: Les Dessous Chocs*, France: Premières lignes.

de las Rivas Sanz, Juan Luis (2017), 'Placemaking or making places? Ambiguity of luxury and the design of urban public spaces', in M. Paris (ed.), *Making Prestigious Places: How Luxury Influences the Transformation of Cities*, New York: Routledge, pp. 129–46.

Delap, Leanne (2017), 'Toronto's fashion war', *Toronto Star*, 28 August, https://www.thestar.com/entertainment/2017/08/28/toronto-fashion-week-set-to-strut-its-stuff.html. Accessed 31 July 2019.

Dembicki, Geoff (2009), 'Over-budget convention centre an "economic powerhouse": Premier', *Tyee*, 3 April, https://thetyee.ca/Blogs/TheHook/Olympics2010/2009/04/03/convention-centre-expansion/. Accessed 1 September 2019.

Demetrios, Eames (2013), *An Eames Primer*, New York: Universe.

Dene Nahjo (2015), 'Hide tanning and tool making', https://www.denenahjo.com/post/hide-tanning-and-tool-making. Accessed 10 October 2020.

Devlen, Balkan (2020), 'The leadership Canadians expect in the post-COVID world order', MacDonald-Laurier Institute, Ottawa, https://macdonaldlaurier.ca/files/pdf/202010229_LeaderShipCanadiansExpect_Devlen_COMMENTARY_FWeb.pdf. Accessed 20 December 2020.

Diffus (studio) (2017), interview by V. Lamontagne, 22 February, Copenhagen, Denmark/Montréal, Canada (via Skype).

Dillon, Phyllis and Godley, Andrew (2012), 'The evolution of the Jewish garment industry, 1840-1940', in R. Kobrin (ed.), *Chosen Capital: The Jewish Encounter with American Capitalism*, New Brunswick: Rutgers University Press, pp. 35–61.

Dior (2020), 'Sauvage, the new parfum', https://www.dior.com/en_ca/fragrance/mens-fragrance/sauvage. Accessed 26 January 2020.

DiSalvo, Carl (2012), *Adversarial Design*, Cambridge, MA: MIT Press.

Dosekun, Simidele and Iqani, Mehita (eds) (2019a), *African Luxury: Aesthetics and Politics*, Bristol: Intellect.

Dosekun, Simidele and Iqani, Mehita (2019b), 'Introduction: The politics and aesthetics of luxury in Africa', in S. Dosekun and M. Iqani (eds), *African Luxury: Aesthetics and Politics*, Bristol: Intellect, pp. 1–16.

Drees, Laurie Meijer (1993), '"Indian's bygone past": The Banff Indian Days, 1902-1945', *Past Imperfect*, 2, pp. 7–28.

Dubinsky, Karen (1999), *The Second Greatest Disappointment: Honeymooning and Tourism at Niagara Falls*, Toronto: Between the Lines Press.

Dumont, Marilyn (1996), 'Helen Betty Osborne', in *A Really Good Brown Girl*, London: Brick Books, p. 20.

Dunne, Anthony (1999), *Hertzian Tales: Electronic Products, Aesthetic Experience, and Critical Design*, Basel: MIT Press.

Dunne, Anthony and Raby, Fiona (2001), *Design Noir: The Secret Life of Electronic Objects*, Basel: Birkhäuser.

Dunne, Anthony and Raby, Fiona (2013), *Speculative Everything: Design, Fiction, and Social Dreaming*, Cambridge, MA: MIT Press.

Dyhouse, Carol (2010), *Glamour: Women, History, Feminism*, London: Zed.

Edelkoort, Lidewij (2015), *Anti-Fashion Manifesto: A Manifesto for the Next Decade*, New York: Trend Union.

Editorial (2021), 'The children can no longer be ignored', *Winnipeg Free Press*, 7 June, https://www.winnipegfreepress.com/opinion/editorials/the-children-can-no-longer-be-ignored-574577262.html. Accessed 10 June 2021.

Elan, Priya (2020), 'Italian fashion needs to confront its racism, say industry insiders', *The Guardian*, 29 June, https://www.theguardian.com/fashion/2020/jun/29/italian-fashion-needs-to-confront-its-racism-say-industry-insiders. Accessed 3 July 2020.

Elliott, Alicia (2018) 'The Indigenous renaissance was truly here in 2018 – and it's not going anywhere', *CBC Arts*, 27 December, https://www.cbc.ca/arts/the-indigenous-renaissance-was-truly-here-in-2018-and-it-s-not-going-anywhere-1.4955973. Accessed 23 December 2020.

Elliott, Kimberly (2013), 'The evolution of Toronto Fashion Week', *Kimberly Elliott*, April, https://kimberlylelliott.files.wordpress.com/2013/04/the-evolution-of-toronto-fashion-week-kimberly-elliott.pdf. Accessed 31 July 2019.

Elliott, Nancy (1966), 'There'll be no more passports to Bohemia', *Maclean's*, 2 July, archive.macleans.ca/article/1966/7/2/therell-be-no-more-passports-to-bohemia. Accessed 31 July 2019.

Elsaesser, Hayley (2019), 'Open letter: Why I'm not doing Toronto Fashion Week', *Hayley Elsaesser*, 5 February, https://www.hayleyelsaesser.com/blogs/hayleys-world/why-im-not-doing-toronto-fashion-week. Accessed 31 July 2019.

Emery, J. C. Herbert and Levitt, Clint (2002), 'Cost of living, real wages and real incomes in thirteen Canadian cities, 1900-1950', *Canadian Journal of Economics*, 35:1, pp. 115–37.

Entwistle, Joanne (2009), *The Aesthetic Economy of Fashion: Markets and Value in Clothing and Modelling*, Oxford: Berg.

Entwistle, Joanne and Rocamora, Agnès (2006), 'The field of fashion materialized: A study of London Fashion Week', *Sociology*, 40:4, pp. 735–51.

Entwistle, Joanne and Rocamora, Agnès (2011), 'Between art and commerce: London Fashion Week as trade fair and fashion spectacle', in B. Moeran and J. S. Pedersen (eds), *Negotiating Values in the Creative Industries: Fairs, Festivals and Competitive Events*, Cambridge: Cambridge University Press, pp. 249–69.

Evasuk, Stasia (1968), 'Way out new styles born in boutiques', *Toronto Daily Star*, 26 September, p. 35.

Faiers, Jonathan (2014), 'Editorial introduction', *Luxury: History, Culture, Consumption*, 1:1, pp. 5–13.

Faiers, Jonathan (2016a), 'Sartorial connoisseurship, the t-shirt and the interrogation of luxury', in J. Armitage and J. Roberts (eds), *Critical Luxury Studies: Art, Design, Media*, Edinburgh: Edinburgh University Press, pp. 177–98.

Faiers, Jonathan (2016b),' "In a galaxy far, far away …": C-3PO, mink, and the promise of disruptive luxury', *Cultural Politics*, 12:1, pp. 83–97.

Faiers, Jonathan (2020), *Fur: A Sensitive History*, New Haven: Yale.

Fashion Design Council of Canada (2012), 'Fashion Design Council of Canada reveals first details of World MasterCard Fashion Week in Toronto', *Canada Wears*, 13 February, http://canadawears.ca/press/pr-00000003.php. Accessed 31 July 2019.

Featherstone, Mark (2016), '*Luxus*: A thanatology of luxury from Nero to Bataille', *Cultural Politics*, 12:1, pp. 66–82.

Featherstone, Mike (2014), 'Luxury, consumer culture and sumptuary dynamics', *Luxury*, 1:1, pp. 47–69.

Featherstone, Mike (2016), 'The object and art of luxury consumption', in J. Armitage and J. Roberts (eds), *Critical Luxury Studies: Art, Design, Media*, Edinburgh: Edinburgh University Press, pp. 108–28.

Ferrier Mackay, Susan (2014), 'Designer Pat McDonagh brought Carnaby Street to Toronto', *Toronto Star*, 4 July, https://www.theglobeandmail.com/life/fashion-and-beauty/designer-pat-mcdonagh-brought-carnaby-street-to-toronto/article19475112/. Accessed 31 July 2019.

Fiedler, Susan (2012), 'East Van Cross Project', Susan Fiedler, http://susanfiedler.com/projects/east-van-cross-project. Accessed 15 April 2015.

Finkelpearl, Tom (ed.) (2000), 'Introduction: The city as site', in T. Finkelpearl (ed.), *Dialogues in Public Art*, Cambridge, MA: MIT Press, pp. 2–51.

Ford, Tanisha (2017), *Liberated Threads: Black Women, Style, and the Global Politics of Soul*, Chapel Hill: University of North Carolina Press.

Forster Rohner (n.d.), 'Fashion through creation, innovation and tradition', http://www.forsterrohner.com/en/. Accessed 28 September 2019.

Frager, Ruth A. (1992a), 'Class, ethnicity, and gender in the Eaton strikes of 1912 and 1934', in M. Valverde and F. Iacovetta (eds), *Gender Conflicts: New Essays in Women's History*, Toronto: University of Toronto Press, pp. 189–228.

Frager, Ruth A. (1992b), *Sweatshop Strife: Class, Ethnicity, and Gender in the Jewish Labour Movement of Toronto, 1900-1939*, Toronto: University of Toronto Press.

Frager, Ruth A. (2008), '"Mixing with people on Spadina": The tense relations between non-Jewish workers and Jewish workers', in B. Walker (ed.), *The History of Immigration and Racism in Canada: Essential Readings*, Toronto: Canadian Scholars' Press, pp. 142–57.

Freed (2019), 'Toronto Fashion Week', *Freed Developments*, https://www.freeddevelopments.com/article/toronto-fashion-week. Accessed 31 July 2019.

Freeman, Joshua B. (2018), *Behemoth: A History of the Factory and the Making of the Modern World*, New York: W. W. Norton & Co.

Friesen, Gerald (1984), *Canadian Prairies: A History*, Toronto: University of Toronto Press.

Fulsang, Deborah (2004), 'The fashion of writing, 1985-2000: Fashion-themed television's impact on the Canadian fashion press', in A. Palmer (ed.), *Fashion: A Canadian Perspective*, Toronto: University of Toronto Press, pp. 315–38.

Gans, Joshua (2019), interview by K. Christensen, *Rotman Magazine*, Winter, pp. 7–11.

Gaugele, Elke and Titton, Monica (2019), 'Fashion and postcolonial critique: An introduction', in E. Gaugele and M. Titton (eds), *Fashion and Postcolonial Critique*, Berlin: Sternberg, pp. 10–37.

Geczy, Adam and Karaminas, Vicki (2018), *Critical Fashion Practice: From Westwood to van Beirendonck*, London: Bloomsbury Academic.

Genova, Aneta and Moriwaki, Katherine (2016), *Fashion and Technology: A Guide to Materials and Applications*, London: Fairchild.

Georgijevic, Anya (2016), 'Off the runway', *Globe and Mail*, 13 October, https://www.theglobeandmail.com/life/fashion-and-beauty/fashion/off-the-runway-how-torontos-fashion-week-fell-apart/article32354808/. Accessed 31 July 2019.

Gershenfeld, Neil A. (2005), *FAB: The Coming Revolution on Your Desktop – From Personal Computers to Personal Fabrication*, New York: Basic Books.

Gibson, William H. (1876), *The Complete American Trapper*, New York: James Miller.

Gilbert, David (2006), 'From Paris to Shanghai: The changing geographies of fashion's world cities', in C. Breward and D. Gilbert (eds), *Fashion's World Cities*, London: Bloomsbury Academic, pp. 3–32.

Gilbert, David (2013), 'A new world order? Fashion and its capitals in the twenty-first century', in S. Bruzzi and P. Church Gibson (eds), *Fashion Cultures Revisited: Theories, Explorations and Analysis*, London: Routledge, pp. 11–30.

Girod, Stéphane J. G. (2020), 'Five new trends that will reshape luxury after Covid-19', *Forbes*, 19 April, https://www.forbes.com/sites/stephanegirod/2020/04/19/five-inflection-points-that-will-reshape-luxury-with-covid-19/#18ee90014eb1. Accessed 20 June 2020.

Giroux, Henry (2008), 'Beyond the biopolitics of disposability: Rethinking neoliberalism in the New Gilded Age', *Social Identities: Journal for the Study of Race, Nation & Culture*, 14:5, pp. 587–620.

Godart, Frédéric (2012), *Unveiling Fashion: Business, Culture, and Identity in the Most Glamorous Industry*, New York: Palgrave Macmillan.

Goffman, Erving (1959), *The Presentation of Self in Everyday Life*, New York: Anchor.

Goffman, Erving (1974), *Frame Analysis: An Essay on the Organization of Experience*, London: Harper & Row.

Grant, Jean (2019), 'Inside Over the Rainbow's swanky new location in Yorkville', *Toronto Life*, 23 May, https://torontolife.com/style/shopping/inside-over-the-rainbow-the-iconic-denim-sellers-new-location-in-yorkville/. Accessed 8 March 2020.

Greenberg, Clement (1961), 'Avant-garde and kitsch', in *Art and Culture: Critical Essays*, Boston: Beacon, pp. 3–21.

Haehnel, Birgit (2019), 'Fashionscapes, hybridity, and the white gaze', in E. Gaugele and M. Titton (eds), *Fashion and Postcolonial Critique*, Berlin: Sternberg, pp. 170–85.

Hall, Casey (2020), 'Fashion looks to China for a glimpse of its future', in *The State of Fashion 2020: Coronavirus Update*, Business of Fashion and McKinsey & Co., pp. 36–40.

Hall, Stuart (1991), 'The West and the rest: Discourse and power', in S. Hall and B. Gieben (eds), *The Formations of Modernity: Understanding Modern Societies*, Cambridge: Polity, pp. 275–331.

Halliday, Rebecca (2020), 'New York Fashion Week as mediatized environment', in T. Ferrero-Regis and M. Lindquist (eds), *Staging Fashion: The Fashion Show and Its Spaces*, London: Bloomsbury, pp. 192–204.

Hanquinet, Laurie (2016), 'Place and cultural capital: Art museum visitors across space', *Museum and Society*, 14:1, pp. 65–81.

Hartman, Kate (2014), *Make: Wearable Electronics: Design, Prototype, and Wear Your Own Interactive Garments*, Sebastopol, CA: Maker Media.

Hayles, N. Katherine (2012), *How We Think: Digital Media and Contemporary Technogenesis*, London: University of Chicago Press.

Heber, R. Wesley (2011), 'Aboriginal people and the fur trade', in C. J. Voyageur, D. R. Newhouse and D. Beavon (eds), *Hidden in Plain Sight: Contributions of Aboriginal Peoples to Canadian Identity and Culture*, vol. 2, Toronto: University of Toronto Press, pp. 15–31.

Henderson, Stuart (2011), *Making the Scene: Yorkville and Hip Toronto in the 1960s*, Toronto: University of Toronto Press.

Hermès (n.d.), 'Hermès Éditeur: Hiroshi Sugimoto', https://www.hermes.com/us/en/story/245496-hiroshi-sugimoto/. Accessed 1 February 2021.

Hiebert, Daniel (1993), 'Jewish immigrants and the garment industry of Toronto, 1901–1931: A study of ethnic and class relations', *Annals of the Association of American Geographers*, 83:2, pp. 243–71.

Hill, Gord (2009), 'Why protest Vancouver's 2010 Olympics?', *Georgia Straight*, 16 March, https://www.straight.com/article-206237/gord-hill-why-protest-vancouvers-2010-olympics. Accessed 1 September 2019.

Hitchcock, Lucy (2016), 'A lack of luxury? Contemporary luxury fashion in Sri Lanka', *Luxury: History, Culture, Consumption*, 3:1&2, pp. 63–82.

Holition (2019), https://www.holition.com/. Accessed 6 November 2019.

Hoskins, Tansy E. (2014), *Stitched Up: The Anti-Capitalist Book of Fashion*, Halifax: Fernwood.

Howard, John Robert (1969), 'The flowering of the hippie movement', *Annals of the American Academy of Political and Social Science*, 382, pp. 43–55.

Hundert, Edward (2002), 'Mandeville, Rousseau and the political economy of fantasy', in M. Berg and E. Eger (eds), *Luxury in the Eighteenth Century: Debates, Desires and Delectable Goods*, Basingstoke: Palgrave Macmillan, pp. 28–40.

Hunt, Sarah and Holmes, Cindy (2015), 'Everyday decolonization: Living a decolonizing queer politics', *Journal of Lesbian Studies*, 19:2, pp. 154–72.

Innis, Harold A. (1930), *The Fur Trade in Canada: An Introduction to Canadian Economic History*, New Haven: Yale University Press.

Jasen, Patricia (1995), *Wild Things: Nature, Culture, and Tourism in Ontario, 1790-1914*, Toronto: University of Toronto Press.

Jaworski, Adam and Thurlow, Crispin (2010), 'Introducing semiotic landscapes', in A. Jaworski and C. Thurlow (eds), *Semiotic Landscapes: Language, Image, Space*, London: Bloomsbury, pp. 1–40.

Jennings, Jeremy (2007), 'The debate about luxury in eighteenth- and nineteenth-century French political thought', *Journal of the History of Ideas*, 68:1, pp. 79–105.

Jenson, Jane (1999), 'From silence to communication? What Innisians might learn by analysing gender relations', in C. R. Acland and W. J. Buxton (eds), *Harold Innis in the New Century: Reflections and Refractions*, Montréal: McGill-Queen's University Press, pp. 177–95.

Johnston, Ian (2017), 'Bloor among world's most expensive streets', *BISNOW*, 17 November, https://www.bisnow.com/toronto/news/retail/bloor-among-worlds-most-expensive-streets-81687. Accessed 31 July 2019.

Johnston, Russell (2005), 'The Murray scheme: Advertising and editorial independence in Canada, 1920', *Media, Culture & Society*, 27:2, pp. 251–70.

Jones, Sam (2019), 'Mexico accuses designer Carolina Herrera of cultural appropriation', *The Guardian*, 13 June, https://www.theguardian.com/world/2019/jun/13/mexico-carolina-herrera-fashion-designer-cultural-appropriation. Accessed 23 December 2020.

Jung, E. Alex (2020), 'The revolution will not be branded', *Vulture*, 2 June, https://www.vulture.com/2020/06/the-revolution-will-not-be-branded.html. Accessed 20 June 2020.

Kaiser, Susan B. (2012), *Fashion and Cultural Studies*, London: Berg.

Kapferer, Jean-Noël and Bastien, Vincent ([2009] 2012), *The Luxury Strategy: Breaking the Rules of Marketing to Build Luxury Brands*, London: Kogan Page.

Kapferer, Jean-Noël and Bastien, Vincent (2009), 'The specificity of luxury management: Turning marketing upside down', *Journal of Brand Management*, 16, pp. 311–22.

Kapferer, Jean-Noël and Valette-Florence, Pierre (2016), 'Beyond rarity: The paths of luxury desire: How luxury brands grow yet remain desirable', *Journal of Product & Brand Management*, 25:2, pp. 120–33.

Kaplan, Ken (2015), 'Robotic Spider Dress powered by Intel smart wearable technology', *iQ by Intel*, 6 January.

Kardulias, P. Nick (1990), 'Fur production as a specialized activity in a world system: Indians in the North American fur trade', *American Indian Culture and Research Journal*, 14:1, pp. 25–60.

Kawamura, Yuniya (2004), *Fashion-ology: An Introduction to Fashion Studies*, Oxford: Berg.

Keene, Adrienne (2016), 'Engaging Indigeneity and avoiding appropriation: An interview with A. Keene', *English Journal*, 106:1, pp. 55–57.

Keys, Barbara (2018), 'Harnessing human rights to the Olympic Games: Human Rights Watch and the 1993 "Stop Beijing" campaign', *Journal of Contemporary History*, 53:2, pp. 415–38.

Kirsch, Jen (2018), 'Yorkville Village: How a former strip mall has become Toronto's hub for Movers and Shakers', *Storeys*, 6 September, https://storeys.com/yorkville-village-toronto/. Accessed 8 June 2021.

King, Thomas (1990), *All My Relations: An Anthology of Contemporary Canadian Native Prose*, Toronto: McClelland & Stewart.

King, Thomas (2013), *The Inconvenient Indian: A Curious Account of Native People in North America*, Minneapolis: University of Minnesota Press.

King, William Lyon Mackenzie (1897), 'Foreigners who live in Toronto', *Daily Mail and Empire*, 25 September, p. 7.

Knight, Charles (1867), *Arts and Sciences; or Fourth Division of 'The English Encyclopedia'*, London: Bradbury, Evans, & Co.

Knowles, Richard Paul (2004), *Reading the Material Theatre*, Cambridge: Cambridge University Press.

König, René (1974), *A La Mode: On the Social Psychology of Fashion* (trans. F. Bradley), New York: Seabury.

Kovach, Margaret (2009), *Indigenous Methodologies: Characteristics, Conversations and Contexts*, Toronto: University of Toronto Press.

Kovesi, Catherine (2016), 'The aura of luxury: Cultivating the believing faithful from the age of saints to the age of luxury brands', *Luxury: History, Culture, Consumption*, 3:1&2, pp. 105–22.

Kucheran, Riley (2016), 'Maadaadizi (to start a journey): Strategies for Indigenous luxury fashion designers', MA thesis, Toronto: Ryerson University.

Kucheran, Riley (2018), 'Luxury place-making in the city', *Cultural Politics*, 14:3, pp. 410–12.

Kucheran, Riley (2019a), 'Decolonizing methodologies in fashion and luxury studies', Northeast Modern Language Association, Washington, DC, 21–24 March.

Kucheran, Riley (@rskucheran) (2019b), 'The Indigenous resistance will be MAJOR', Instagram, 9 November, https://www.instagram.com/p/B4q5Z1IFGv0/. Accessed 19 December 2019.

Kwandibens, Nadya (2018) 'Designer: Tania Larsson, model: Cleo Keahna', Facebook, 4 June, https://www.facebook.com/IFWtoronto/photos/a.325981304601821/325983171268301. Accessed 19 December 2019.

Lamontagne, Valérie (2011), 'Open design practices + wearables + 3lectromode', *International Symposium on Electronic Art*, Istanbul, Turkey, 14–21 September.

Lamontagne, Valérie (2017), 'Performative wearables: Bodies, fashion and technology', Ph.D. dissertation, Montréal: Concordia University, https://spectrum.library.concordia.ca/982473/1/Lamontagne_PhD_S2017.pdf. Accessed 9 January 2020.

Laurence, Robin (2005), 'Ken Lum: A tale of two children', *Georgia Straight*, 3 November, https://www.straight.com/article/ken-lum-a-tale-of-two-children. Accessed 1 September 2019.

Laurence, Robin (2010), 'Ken Lum's *from shangri-la to shangri-la* and Michael Lin's *A Modest Veil*', *Georgia Straight*, 3 February, https://www.straight.com/article-284436/vancouver/shacks-sit-stark-contrast-luxe-shangrila. Accessed 1 September 2019.

Lefebvre, Henri ([1974] 1991), *The Production of Space* (trans. D. Nicholson-Smith), Oxford: Blackwell.

Lehmann, Ulrich (2016), 'The luxury duality: From economic fact to cultural capital', in J. Armitage and J. Roberts (eds), *Critical Luxury Studies: Art, Design, Media*, Edinburgh: Edinburgh University Press, pp. 67–87.

Leong, Nancy (2013), 'Racial capitalism', *Harvard Law Review*, 126:8, pp. 2151–226.

Lescarbot, Marc (1609), *Noua Francia: Or the Description of That Part of New France*, London: Eliot's Court.

Ley, David and Dobson, Cory (2008), 'Are there limits to gentrification? The contexts of impeded gentrification in Vancouver', *Urban Studies*, 45:12, pp. 2471–98.

Lezama, Nigel (2021), 'Review: Indigenous Fashion Week Toronto 2020', *Fashion Studies*, 3:2, pp. 1–6.

Lipovetsky, Gilles (1994), *The Empire of Fashion: Dressing Modern Democracy*, Princeton: Princeton University Press.

Lipovetsky, Gilles (2003), 'La Société d'hyperconsommation', *Le Débat*, 2:124, pp. 74–98.

Lipovetsky, Gilles (2005), *Hypermodern Times* (trans. A. Brown), Cambridge: Polity.

Liverant, Bettina (2018), *Buying Happiness: The Emergence of Consumer Consciousness in English Canada*, Vancouver: UBC Press.

Lowenstein, Steven M. (1984), 'Governmental Jewish policies in early nineteenth century Germany and Russia: A comparison', *Jewish Social Studies*, 46:3&4, pp. 303–20.

Lury, Celia (2004), *Brands: The Logos of the Global Economy*, London: Routledge.

Mansvelt, Juliana, Breheny, Mary and Hay, Iain (2016), '"Life's little luxuries?" The social and spatial construction of luxury', in J. Armitage and J. Roberts (eds), *Critical Luxury Studies: Art, Design, Media*, Edinburgh: Edinburgh University Press, pp. 88–107.

Manuel, Arthur and Derrickson, Ronald M. (2017), *The Reconciliation Manifesto: Recovering the Land, Rebuilding the Economy*, Toronto: Lorimer.

Martineau, Harriet (1838), *Retrospect of Western Travel*, vol. 1, New York: Charles Lohman.

Marx, Karl ([1867] 1972), *Capital: Critique of Political Economy*, Vol. 1: *The Process of Capitalist Production*, New York: International.

Mason, Courtney W. (2008), 'The construction of Banff as a "natural" environment: Sporting festivals, tourism, and representations of Aboriginal peoples', *Journal of Sport History*, 35:2, pp. 221–39.

Mason, Courtney W. (2014), *Spirits of the Rockies: Reasserting an Indigenous Presence in Banff National Park*, Toronto: University of Toronto Press.

Mason, Donna (1968), 'Beautiful girls of Yorkville', *Toronto Daily Star*, 29 July, p. 39.

Mason, Otis Tufton (1889), *Aboriginal Skin Dressing: A Study Based on Material in the United States National Museum*, Washington: Government Printing Office.

Massey, Doreen and Rose, Gillian (2003), *Personal Views: Public Art Research Project, Milton Keynes*, Milton Keynes: Art Point Trust and Milton Keynes Council.

Matthews David, Alison (2015), *Fashion Victims: The Dangers of Dress Past and Present*, London: Bloomsbury.

Maynard, Margaret (2002), 'Blankets: The visible politics of Indigenous clothing', in W. Parkins (ed.), *Fashioning the Body Politic: Dress, Gender, Citizenship*, Oxford: Berg, pp. 189–204.

McDonagh, Pat (1997), 'Something happened here', *Globe and Mail*, 21 June, p. C12.

McDowell, Maghan (2019), 'Analytics are reshaping fashion's old-school instincts', *Vogue Business*, 7 February, https://www.voguebusiness.com/technology/data-trend-forecasting-google-tracking-tools. Accessed 19 August 2019.

McIntosh, Robert (1993), 'Sweated labour: Female needleworkers in industrializing Canada', *Labour/Le Travail*, 32, pp. 105–38.

McKinsey & Co., Apparel, Fashion & Luxury Group (2018), *The Age of Digital Darwinism: Enhance the Customer Experience and Transform Your Business to Survive and Prosper in the Luxury Digital Era*, New York: McKinsey & Co.

McKinsey, Elizabeth (1985), *Niagara Falls: Icon of the American Sublime*, New York: Cambridge University Press.

McNeil, Peter and Riello, Giorgio (2016), *Luxury: A Rich History*, Oxford: Oxford University Press.

Mercer (2019), 'Quality of living city ranking', *Mercer*, 13 March, https://www.mercer.com/newsroom/2019-quality-of-living-survey.html. Accessed 1 September 2019.

Micallef, Shawn (2010), *Stroll: Psychogeographic Walking Tours of Toronto*, Toronto: Coach House.

Michael, Souzan (2010), 'Roots x Douglas Coupland', *Chatelaine*, 8 July, https://www.chatelaine.com/style/roots-x-douglas-coupland/. Accessed 1 September 2019.

Mignolo, Walter and Walsh, Catherine (2018), *On Decoloniality: Concepts, Analytics, Praxis*, Durham: Duke University Press.

Milton-Smith, John (2002), 'Ethics, the Olympics and the search for global values', *Journal of Business Ethics*, 35:2, pp. 131–42.

Mok, Tanya (2018), 'Uncle Otis', *blogTO*, 27 October, https://www.blogto.com/fashion/uncle-otis-spadina-toronto/. Accessed 8 March 2020.

Moreau, Marie (1967), 'Modesty to mod labels ROM century of fashion mod girls visit museum', *Toronto Daily Star*, 4 May, p. 61.

Morgan, Cecilia Louise (2016), *Commemorating Canada: History, Heritage, and Memory, 1850s-1990s*, Toronto: University of Toronto Press.

Mortelmans, Dimitri (2005), 'Sign values in processes of distinction: The concept of luxury', *Semiotica*, 157, pp. 497–520.

Mount, Nicholas James (2017), *Arrival: The Story of CanLit*, Toronto: House of Anansi.

Muirhead, James Fullarton (1898), *America, the Land of Contrasts: A Briton's View of His American Kin*, London: Bodley Head.

Mumford, Lewis (1934), *Technics and Civilization*, New York: Harcourt, Brace and Co.

Murphy, Robert (2004), 'Schlaepfer's century of fabrics', *Women's Wear Daily*, 31 August, https://wwd.com/fashion-news/textiles/schlaepfer-8217-s-century-of-fabrics-702386/. Accessed 20 September 2019.

Museum at FIT (2015), *Global Fashion Capitals*, https://exhibitions.fitnyc.edu/global-fashion-capitals/. Accessed 31 July 2019.

Nadeau, Chantal (2001), *Fur Nation: From the Beaver to Brigitte Bardot*, London: Routledge.

Naskapi Nation of Kawawachikamach (n.d.), 'Our community', http://www.naskapi.ca/en/History. Accessed 15 May 2020.

Naylor, Robin T. (2011), *Crass Struggle: Greed, Glitz, and Gluttony in a Wanna-Have World*, Montréal: McGill-Queen's University Press.

Niessen, Sandra (2003), 'Afterword: Re-orienting fashion theory', in S. Niessen, A. M. Leshkowich, and C. Jones (eds), *Re-Orienting Fashion: The Globalization of Asian Dress*, Oxford: Berg, pp. 243–66.

Noris, Alice, Kalbaska, Nadzeya and Cantoni, Lorenzo (2018), 'When fashion meets social commitment: The case of Ara Lumiere', *Luxury: History, Culture, Consumption*, 5:3, pp. 281–88.

O'Brien, Jean M. (2016), 'Historical sources and methods in Indigenous studies: Touching on the past, looking to the future', in C. Andersen and J. M. O'Brien (eds), *Sources and Methods in Indigenous Studies*, London: Routledge, pp. 15–22.

O'Mahony, Marie (2014), phone interview with M. Leuthold, November.

O'Mahony, Marie (2018), 'Craft + technology in the work of Iris van Herpen + Philip Beesley', *Studio Magazine*, Fall, https://www.studiomagazine.ca/issues/2018/vol-13-no-2. Accessed 21 March 2020.

O'Mahony, Marie (2019), 'When innovation succeeds', *Advanced Textiles Source*, 10 June, https://advancedtextilessource.com/2019/06/10/when-innovation-succeeds/. Accessed 20 September 2019.

Openshaw, Jonathan (2015), *Postdigital Artisans: Craftsmanship with a New Aesthetic in Fashion, Art, Design and Architecture*, Amsterdam: Frame.

Otahpiaaki Fashion Week Website (2019), Home page, https://otahpiaakifashionweek.com/. Accessed 30 March 2020.

Owram, Doug R. (1999), 'Canada and the Empire', in R. Winks (ed.), *The Oxford History of the British Empire,* Vol. 5: Historiography, New York: Oxford University Press, pp. 146–62.

Pakhchyan, Syuzi (2008), *Fashioning Technology: A DIY Intro to Smart Crafting,* Sebastopol, CA: O'Reilly Media.

Palmer, Alexandra (2004a), 'The Association of Canadian Couturiers', in A. Palmer (ed.), *Fashion: A Canadian Perspective*, Toronto: University of Toronto Press, pp. 90–109.

Palmer, Alexandra (2004b), 'Introduction', in A. Palmer (ed.), *Fashion: A Canadian Perspective*, Toronto: University of Toronto Press, pp. 3–14.

Paris, Mario (ed.) (2017), *Making Prestigious Places: How Luxury Influences the Transformation of Cities*, New York: Routledge.

Paris, Mario and Fang, Li (2017), 'From luxury to prestigious place-making', in M. Paris (ed.), *Making Prestigious Places: How Luxury Influences the Transformation of Cities*, New York: Routledge, pp. 1–20.

Parker, Odessa Paloma (2016a), 'Full steam ahead', *Globe and Mail*, 22 July, http://www.theglobeandmail.com/life/fashion-and-beauty/fashion/full-steam-ahead-what-should-happen-now-that-toronto-fashion-week-isgone/article31078660/. Accessed 31 July 2019.

Parker, Odessa Paloma (2016b), 'Toronto Fashion Week is dead: Long live Toronto Fashion Week', *Globe and Mail*, 7 July, http://www.theglobeandmail.com/life/fashion-and-beauty/fashion/toronto-fashion-week-is-dead-long-live-toronto-fashion-week-1/article30815183/. Accessed 31 July 2019.

Parkins, Wendy (ed.) (2002), *Fashioning the Body Politic: Dress, Gender, and Citizenship*, London: Berg.

PavCo (2009–10), *B.C. Pavilion Corporation: Annual Report*, 1 April 2009–31 March 2010, Vancouver: B.C. Pavilion Corporation, http://www.bcpavco.com/pdfs/PavCoAnnualReportFiscal2010.pdf. Accessed 1 September 2019.

Payette-Daoust, Michelle (1986), 'The Montreal garment industry, 1871–1901', MA thesis, Montréal: McGill University.

Pentifallo, Caitlin and VanWynsberghe, Robert (2015), 'Mega-event impact assessment and policy attribution: Embedded case study, social housing, and the 2010 Winter Olympic Games', *Journal of Policy Research in Tourism*, 7:3, pp. 266–81.

Pickering, Andrew (1995), *The Mangle of Practice: Time, Agency, and Science,* Chicago: University of Chicago Press.

Picketty, Thomas ([2019] 2020), *Capital and Ideology* (trans. A. Goldhammer), Cambridge, MA: Harvard University Press.

Podruchny, Carolyn and Peers, Laura Lynn (eds) (2010), *Gathering Places: Aboriginal and Fur Trade Histories*, Vancouver: UBC Press.

Pohlmann, Tim (2019), 'Patent and litigation trends for 3D printing technologies', iam-media, 12 March, https://www.iam-media.com/patent-and-litigation-trends-3d-printing-technologies. Accessed 28 September 2019.

Polhemus, Ted and Procter, Lynn (1978), *Fashion & Anti-Fashion: Anthropology of Clothing and Adornment*, New York: Thames and Hudson.

Poutanen, Mary Anne (1985), 'For the benefit of the master: The Montreal needle trades during the transition, 1820-1842', MA thesis, Montréal: McGill University.

Public Art Registry, City of Vancouver (2010a), 'Digital Orca', https://covapp.vancouver.ca/PublicArtRegistry/ArtworkDetail.aspx?ArtworkId=521. Accessed 1 September 2019.

Public Art Registry, City of Vancouver (2010b), 'Monument for East Vancouver', https://covapp.vancouver.ca/PublicArtRegistry/ArtworkDetail.aspx?ArtworkId=441. Accessed 1 September 2019.

Rantisi, Norma M. (2011), 'The prospects and perils of creating a viable fashion identity', *Fashion Theory: The Journal of Dress, Body & Culture*, 15:2, pp. 259–66.

Rantisi, Norma M. (2014), 'Gendering fashion, fashioning fur: On the (re)production of a gendered labor market within a craft industry in transition', *Environment and Planning D: Society and Space*, 32:2, pp. 223–39.

Rappaport, Erika (2000), *Shopping for Pleasure: Women in the Making of London's West End*, Princeton: Princeton University Press.

Ray, Arthur (1990), *The Canadian Fur Trade in the Industrial Age*, Toronto: University of Toronto Press.

Regal Tents & Structures (2020), 'Toronto Fashion Week', Regal Tents & Structures, https://www.regaltent.com/portfolio/toronto-fashion-week/. Accessed 22 June 2020.

Rich, E. E. (1967), *The Fur Trade and the Northwest to 1857*, Toronto: McClelland & Stewart.

Richardson, John (1829), *Fauna Boreali-Americana or the Zoology of the Northern Parts of British America*, London: John Murray.

Richardson, Robbie (2018), *The Savage and Modern Self: North American Indians in Eighteenth-Century British Literature and Culture*, Toronto: University of Toronto Press.

Riello, Giorgio (2016), 'Luxury or commodity? The success of Indian cotton cloth in the first global age', in K. Hofmeester and B. S. Grewe (eds), *Luxury in Global Perspective: Objects and Practices, 1600-2000*, Cambridge: Cambridge University Press, pp. 138–68.

Roach, Joseph (2007), *It*, Ann Arbor: University of Michigan Press.

Rocamora, Agnès (2009), *Fashioning the City: Paris, Fashion and the Media*, London: I. B. Tauris.

Rosenberg, Louis ([1939] 1993), *Canada's Jews: A Social and Economic Study of Jews in Canada in the 1930s*, Montréal: McGill-Queen's University Press.

Rosier, James (1605), *A True Relation of the Most Prosperous Voyage Made This Present Yeere 1605, by Captaine George Waymouth*, London: Eliot's Court.

Ross, Robert (2008), *Clothing: A Global History, or, The Imperialists' New Clothes*, Cambridge: Polity.

Roux, Élyette (2009), 'Le luxe au temps des marques', *Géoéconomie*, 2:49, pp. 19–36.

Said, Edward (1978), *Orientalism*, New York: Pantheon.

Sala, George Augustus (1865), *My Diary in America in the Midst of War*, vol. 1, London: Tinsley Brothers.

Sandals, Leah (2016), 'Why Art21 thinks Vancouver is Canada's top art city', *Canadian Art*, 12 September, https://canadianart.ca/features/some-thoughts-on-why-vancouver-is-canadas-top-art-city/. Accessed 1 September 2019.

Sandals, Leah (2019), '15 Canadian sites make international art destinations list', *Canadian Art*, 16 January, https://canadianart.ca/news/15-canadian-sites-make-international-art-destinations-list/. Accessed 1 September 2019.

Sangster, Joan (2007), 'Making a fur coat: Women, the labouring body, and working-class history', *International Review of Social History*, 52:2, pp. 241–70.

Schelling, Steven (2013), 'Festival des Métiers: Hermès pulls back the curtain on Craftsmanship', *Nuvo Magazine*, 27 September, https://nuvomagazine.com/magazine/autumn-2013/festival-des-metiers. Accessed 16 September 2019.

Scholze, Jana (2015), *What is Luxury?*, V&A Museum, London, 25 April–27 September.

Sekhon, Yasmin K. (2015), 'Sacred and treasured luxury: The meaning and value of luxury possessions amongst second-generation Asian Indian immigrants', *Luxury: History, Culture, Consumption*, 2:2, pp. 71–89.

Sekora, John (1977), *Luxury: The Concept in Western Thought, Eden to Smollett*, Baltimore: Johns Hopkins University Press.

Sennett, Richard (2008), *The Craftsman*, New Haven: Yale University Press.

Serdari, Thomaï (2016), 'Experiments in suchness: Hiroshi Sugimoto's silk *shiki* for Hermès', in J. Armitage and J. Roberts (eds), *Critical Luxury Studies: Art, Design, Media*, Edinburgh: Edinburgh University Press, pp. 131–50.

Serdari, Thomaï (2020), *Rethinking Luxury Fashion: The Role of Cultural Intelligence in Creative Strategy*, Cham: Palgrave Macmillan.

Shannon, Sarah (2019), 'Why Browns is closing its London flagship and moving around the corner', *Business of Fashion*, 4 June, https://www.businessoffashion.com/articles/intelligence/why-browns-is-closing-its-london-flagship-and-moving-around-the-corner. Accessed 6 November 2019.

Sharr, Adam (2016), 'Libeskind in Las Vegas: Reflections on architecture as a luxury commodity', in J. Armitage and J. Roberts (eds), *Critical Luxury Studies: Art, Design, Media*, Edinburgh: Edinburgh University Press, pp. 151–76.

Siegel, Andre and Hull, James (2014), 'Made-in-Canada! The Canadian Manufacturers' Association's promotion of Canadian-made goods, 1911-1921', *Journal of the Canadian Historical Association*, 25:1, pp. 1–31.

Simpson, Leanne Betasamosake (2011), *Dancing on Our Turtle's Back: Stories of Nishnaabeg Re-Creation, Resurgence and a New Emergence*, Winnipeg: ARP.

Simpson, Leanne Betasamosake (2017), *As We Have Always Done: Indigenous Freedom through Radical Resistance*, Minneapolis: University of Minnesota Press.

Simpson, Leanne Betasamosake (2020), 'The brilliance of beavers: Learning from an *Anishinaabe* world', *CBC Ideas*, https://www.cbc.ca/radio/ideas/the-brilliance-of-the-beaver-learning-from-an-anishnaabe-world-1.5534706. Accessed 10 October 2020.

Skov, Lise (2005), 'The return of the fur coat: A commodity chain perspective', *Current Sociology*, 53:1, pp. 9–32.

Smart, Reginald G. and Jackson, David (1969), *The Yorkville Subculture: A Study of the Life Styles and Interactions of Hippies and Non-Hippies, Prepared from the Field Notes of Gopala Alampur*, Toronto: Addiction Research Foundation.

Smith, Linda Tuhiwai (1999), *Decolonizing Methodologies: Research and Indigenous Peoples*, New York: Zed.

Sombart, Werner ([1913] 1967), *Luxury and Capitalism* (trans. W. Dittmar), Ann Arbor: University of Michigan Press.

Sorensen, Chris (2007), 'Revisiting the Summer of Love', *Toronto Star*, 3 June, https://www.thestar.com/entertainment/2007/06/03/revisiting_the_summer_of_love.html. Accessed 3 June 2021.

Stapleton, Betty (1969), 'Fashion explodes into print', *Toronto Daily Star*, 21 August, p. A59.

Stead, Lisa, Goulev, Peter, Evans, Caroline and Mandani, Ebrahim (2004), 'The emotional wardrobe', *Personal and Ubiquitous Computing*, 8:3, pp. 282–90.

Steedman, Mercedes (1997), *Angels of the Workplace: Women and the Construction of Gender Relations in the Canadian Clothing Industry, 1890-1940*, Toronto: University of Toronto Press.

Steele, Valerie (2017), *Paris Fashion: A Cultural History*, 3rd ed., New York: Bloomsbury.

Steele, Valerie (2000), 'Fashion yesterday, today and tomorrow', in I. Griffiths and N. J. White (eds), *The Fashion Business: Theory, Practice, Image*, Oxford: Berg, pp. 7–22.

Sturken, Marita and Cartwright, Lisa (2009), *Practices of Looking: An Introduction to Visual Culture*, 2nd ed. Oxford: Oxford University Press.

Styles, John (2000), 'Product innovation in early modern London', *Past and Present*, 168, pp. 124–69.

Svadja, Hep (2014), 'Anouk's new creation: Intel Edison based Spider Dress 2.0', *Makezine*, 19 December, https://makezine.com/2014/12/19/anouks-new-creation-the-spider-dress/.

Szeman, Imre (2000), 'The rhetoric of culture: Some notes on magazines, Canadian culture and globalization', *Journal of Canadian Studies*, 35:3, pp. 212–30.

Tang, Colleen (2010), 'Douglas Coupland's digital orca captures the spirit of Vancouver harbour', *BC Living*, 6 August, https://www.bcliving.ca/douglas-couplands-digital-orca-captures-the-spirit-of-vancouver-harbour. Accessed 1 September 2019.

Taylor, C. J. (2007), 'The changing habitat of Jasper tourism', in I. S. MacLaren (ed.), *Culturing Wilderness in Jasper National Park: Studies in Two Centuries of Human History in the Upper Athabasca River Watershed*, Edmonton: University of Alberta Press, pp. 199–232.

Tennant, Chris (1994), 'Indigenous peoples, international institutions, and the international legal literature from 1945-1993', *Human Rights Quarterly*, 16:1, pp. 1–57.

The T. Eaton Company Limited (1896), T. Eaton Co. Catalogue [English edition] Fall-Winter 1896–97, no. 34.

The T. Eaton Company Limited (1921), T. Eaton Co. Catalogue [English edition] Spring-Summer 1921.

The T. Eaton Company Limited (1923), T. Eaton Co. Catalogue [English edition] Spring-Summer 1923.

The T. Eaton Company Limited (1924), T. Eaton Co. Catalogue [English edition] Fall-Winter 1924–25.

Thomas, Dana (2007), *Deluxe: How Luxury Lost Its Luster*, London: Penguin.

Toronto Fashion Week (2020), 'An announcement about Toronto Fashion Week', Twitter, 14 January, https://twitter.com/tofashionwk/status/1217086599785263105. Accessed 8 March 2020.

Truth and Reconciliation Commission of Canada (2015), 'Honouring the truth, reconciling for the future. Summary of the final report of the Truth and Reconciliation Commission of Canada', 23 July, http://www.trc.ca/assets/pdf/Honouring_the_Truth_Reconciling_for_the_Future_July_23_2015.pdf. Accessed 1 June 2021.

Tuan, Yi-Fu (1977), *Space and Place: The Perspective of Experience*, Minneapolis: University of Minnesota Press.

Turner, Victor (1967), 'Betwixt and between: The liminal period in "rites de passage"', in *The Forest of Symbols*, Ithaca, NY: Cornell University Press, pp. 93–111.

Turner, Victor (1974), 'Liminal to liminoid in play, flow, and ritual: An essay in comparative symbology', *Rice University Studies*, 60:3, pp. 53–92.

Turunen, Linda Lisa Maria (2017), *Interpretations of Luxury: Exploring the Consumer Perspective*, Cham, Switzerland: Palgrave MacMillan.

van Kirk, Sylvia (1980), *Many Tender Ties: Women in Fur-Trade Society, 1670-1870*, Winnipeg: Watson & Dwyer.

Veblen, Thorstein ([1899] n.d.), 'The Theory of the Leisure Class', http://moglen.law.columbia.edu/LCS/theoryleisureclass.pdf. Accessed 29 November 2016.

Vigod, Bernard L. (1984), *The Jews in Canada*, Ottawa: Canadian Historical Association.

Voyageur, Cora J. (2016), 'First Nations women in the fur trade: From essential to redundant', *Canadian Issues*, pp. 15–18.

Walji, Nazima (2012), 'Toronto Fashion Week launching Canadian designers onto world stage', *CBC*, 16 March, https://www.cbc.ca/news/canada/toronto-fashion-week-launching-canadian-designers-onto-world-stage-1.1293675. Accessed 31 July 2019.

Wallace, Keith (2011), 'A particular history: Artist-run centres in Vancouver', in S. Douglas (ed.), *Vancouver Anthology: A Project of the Or Gallery*, Vancouver: Talonbooks and Or Gallery, pp. 29–51.

White, Nicola J. (2000), 'Italy: Fashion, style and national identity, 1945-65', in N. J. White and I. Griffiths (eds), *The Fashion Business: Theory, Practice, Image*, Oxford: Berg, pp. 183–203.

Wiesing, Lambert (2018), 'Towards a phenomenology of luxury', *Cultural Politics*, 14:1, pp. 78–89.

Williams, Robert and Hong, Jinshan (2020), ' "Revenge spending" spurs Chinese luxury rebound from virus', *Bloomberg*, 12 March, https://www.bloomberg.com/news/articles/2020-03-12/luxury-shoppers-in-china-emerge-from-quarantine-to-buy-again. Accessed 20 June 2020.

Williams, Roger (1643), *A Key into the Language of America*, London: Gregory Dexter.

Wilson, Elizabeth (2000), *Bohemians: The Glamorous Outcasts*, London: I. B. Taurus.

Wilson, Elizabeth (2014), 'Luxury', *Luxury: History, Culture, Consumption*, 1:1, pp. 15–21.

Wilson, Shawn (2008), *Research Is Ceremony: Indigenous Research Methods*, Halifax: Fernwood.

Wipprecht, Anouk (2017), interview by V. Lamontagne, 28 April, Toronto, Canada.

Wood, William (2011), 'Some are weather-wise; some otherwise: Criticism and Vancouver', in S. Douglas (ed.), *Vancouver Anthology: A Project of the Or Gallery*, Vancouver: Talonbooks and Or Gallery, pp. 137–71.

Wright, Cynthia (1992), ' "Feminine trifles of vast importance": Writing gender into the history of consumption', in F. Iacovetta and M. Valverde (eds), *Gender Conflicts: New Essays in Women's History*, Toronto: University of Toronto Press, pp. 229–60.

XS Labs and Joanna Berzowska (2017), interview by V. Lamontagne, 26 January, Montréal, Canada.

Contributors

Jessica P. Clark is a historian of Britain and empire, with a focus on gender, consumption and labour. She is the author of *The Business of Beauty: Gender and the Body in Modern London* (2020). Her work has also appeared in such publications as the *Women's History Review, Victorian Periodicals Review* and *Gender and Material Culture in Britain since 1600* (2015). She is an associate professor of history at Brock University in St. Catharines.

Kathryn Franklin is an arts and science postdoctoral fellow in the English Department at the University of Toronto. She holds a Ph.D. from the graduate programme in Humanities at York University, and her dissertation focused on the concept of glamour as an expression of Toronto's urban imaginary. Her current research explores the relationship between glamour and the popularization of the urban Canadian middlebrow novel in the 1950s and 1960s. Her work has appeared in *Imaginations, International Journal of Fashion Studies* and *World Film Locations: Berlin* (2012). She also served as a co-editor for the Canadian literary publication *Descant*.

Rebecca Halliday has a Ph.D. in communication and culture from York University (joint program with Ryerson University) and an MA in theatre and performance studies, also from York. As of 2021–22, she is an assistant professor (limited-term) in the School of Professional Communication at Ryerson University and has also taught in the School of Fashion at Ryerson. Her research at the intersection of digital media and fashion has been published in the journals *Comunicazioni Sociali, Imaginations* and *TranscUlturAl*, as well as in numerous edited volumes. Her manuscript on the mediatization of fashion shows is forthcoming from Bloomsbury.

Riley Kucheran is an assistant professor of design leadership at Ryerson University's School of Fashion and associate director of the Saagajiwe Centre for Indigenous Research and Creation in the Faculty of Communication and Design.

As an Indigenous fashion researcher, he supports the global movement towards cultural and economic resurgence through design. With experience in fashion retail and entrepreneurship, he draws on Indigenous theory to propose that fashion is a powerful tool for decolonization. He is a member of Biigtigong Nishnaabeg (Pic River First Nation) and is working with the community to promote artisanal products and land-based design education.

VALÉRIE LAMONTAGNE was a Montréal artist-designer and curator and held a Ph.D. in 'Performative wearables: Bodies, fashion and technology' from Concordia University. She was the owner and designer at 3lectromode, a wearables electronics atelier, and founder of the Fashiontech Festival in Montréal. Valérie curated and collaborated on design and media arts exhibitions and events such as: *Fashiontech Festival*, McCord Museum, Montréal, Canada (2017); *Tech-à-porter*, MUTEK IMG, Montréal, Canada (2016); *The Future of Fashion Is Now*, Museum Boijmans van Beuningen, Rotterdam, Netherlands (2014); and *TechnoSensual*, MuseumsQuartier, Vienna, Austria (2012). Valérie passed away in 2019.

NIGEL LEZAMA is an associate professor in the Modern Languages, Literatures and Cultures Department of Brock University. Examining how marginalized and peripheral fashion and luxury practices transform dominant culture, he works at the intersection of fashion, luxury, literary and cultural studies. He is a member of the editorial board for *Fashion Studies* and the new *In Pursuit of Luxury* journal. His work has appeared in such publications as *Luxury, Fashion, Society and the First World War: International Perspectives* (2021), *Fashion, Dress, and Post-Post Modernism* (2021) and *Fashioning Horror: Dressing to Kill on Screen and in Literature* (2017).

MARIE O'MAHONY is an industry consultant, author and academic. She is the author of several books on advanced and smart textiles published by Thames and Hudson and visiting professor at the Royal College of Art (RCA), London.

JULIA POLYCK-O'NEILL is an artist, curator, critic, poet and writer. A former visiting lecturer at the Obama Institute at Johannes Gutenberg Universität Mainz (2017–18) in Germany, she is currently a Social Sciences and Humanities Research Council (SSHRC) postdoctoral fellow in the department of Art History and Visual Art and the Sensorium Centre for Digital Arts and Technology at York University (Toronto).

Index